the fateful question of culture

the fateful question of culture

Geoffrey H. Hartman

The Wellek Library Lecture Series

at the University of California, Irvine

columbia university press

NEW YORK

PN94
.H344
1997

Columbia University Press
Publishers Since 1893
New York   Chichester, West Sussex

Copyright © 1997 Columbia University Press
All rights reserved

Library of Congress Cataloging-in-Publication Data
Hartman, Geoffrey H.
    The fateful question of culture / Geoffrey H. Hartman.
        p.   cm. — (The Wellek Library lecture series at the
    University of California, Irvine)
        Includes index.
        ISBN 0–231–08490–0 (alk. paper)
        1. Criticism—History—20th century.   2. Culture.   I. Title.
    II. Series.
    PN94.H344   1997
    801'.95'0904—dc21   97–16846
                                                                            CIP

Casebound editions of Columbia University Press books are
printed on permanent and durable acid-free paper.

Printed in the United States of America
c 10 9 8 7 6 5 4 3 2 1

The author is grateful for permission to quote nine lines from *The Aeneid*
by Vergil, trans. Robert Fitzgerald (New York: Random House, 1983)
© Random House 1993.

editorial note

The Wellek Library Lectures in Critical
Theory are given annually at the University
of California, Irvine, under the auspices of
the Critical Theory Institute. The following
lectures were given in June 1992.

The Critical Theory Institute
John Carlos Rowe, Director

For Murray Krieger
critic, scholar, founder

The fateful question for the human species seems to me to be whether and to what extent their cultural development will succeed in mastering the disturbance of their communal life by the human instinct of aggression and self-destruction. It may be that in this respect precisely the present time deserves a special interest. Men have gained control over the forces of nature to such an extent that with their help they would have no difficulty in exterminating one another to the last man. They know this, and hence comes a large part of their current unrest, their unhappiness and their mood of anxiety. And now it is to be expected that the other of the two "Heavenly Powers," eternal Eros, will make an effort to assert himself in the struggle with his equally immortal adversary. But who can foresee with what success and with what result?

— SIGMUND FREUD, *Civilization and Its Discontents*

In spite of difference of soil and climate, of language and manners, of laws and customs, in spite of things silently gone out of mind and things violently destroyed, the poet binds together by passion and knowledge the vast empire of human society.

— WORDSWORTH, PREFACE (1802) TO *Lyrical Ballads*

contents

acknowledgments

Conversations with many people have
helped me. I thank especially Kevis Goodman, Thomas and
Liliane Greene, Paul Fry, Helen Elam, Cathy Caruth, Richard
Weisberg, Victor Gourevitch, Richard and Carol Bernstein, Rob-
ert Griffin, Elizabeth Freund, Sandy and Emily Budick, Simone
and Carlo Barck, Anselm Haverkamp, and Winfried Menning-
haus. Thanks are also due to the fellows of the Woodrow Wilson
Center in Washington, D.C., and its director, Charles Blitzer,
who became sounding boards in the winter and spring of 1994/95.
The core of these reflections was presented as part of the René
Wellek Library Lectures at the University of California, Irvine;
Mark Poster was the chair of the committee that invited me and
Murray Krieger encouraged me to take up the theme of culture
despite my reluctance to enter a crowded field. The dedication of
this book expresses my gratitude for acts of support and friendship
that began at the University of Iowa in 1962. My debts to scholarship, new and old, are clearly indicated in the book itself.

the fateful question of culture

chapter one
Introduction

Art has always enjoyed some autonomy because of its ability to put into play a sympathetic imagination independent of political directives and social decorum. Literature (my special concern) can reach vastly different kinds of people, even across national boundaries. It has that power to move—and offend—as well as instruct.

But art has also been denounced for its supposed elitist status. Because art is so various, it is difficult to generalize about it; recently, however, the attempt to control it through cultural or political steering or other functional criteria has become the subject of intense debate. Defenders have had to meet challenges coming even from liberal sources: everyone, it seems, wants to make art more accountable, to prove its social or material effectiveness. There has been a shift from aesthetics, or art studied within its own institutional history, to what might be called "culturalism," the effort to use art to diagnose or affirm particular cultures. Can we still understand Hannah Arendt's paradox, that works of art are "the worldliest of things" in their staying power yet "the only things without function in the life process of society"?[1]

In *The Fateful Question of Culture*, my focus is initially on the word "culture" and the growth of cultural studies in the last fifty years. I look home to the academy before tackling the larger issue of the fateful militancy "culture" has achieved in the world. However far literature and cultural reflections seem from the wars that have afflicted this century, it is worth recalling Julien Benda's sardonic remark in *The Treason of the Intellectuals* (1927): "That political war should imply cultural wars is truly an invention of our time, and which assures it a notable place in the moral history of humanity."[2]

Given the expansion of culture, as both word and academic subject, what is the present status of literature and literary studies? "Literature" has not expanded; if anything, the vigor and affect of the word are now overshadowed. Ironically, the adoption in anthropology and cultural history of what Clifford Geertz called the "text analogy"—which enables a "thicker" description of the religious or social rituals of particular societies—seems to take from rather than add to the discipline of literary studies. If "man is an animal suspended in webs of significance he himself has spun,"[3] if social, ritual, and symbolic process is the text, how is the textuality of the literary artifact to be distinguished?

The text analogy has functioned, in effect, to place art on the level of all other activities and to encourage views that either demystify it or reduce it to an illustration. After a heady period during which the semiotic theory of culture drew every human activity into its net, students and scholars of literature are no longer sure what they profess. Many sense that literature as we have known it is being relegated to the past, to an obsolete realm characterized by the dominance and privilege of print literacy and within that to a reactionary, because distinctively aesthetic, body of works. Both theory and temperament militate at present against what appears to be a Ptolemaic universe (canonical literature) that is giving way not just to a Copernican model but to a plurality of worlds, cultures that either have their own "sun," their own identity principle, or, lacking a firm center, create it through the artificial glare of publicity.

In chapter 2 I explain the appeal of "culture," how our time has made it a more complex word, how it has accrued a pathos that may seem trivial yet expresses an important need. But my main purpose is to restore literature's specificity as a focus for thinking about culture and as a force that challenges a monolithic or complacent culturalism.

The conflict between art and culture is both obvious and easily overlooked. Politics is a mode of interpretation as well as of action, and art is often pressed into duty. The stakes are large: from quarrels about moral standards to issues of cultural identity. Cultural nationalism of one sort or another occupies our thinking and a good part of our life; culture wars, as they are now called, are pursued globally as well as locally.[4] Blood and spirit mingle in the quest for cultural identity, which often exploits relics of ancient art while reviving much in the literary past and rescuing it from oblivion. We cannot be indifferent to how culture is defined, and I want to anticipate here, by a sort of "overture," how complex and precarious the links are between artistic genius and cultural self-definition.

The strong reliance of cultural nationalism on art comes about because it is taken for granted that a great nation will also be great in its art. The historical record, that is, should provide proof not only of past independence or ethnic unity but of imaginative vigor. While Latin writers already borrow from and accommodate Greek precursors, marrying, as it were, into their greatness, this process intensifies in the European Renaissance, where underdeveloped vernaculars seek to become national literatures and enrich themselves by imitating or "translating" classical genres, images, and tropes. They practice high-class theft under the patronage of Hermes. Later, with the romantics, the claim arises that the new literary languages are simply stealing back (reappropriating) their own goods, just as today a Black Moses or Black Athena is affirmed.

Romanticism, as a movement, is far less interested in nationalizing classical models than in discovering distinctive native sources of poetical energy attributed to the genius loci. Though artistic glory remains a motivating theme, it has to be different in character from that of the classics. After being reduced to the status of minor deity in neoclassical verse, to the merely picturesque and decorative, the genius loci, or spirit of place, evolves in a radical direction to figure as muse and guardian of each nation's collective memory. The romantic poets are the beneficiaries of a sense of literary history based on the older classics *and* on competitive modern works that in less than two centuries had assumed the look of native classics.[5]

In their cultural politics, therefore, the romantics express anxiety as well as hope. There is hope in the continued greatness of a characteristic national genius, but it is darkened by anxiety about their individual genius. Can they add to the legacy of the Renaissance, or does the recession of great poetry in the Enlightenment indicate the party is over? The Renaissance poets could still tap into archaic strength, into romance or vision, yet by the middle of the next century a progress of poetry was in doubt. William Collins declared that the "God-like gift" inspiring Spenser, Shakespeare, and Milton was now "curtain'd close from ev'ry future View."[6]

What saves romantic poetry from depression is a revivalist idea: there will be a *second* Renaissance, this time creating a nonclassical (or radically classical)[7] literature, a poetry of our climate. This aspiration finds support, as I have mentioned, in the genius loci notion, often linked to that of a collective (folk) memory composed of popular legends and songs. Poems are valued as the emanation of particular places or regions. The relation of poetry to place—the inspiring or organic relation—may be a superstition or at best a generous error, but to celebrate one's native land or to lament its loss has always fostered national sentiment.

At the same time, in the most original poetry of the romantic period, genius as individual talent separates off from the genius loci, which stands against it as the self-incurred burden of tradition, as what poetic genius has itself—imperfectly—engendered. Wordsworth begins his autobiographical poem on the growth of a poet's mind with an outburst invoking and celebrating "Dear Liberty!" yet the "correspondent breeze" roused by "the sweet breath of heaven" blowing on him, which should have led to further composition, escalates from a "quickening virtue" into "a tempest, a redundant energy, / Vexing its own creation."[8] Both breezes, adds the poet, break up an inner frost, but the hint that, as Keats will say, "The creative must create itself" is there, and an ambiguity in "Vexing its own creation" suggests that the poem itself, or whatever was created, may not satisfy the inner, engendering force. In Emerson, moreover, genius, even as it seeks to identify itself with the genius loci, with America as a new origin, stands in even greater tension to any fixed deliverance to the emanated work. Richard Poirier remarks that if with Emerson's help you try to discover the evidence of "genius" in a text, "you would quickly find that the text had to surrender its wording and become in some way volatile." He goes on to cite Emerson's remarkable *Journal* entry for 18 May 1840: "Criticism must be transcendental, that is it must consider literature ephemeral & easily entertain the supposition of its entire disappearance."[9]

Such skepticism about cultural monumentality may have had its influence on Nietzsche. It is with Nietzsche, in any case, that a different and more critical understanding of the relation among nation, art, genius, and culture becomes overt. He was outraged by claims that the German victory over France in the Franco-Prussian war of 1871 was a success story of "German culture." He mocks this kind of cultural nationalism as a gross simplification abetted by a conspiracy of journalistic, historical, and literary fabricators who seek to control the leisure time of readers. He calls their cultural and exploitative claims a defeat, not a victory: "a defeat, even extirpation of the German spirit in favor of the 'German *Reich*.' "[10] Nietzsche does not deny the existence of something "German," but it does not yet exist, he says, in the form of a culture; it is too new in Europe (especially when compared to French culture). Germany's premature nationalization of *Geist* was the worst fate that could befall it.

> Cursed *folk*-soul! When we talk of the *German spirit*, we mean Luther, Goethe, Schiller and a few more. . . . We should be careful about calling anything German: it is, first of all, the *language*; but to understand that as an expression of national character is nothing but a cliché, and has everywhere led to fatal equivocations [*Unbestimmtheiten*] and turns of speech. . . . To give predicates to a nation [*Volk*] is always dangerous: things are so mixed and mingled that it is only later that a unity can establish itself in the language, or an illusion of unity. Germans, yes! The German *Reich*! That is something. German speech also. But race-Germans

[Rasse-Deutsche]! German as artistic unity of style is still to be *found*.

Nietzsche is trying to get away from two confusions: of cultural with racial and of cultural with nationalistic-political. These have continued to plague postromantic writers in one form or another. What he does not deny, indeed what he seeks to affirm, is the link of the idea of culture with "style," style as a quality that permeates the habits and mentality of a people and, in that sense and that alone, can be said to bestow unity. The achievement of cultural style would be a victory: of the Germans over themselves, their crudeness, their boastfulness, their prejudices, their anti-Semitism. But the fact is that Germanity so conceived does not yet exist; it must still come into being. Nietzsche adds, ominously from our point of view, "every birth is painful and violent."[11]

The notion of culture as a certain "style" of life, not given by nature or destined by history but formed of an assemblage of living institutions that are—as Emerson said—the lengthened shadow of exceptional human beings, approaches the only idea of culture that is not, in Nietzsche's view, deadly. Nietzsche believed the Greeks had attained such an encompassing cultural style at one point. However that may be, this beneficial and peaceable rather than militant concept has become rare in modernity.

Even Nietzsche's "aesthetic" hope for unity is not without its problems, however. While rejecting popular chauvinism and *état-isme*, Nietzsche sees genuine culture as the result of the mental fight of great individuals and so preserves the genius concept at the level of the agonistic personality. While he attacks the myth of a historically manifest destiny he does not give up the cult of genius. After quoting Hegel's "What happens to a people and what comes from within its ongoing life has its essential meaning in relation to the state; the mere particularities of individuals are at the furthest distance from the subject matter proper to history," he comments: "But the state is always only the means of preserving many individuals: how could it be the end! It is our hope that through the preservation of so many inferior types [*Nieten*; more colloquially, "los-ers"] a few individuals in whom humanity culminates will be protected."[12] This antidemocratic cult of genius will be exploited by a Nazism that ignored, needless to say, Nietzsche's firm rejection of the state as the exclusive bearer of a nation's significance.

I will show in chapters 3 and 5 that the work of a great artist can have a strong and long-range impact on the way we look at ourselves as a culture. This impact goes beyond inculcating a firmer sense of national character (or reforming it). The original genius among literary artists is quite literally creative. I argue that Wordsworth, writing near the beginning of the industrial revolution, achieves a precarious cultural transfer (*translatio*) of English rural life—or rather of its spirit, given that literary culture was, and continued to be, an urban phenomenon. Unlike the older *translatio studii*, his transfer moves neither across a geographical expanse nor across historical time (from ancient Rome to the Holy Roman Empire, from England to America). It does something more subtle and less overtly deliberate: it gives representation to what in English culture was previously unrealized or semi-articulate, a potentiality only. Wordsworth's poetry does not reflect in any simple way an existing situation; it surrounds it, rather, with an imaginative aura (the French have the word *imaginaire*) that helped to create the sense of a particularly *English* culture. I speculate that this saved English politics from the virulence of a nostalgic political ideal centering on rural virtue, which led to serious ravages on the continent.[13]

Since Wordsworth's poetry is only one example, and I do not test other explanations for the specific influence it exerted in England, I claim for my thesis no more than heuristic value. But were my conjectures to be disproved or shown incapable of being proved, I would continue to feel as Mrs. Henshaw does, in Willa Cather's *My Mortal Enemy*: "How the great poets do shine on . . . ! Into all the dark corners of the world. They have no night."

Several issues broached in this book are described rather than resolved. In chapter 6, especially, I draw attention to an impasse that toward the end of the eighteenth century affects a new or conceptually clarified idea of culture. As industrialism becomes a shaping force of nations and the sense arises that residual feudal institutions are finally being swept away, the question is raised, often with premature nostalgic force, of what will be lost in the transition. While progress, enlightenment, and modernity continue to be linked, there is a fear concerning the gulf that might open up as new political and belief structures are worked out. It is now that the concept of an uncertain interim or "Age of Transition" takes hold. Matthew Arnold's famous verses concerning the modern pilgrim, "Wandering between two worlds, one dead / The other powerless to be born" catch perfectly that uncertain mood.[14]

Implicit here is the thought that the new world must be helped into existence by the imaginative intellect of the artist, belated and conflicted as he is. In Schiller that impasse, that sense of coming too late to have a future, is at least philosophically transformed. "Culture" (sometimes "art," in the sense of artifice) designates in his *Letters on Aesthetic Education* progress toward a distinctively modern society with its compartmentalization of fields of knowledge and its social or bureaucratic division of labor.[15] At the same time, "culture" denotes whatever cures the alienation and loss of community inflicted by society's emergence from a more primal and unreflected unity. In postmodernity, however, this paradox shows its consequences. If culture is associated with the search (however fantasy-driven) for a lost unity, then culture cannot remain a separate activity. To recover that unity, or a simulacrum of it, culture will have to deny its own separate status. "Culture," writes Guy Debord, "is the site of the search for the lost unity. In this search for unity, culture as a separate sphere is obliged to negate itself."[16]

What can this obligation of culture to negate itself mean? What kind of vanishing act or abdication is involved? Perhaps Debord hints at a return of the repressed, at the transcendent, even anarchic individuality of genius that Emerson intuited and Arnold feared. This genial energy may lead to the sophistication of self-consuming artifacts or to mass culture's centrifugal and conspicuous consumption. What is equally dangerous, however, is making the arts disappear by instrumentalizing them: seeing them only as "cultural work," for example. For this leaves them open to being administered, as well as to the argument that they are expendable: socially, functionally, are there not things of better value? Even art's countercultural resistance could then be likened to that of the clown in a royal court: a vaguely restitutive, irrational entertainment. Art is not shielded by a sacred or institutional matrix nor, today, by qualities that are aesthetic in the older sense of the word: that come from art's relation to sense perception and its quasi-Kantian immunity to teleological concepts. It is not melodramatic to talk once more of the death or dissolution of art.

No wonder Schiller postulates an interim of indefinite length characterized by "aesthetic education." It removes our anxiety about a transition: a transition governed by culture and art to a world that has outlived them. Schiller, one suspects, knows that this aesthetic state contains as much autonomy, as much freedom from instinctual drives or government power, as we will ever enjoy. For Nietzsche, too, the aesthetic illusion is valuable, and the unity of a culture cannot be guaranteed by the state. As long as we still appreciate the surprise of the senses[17] and tolerate the excess of life over meaning and as long as freedom (as in Schiller) is an idea as well as an illusion, the question "How German/French/English/American is it?" depends for its answer on genial individuals and never on government authority. At the same time, if nations are "imagined communities," the imagination required to sustain such collectivities will not neglect nature as habitat or any other basic orientation.[18]

Recent pressures have introduced two further complications. As we turn away not only from statism but also from "high culture" in order to legitimate creative energies coming from a more diffused center *and* use everything cultural as fodder for spectacle and entertainment, the seriousness of the concept of "culture" seeks shelter from inauthenticity and trivialization in that of "*a* culture." For otherwise we risk losing entirely the idea of radical *poiesis*: that man is made by what he makes, that art too, even if "play" rather than "work," has transformative potential.

A second complicating factor is that once the nation-state has been firmly established, often with the help of cultural convictions, the concepts of nation and culture may diverge once again, as multiculturalism arises within that framework. The result is that culture as a cosmopolitan or universalistic ideal dissipates. Yet we cannot return to a self-evident and unreflective localism.[19] What takes the place of the universalist idea are subcultures, each of which makes an identity claim in the form of an intensely conscious and ideologized localism. The indefinite article in "*a* culture" then points to something as definite as the definitive absence of any article preceding "culture." The traditional antithesis of culture and nature gives way to an opposition between culture and cultures.

Ideologically, this diversification of the nation, or diversity of cultures within the nation, links up less with pluralism than with a revolt against a superficial and often snobbish universalism. In Europe, cultures used to mask their exclusiveness by claiming they were or should be universal. They sought to furnish educated people everywhere with a *parole* or password, as Dr. Johnson said of the classics. Even in a more liberal, education-oriented age, culture is generally defined as "the best that has been said or thought" (Matthew Arnold) and becomes evangelical or even coercively didactic, a purveyor of truth to nation and world. (Arnold, aware of that coerciveness, carefully distinguished culture from religion.) But pluralism may not result from diversification when "a culture" becomes purely affirmative in its ideology, when it is simply *not yet* expansionist or domineering. Often a minority culture in its quest for identity not only declares its own way of life but insists on its members' conformity to that way of life (comprising ceremonies, dress, diction, rules of participation, association, and marriage). It may have good reasons for that attitude (the disciplined cohesion necessary to achieve a political end, for example, or a visible taunt to the majority), but we should recognize that identity politics challenges not only the state but civil society itself, that "marketplace of ideas" or "republic of letters" that frees discussion and expression from political regulation or extreme sociopolitical pressure. The energies that develop civil society, energies we designate as "cultural," can also threaten that same society in the name of a more exigent unity.[20]

I come, then, to a related and unresolved issue. It concerns the political effect of "ideas," of formalized thoughts that are teased out, disputed, passionately or casually elaborated in a university setting or in civic forums but lose their innocence or flexibility outside of that context.[21] There is an academic suspension of the teleological in which aesthetic experience participates, because it has already instituted its own donation of (nonpolitical) worldliness. Thus Václav Havel is also the name of an experiment: whether democratic concepts developed by a literary sensibility and favoring the civic ideals of Charter 77 can survive power politics and the remaking of the Czech state.

This experiment does not take place in a vacuum. There are those who feel that the free development of such ideas is too permissive. Reverting to the 1920s and 1930s, they connect the structures that foster such dangerous freedom with parliamentary democracy as an inherently feeble system destructive of national unity in a hostile world of nations: as nothing, basically, but disputes by parties representing vested interests. Thus the very idealism of certain political ideals disseminated by the American and French Revolutions—the usual term of opprobrium attached to those ideals is "abstract"—is held to make them dangerous. The resurgence of narrowly nationalist and xenophobic politics in Central Europe is then supported by concepts of a unified culture that must be protected and restored. Ethnic group or cultural nation revives as the viable middle term between vested local interest and an unworldly or else subversive cosmopolitanism.

Yet ethnic cleansing makes its appearance in this very context. My book is haunted by the fact—which the Holocaust as a totalized and technologized genocide made terrifyingly clear—that ideals can become pathological, that they can be used to rationalize state-supported immoral and deadly acts. Chapter 4, "Language and Culture After the Holocaust," tries to come to grips with that fact. While the extremity of that event warns us not to aestheticize politics, it also teaches us to appreciate the aesthetic in itself, to develop it as a precious and sustainable experience, a vitality apart that challenges political monomania. When Wordsworth writes, "The sunshine is a glorious birth," he need not be thinking of politics because he also wrote, about the French Revolution, "Bliss was it in that dawn to be alive."

My last item of unfinished business is the disputed status of literature itself. Two types of terrorism (to employ Jean Paulhan's word) direct themselves against literary speaking and thinking. The first attacks literary language in the name of clarity, understood as logical clarity, or a common sense without figures, tropes, "flowers of speech." It insists on the short-term profitability of language, on an immediate yield for nation and culture.

A second type of terrorism seeks to purify art in the name of a more complex ideal: that of a sacred language, an adamic or archaic "universal character." As a father tongue it may lead to purity of diction but as a recovered and vernal mother tongue, as Dante's "illustrious vernacular," it sets the pattern for the development of national literatures in the Renaissance.[22] Heidegger's language of Being is a mixed case: innovative in Heidegger's practice yet dangerous in theory, for it could be used to support a linguistic nationalism seeking to purge from the mother tongue "impure" historical accretions, including foreign words, described by Adorno sardonically as "the Jews of language."

Both language critiques combine with other motivations wishing to keep speech "honest." That honesty is constantly impugned (Hamlet to Ophelia: "Are you honest?") as if language *in the world* were necessarily insincere or equivocal, a false confession or a hypocritical, entrapping rhetoric. The very multiplication of discourses, and our exacerbated awareness of the mediated nature of significance, increases the subversive feeling that all is rhetoric, an unreal rhetoric of the unreal.[23] Culture talk would then be the latest, most formalized instance of such rhetoric.

Realism in modern art fights that unreality. Yet the very attempt to be as realistic as possible, to represent extreme experiences, has made the issue of *silence* (the withholding of speech because of terror, trauma, or disgust) a constant topic of literary reflection. So Maurice Blanchot, aware of the stifling effect of trauma, and especially of political terror, tries to formulate what is involved in writing about disaster: "One must in the end speak dangerously and dangerously remain silent in the very act of breaking this silence."[24]

Sentences like that receive a special pathos from the European experience, from speech that has had to function under foreign occupation and a dictatorial regime. I ask readers to consider that experience, though England and the United States have escaped it. The alternative to making a virtue out of duress and producing equivocal or enigmatic modes of expression is to develop a style that overcomes muteness but not "the reticent domain that is the source of what has to be thought."[25] However, the desire for that kind of integrity often associates itself with a lost relationship to earth, land, rural virtue. In Europe, the pernicious influence on politics of converging pastoral and apocalyptic perspectives usurps the concept of culture and reinforces (as I show specifically in chapter 3) an anti-urban provincialism, or a sentimental belief in a golden age, or other resentful evocations of a prior and original greatness. Yet the link of literature to a more contemplative or aesthetic mode of perception cannot be dismissed, and I try to explain throughout this book the "active silence" of the written word.

In the final analysis, it comes down to the "Question of Our Speech," including the statements by which we justify national institutions and habitual ways of thinking and acting. Not only art itself but the way we value it defines a culture. The authors I discuss are critics in the fullest sense: they examine a *mutual* obligation, the way art and organized cultures interact. But can art become aesthetic education without succumbing to cultural politics?

The task of the critic becomes more difficult as well as fascinating because significant art like Wordsworth's or Thoreau's does not represent what is the case but brings something virtual into existence, which then has the force of imaginative fact. The love Freud conjures up at the end of *Civilization and its Discontents* may also be such a fact. However destabilizing or anarchic it is, genius in art leaves an imprint that changes, perhaps forever, what we see and believe. As Shelley says of Keats's effect on Nature: "There is heard / His voice in all her music." The fateful question, then, is not whether what Freud identifies as a death drive can ever be overcome, for Thanatos is as immortal as Eros and genius partakes of both. The question is whether culture can diminish aggression and tilt the balance toward love. Here aesthetic education has its place and is all the more urgent at a time when "culture" has become an inflammatory word that kindles actual wars.

NOTES

1. "The Crisis in Culture," *Between Past and Future: Six Exercises in Political Thought* (New York: Viking, 1961), 209.

2. "La guerre politique impliquant la guerre des cultures, cela est proprement une invention de notre temps et qui lui assure une place insigne dans l'histoire morale de l'humanité" (*La trahison des clercs* [Paris: Grasset, 1927], 33). Benda's statement may not be literally true, in that older, religiously inspired wars, for example, were also cultural wars, but Benda is influenced by the conception that the First World War was a cultural war, pitting a certain German "mentality" against, in particular, French civilization. Emile Durkheim, for example, in *L'Allemagne au-dessus de tout: La mentalité allemande et la guerre*, first published by the Librairie Armand Colin in 1915 (republished in 1991), claims that there is "an entire mental and moral system that, constituted above all with war in mind, remained during peacetime in the back of people's heads." He then describes this mentality by deriving it from the works of the historian Heinrich von Treitschke.

3. Clifford Geertz, *The Interpretation of Cultures* (London: Hutchinson, 1975), 5.

4. For a recent ambitious speculation, see Samuel P. Huntingdon, *The Clash of Civilizations and the Remaking of World Order* (New York: Simon and Schuster, 1996).

5. Germany is a special case: its belated literary renaissance coincides with romanticism and comes before its unification as a nation-state.

6. William Collins, "Ode on the Poetical Character" (1746).

7. This development is less clear in England than on the Conti-

nent. Some romantic poets, such as Hölderlin, pursue a radical classicism, directed against a previous—usually French—neoclassicism.
The replacement of French cultural hegemony by a native genius
truer to the spirit of the ancients shows the culture-political motive. For
Hölderlin, Germany is classical ground or, more precisely, his "translation" of the spirit of the ancients will reveal that his native German
land is their true successor.

    8. 1850 *Prelude* 1.31–37.

    9. Richard Poirier, *The Renewal of Literature* (New York: Random
House, 1987), 88. For "the antagonism in [Emerson's] writing between what he calls 'genius' and the institutions represented for him
by the word 'culture,' " see Poirier's entire first chapter, "The Question
of Genius."

    10. My translation. In this and what follows I quote from Nietzsche's
1873 "Untimely Observations" ("Unzeitgemäße Betrachtungen").

    11. My choice of Nietzsche to demonstrate the problematic of cul-
ture in modernity is not arbitrary. Consider Robert Musil's comment of
around 1923 on a "symptomatic" Germany: "What has become clear in
the German case—this moral situation that no longer finds a point of
reference in itself, but looks for one in the past (race, nation, religion,
old-fashioned simplicity and strength, uncorrupted goodness)—is the
latent spiritual situation of Europe as a whole. To regard the Germans
as a symptom means, in other words, to raise the whole problem of civilization" (*Precision and Soul: Essays and Addresses*, ed. and trans.
Burton Pike and David S. Luft [Chicago: University of Chicago Press,
1990], 161). In the 1950s, and centering on France, Fanon's postcolonial
appeal is the precise obverse of Musil's understanding of Germany's
incapacity to find "a point of reference in itself." His "On National
Culture," in *The Wretched of the Earth*, rejects not only European cultural models as contaminated or belonging to an outmoded passive resistance ("Quand je cherche l'homme dans la technique et dans le style
européens, je vois une succession de négations de l'homme, une ava-
lanche de meurtres") but also a resuscitation of local color and folklore,
of "coutume," as the deterioration of a destroyed culture or at best the
"revêtement visible" of a subterranean life. Like Nietzsche (though unable to reapply the classics), he evokes the *universalism* of the missing

ideal through the force of his accusatory style: "Décidons de ne pas imiter l'Europe et bandons nous nos muscles et nos cerveaux dans une direction nouvelle. Tâchons d'inventer l'homme total que l'Europe a été incapable de faire triompher" (Frantz Fanon, "Sur la culture nationale" and "Conclusion," *Les damnés de la terre* [Paris: François Maspero, 1961], 240).

12. From the preparatory drafts to "On the Use and Abuse of History," the second of his "Untimely Observations" of 1873. My translation.

13. I should distinguish, however briefly, my concept of cultural causation from that of the New Historicism. In an exemplary thinker of that movement like Louis Montrose, there is a brilliantly demonstrated emphasis on the "dialectical" character of that causation: the work of art, such as a Shakespeare play, is never the passive outcome of socioeconomic factors. The play creates the culture, as well as being created by it: this gives weight to the otherwise overused phrase "cultural production." Montrose's analyses in *The Purpose of Playing: Shakespeare and the Cultural Politics of the Elizabethan Theatre* (Chicago: University of Chicago Press, 1996) intend to convince us of the existence of both formative social forces (reflected in the text as "social text") and the contribution of the text itself, the power of its "shaping fantasies." Yet what is hard to distinguish here is the precise influence of the artist's work: there is often a dialectical blur as Shakespeare becomes a sort of primal historical scene, the paradigm case of a rich interplay that could go on and on, without a clear result except the work of art itself. The so-called dialectic, then, ends in a swollen moment of stasis. My claim for Wordsworth's influence is both more complicated and less modest: the *imaginaire* created is not so much a heightened picture of forces within a specific historical moment as the *transmission* of a *potentiality* whose realism and idealism can no longer be distinguished and that we reclaim, whether it actually existed or not. In Wordsworth's case (here my immodesty shows itself) I argue that there was a beneficial political influence, at least over the long run. In Shakespeare's case, however profoundly he depicts character and politics, new-historical interpreters have not demonstrated the actual sociopolitical impact of his work but rather a theory about its role in at once sharing and shaping the *imaginaire* of his time. It remains

unclear what stabilizes the destabilizing text or makes it endure as a "dramatistic paradigm of social life based upon the interaction of protean players" (209) or a "site of convergence of various and potentially contradictory cultural discourses" (xii). Would a playhouse such as the Globe have been "a new kind of social and cognitive space" (210) without Shakespeare's plays? Did, in fact, the "absolutist theatricality" of the state "become subject to appropriation and destabilization" (210) when performed in the playhouse? Everything tends to become the metonym of everything else in Montrose. The strongest argument for Shakespeare's as for Wordsworth's enduring influence is that they still participate in the way we think and feel, that they hold up a mirror to us, in the present.

14. "Stanzas from the Grande Chartreuse," ll. 85–86. Arnold visited this famous monastery (disestablished after the French Revolution) in 1851, and his poem was published in 1855. The monastery had figured in Wordsworth's Prelude (not published till 1850) as symbol of a venerable aspect of the past that should have remained inviolate.

15. Some of Adorno's remarks on the defamation of imagination and, after Comte's sociology, its repressive compartmentalization ("Abdrängung in einem arbeitsteiligen Spezialbereich") sound wonderfully like the counter-Enlightenment polemics of William Blake. But Adorno has little to say about the romantic reaction, despite the fact that the reification of imagination and that faculty's increasingly abstract position vis-à-vis real life ("ein Urphänomen der Regression bürgerlichen Geistes" [an aboriginal phenomenon of the regressiveness of the bourgeois mentality]) are countered by the visionary labors of poets like Blake. For Adorno, see especially his edition of Der Positivismusstreit in der deutschen Soziologie (Neuwied-Berlin: Luchterhand, 1969).

16. La société du spectacle (Paris: Buchet/Chastel, 1967), 149: "La culture est le lieu de la recherche de l'unité perdue. Dans cette recherche de l'unité, la culture comme sphère séparée est obligée de se nier elle-même." On the impasse in the idea of culture, see also appendix 1.

17. "The wind, the light, the air, the smell of a flower affects me with violent emotions" (letter from Shelley to Claire Clairmont, 16 January 1821).

18. Cf. Benedict Anderson, Imagined Communities, rev. ed. (New

York: Verso, 1991). Anderson sees in the nation a new form of cohesion (as older cultural certainties are declining): the nation links once more "fraternity, power and time." He singles out what he calls "print-capitalism" as an especially effective force for arbitrary and anonymous linkages. My point is somewhat different from his: common sense (in the Kantian meaning of the term) or shared feelings arising from *stabilities* in nature and perception are linked in the eighteenth century to the field of the aesthetic and suggest a different basis (more difficult to nationalize) for community.

19. Cf. David Simpson, *The Academic Postmodern: A Report on Half-knowledge* (New York: Routledge, 1995).

20. This is not to say that a free play of ideas should keep us permanent intellectual playboys. On the contrary, play should be taken as seriously as Huizinga suggests in *Homo Ludens* (1939), a book conscious of the shadow of fascism. Our institutions reflect the spirit of (competitive) play from which they arise, even after their rules have been codified. Art and its cultural ramifications are a reminder, both forceful and delightful, of unbound energies—anarchic, self-pleasuring—behind and within codification. The fading of what Zygmunt Bauman has called the "legislative" (and colonial) role of the intellectuals, has brought a compensation: "Having reached the nadir of their political significance, modern intellectuals enjoy freedom of thought and expression they could not dream of at the time that words mattered politically" (*Intimations of Postmodernity* [New York: Routledge, 1992], 16). Except, he adds, this freedom is then alienated by a new power, the market, the increasing subordination of culture to consumer society.

21. The political effectiveness of ideas depends in the short run—but this can affect millions of people and for several generations—on their seeming unity, on being frozen into truth by ontology or ideology. Here the radically political side of writers like Derrida and Blanchot shows itself. Derrida in *Specters of Marx*, developing Blanchot's essay "The Three Voices of Marx," demonstrates a hidden polyphony, or voices within an apparently unified ideology that continue to haunt it like spectral emanations. He suggests a linking of the democratic process with a respect for the deliverances of time and the liberating if complicating analysis he undertakes. Marx's legacy is—certainly in the long

run—far from univocal: what we come to see and (to an extent) admire is how tenaciously different voices and even contradictions are kept together (synthesized) in a body of writing frayed by ghosts (revenants). "If the readability of a legacy were given, natural, transparent, univocal, if it did not call for and at the same time defy interpretation, we would never have anything to inherit from it. We would be affected by it as by a cause—natural or genetic" (*Specters of Marx: The State of the Debt, the Work of Mourning, and the New International* [New York: Routledge, 1994], 16).

22. Benedict Anderson is correct in seeing that "a particular script-language [which] offered privileged access to ontological truth" is a fundamental cultural conception whose recession is one of the factors necessitating a new concept of "imagined community" (*Imagined Communities*, chapter 2). But the persistence of this hieratic, visionary, quasi-magical *logos* into the era of nationalism shows itself in the disputed status of literature, which often remains ambiguously both on the side of the demotic/secular and that of holiness.

23. See Christine Brooke-Rose, A *Rhetoric of the Unreal: Studies in Narrative and Structure, Especially of the Fantastic* (Cambridge: Cambridge University Press, 1981). It is my sense that Rousseau's positing of a "pure state of nature" and his famous First Discourse on "whether the restoration of the Sciences and Arts has contributed to the purification of morals," which sees them contributing rather to a corruption of morals, is motivated by a contradiction between the honest man and his speech and the "honnête homme" (his socialized equivalent) and his speech. Rousseau's extraordinary self-consciousness as a writer shows him encompassed by, if not trapped in, a rhetorical situation that is bound to compromise him despite his effort at overturning hypocrisy of speech and morals. See chapter 3, "The Question of Our Speech."

24. *The Writing of the Disaster*, trans. Ann Smock (Lincoln: University of Nebraska Press, 1986).

25. Heidegger, quoted in Steven Unger, *Scandal and Aftereffect: Blanchot and France since 1930* (Minneapolis: University of Minnesota Press, 1995). I am indebted to Unger for bringing Heidegger's and Blanchot's statements together. The exact nature of Heidegger's reserve, though partially explored by Derrida and Blanchot (see chapter

4 below) remains obscure. I am not arguing, of course, that this emer-gence of "silence" is reducible to a specific experience, however com-plex—of the war, for example, or the Occupation or the Holocaust—but that these events led to a new and radical thinking about speech and writing.

chapter two
Culture and the Abstract Life

"This is not a real world. This life is not the real life." "But you're really suffering, I said." "Yes," Tang said, "It's a problem, this real suffering in a not-real world." — PHILIP GOUREVITCH, *"The Boat People"*

           I begin with a feeling; then I throw some history after that feeling, hoping it will stick, spark, or make the feeling and its consequences (rather than its causes) more visible.

The feeling is that of being an outsider to life. Not just to social life or a particular group that I aspire to join, although this wish may play a part, but to participation (perhaps always mystical) in life itself. I want to be a part of all I perceive; I want to know myself, not only my processes of knowing. I want to share, be part of, the feelings of others and not simply feel for them, sympathize in an abstract way. The sense, moreover, that someone else (even more uncannily, something else) may be living my life can become psychologically unsettling. The search for identity, which never seems to cease, plays its role in this strong and potentially pathological fantasy that others live my life, a life I want to live—fully—myself.

It is also at the level of *ideological explanation* that I want to intervene, in order to explore how attributions of causes and prescriptions of remedies may have consequences that are destructive rather than creative. But I should first describe this feeling that it is not exaggerated to call a phantomization, one that makes a ghost of us, even a vengeful ghost, while we are still alive, patently flesh and blood. That it can be trivialized, and is found in most popular literature as a belief in ghosts or spirits, that it is *permitted* in this form or gleefully *exploited*, merely shows its inveterate hold. For the purpose of description, however, I turn to examples from canonical poetry and fiction.

Shelley's atheistic mysticism seems to come from an overwhelming sense of powers residing in nature or the cosmos. Intuiting those powers suggests that life on earth is the mere shadow of another world to which fuller access comes with death. Shelley is quite aware of the seduction of this thought, and he cannot always decide whether to follow or to resist it. Despite the Enlightenment he remains unawakened, wrapped in spiritual and ghostly feelings that fail to bring revelation:

> I look on high;
> Has some unknown omnipotence unfurled
> The veil of life and death? Or do I lie
> In dream, and does the mightier world of sleep
> Spread far around and inaccessibly
> Its circles?[1]

In "Adonais," prompted by the death of fellow poet John Keats, this dreamy uncertainty about the intersection of life and eternity—his phrase "the veil of life and death" evokes a mixed or occulted condition—leads him into the overpowering temptation to conjure up, if only in dream vision, what is behind the veil and to merge with it, even if it proves to be the power of blackness:

> The breath whose might I have invoked in song
> Descends on me; my spirit's bark is driven,
> Far from the shore, far from the trembling throng
> Whose sails were never to the tempest given;
> The massy earth and sphered skies are riven!
> I am borne darkly, fearfully, afar.[2]

Shelley becomes his own Charon in a movement that rejects Wordsworth's trivial "sky-canoe" (in *Peter Bell*), anticipates Rimbaud's "drunken boat," and depicts an impulse deriving from inspiration rather than impotence but therefore all the more persuasive and suicidal.

My second example is the plot of one of the most uncanny short stories ever composed. An exemplary Gothic fantasy, its influence reached Dostoyevsky. Friedrich Schiller's *Der Geisterseher* (The visionary) recounts how the prince of a small German state who is visiting Venice begins to experience strange phenomena that rouse his self-awareness. They seem to be accidental or unplanned and therefore impinge on him as omens. Behind their exotic trappings, is there more than a psychological truth, such as our propensity to succumb to what psychoanalysts have called "ideas of reference"?

A troupe of young girls and boys, all in theatrical dress, welcomed us with a dance that was a pantomime. It was inventive; lightness and grace inspired every gesture. Before it was completely finished, the leading dancer, who played a queen, seemed suddenly arrested by an invisible hand. Lifeless she stood, as did everyone around her. The music stopped. In the whole assembly you could not hear a breath, and she stood there, her eyes fixed on the ground, withdrawn, paralyzed. Then, suddenly, with the fury of inspiration, she startled, looked around her wildly—"A King is among us," she cried, tore the crown from her head and . . . laid it at the feet of the Prince. Everyone there now turned to look at him.

Such incidents, which single out the prince as if he were chosen to embody a mysterious destiny, are expertly Gothic, indebted to a late eighteenth-century formula in which preternatural episodes intrigue the reader as well and induce a state of wonderment or suspension of judgment. Is it still possible, given an enlightened age, to believe in the supernatural: in marvelous, extraterrestrial influences? Eventually, of course, the reader's "hesitation," as Todorov calls it in his fine book *The Fantastic*, is resolved. After the permitted shudder, which Schiller extends to paranoid detail and length, strengthening a genre that continues to exert its formulaic charm on Thomas Mann's *Death in Venice* (remember the strange incidents that befall Aschenbach and entice him toward his fate?), the Gothic tale's miraculous parts are then exposed as machinery, not yet that of the artist, but the machination of a mortal and devilish conspiracy. This pattern of the *surnatural expliqué* still dominates, suitably adjusted, modern detective fiction, where the corpse is "explained," laid to rest, as it were, by the plot's ingenious if temporary challenge to the reasoning reason.

In Schiller's mystery story it turns out that the Catholic Church is behind it all: it wished to have this Protestant prince convert to Catholicism, to make him a vassal of Rome and to that end decided that his capacity for wonder had to be renewed as a first step. But the reader easily exits this polemical frame. We know that what is at stake is poetry, or the faculty of wonder itself: the romantics' fear, and ours, that a progressive disenchantment of the world, associated with the Age of Reason, will make outsiders of us all. Indeed, Schiller's paradigmatic story leaves us in limbo, in suspense between two coldnesses, that of a world without its animating supernatural, without gods or ghosts, genii or genial surprises, and a world created by those who engineer spiritual revolutions, who exploit and instrumentalize our obstinate hunger for the wonderful, which remains a dream always ready to enter the waking life. Therefore the Gothic persists in Brockden Brown, Hawthorne, and Melville, in cultic horror movies or science fiction, in Bergman's *The Magician*, Yeats's *A Vision*, or Bunuel's experiments with surrealism.

My third example comprises evocative lines from Wallace Stevens's "The Rock" that point to the passage of time as the abstracting or ghosting principle yet hardly explain why mutability should have this effect:

> It is an illusion that we were ever alive,
> Lived in the houses of mothers, arranged ourselves
> By our own motions in a freedom of air.

It is just this fading or fugacity, moreover, that challenges the poet "as if nothingness contained a métier." From the void of memory or desire or from an absence he calls "the remotest cleanliness of heaven," from this unreal a simulacrum springs, a fiction of the real. It challenges the fallacious, anthropomorphic imagination. "Less and less human, O savage spirit." Whatever the ultimate source of such "Phantomerei," Stevens orchestrates it, draws from it an extraordinary decorum.

Postmodernists will say at this point that Stevens has it the wrong way around: the unreal springs from our accelerating capacity to fashion simulacra. Indeed, Jean Baudrillard challenges the notion of "taking place." Everything tends toward a condition of *non-lieu*, even as our desire for authentic or auratic objects (in Walter Benjamin's sense) is artificially stimulated.[3] But I have said I do not want to speculate on the causes of, or historicize, this acute sense of phantomization. Instead of multiplying instances of it—dramatic exhibits would be Mallarmé's well-publicized struggle with the *Néant* or Virginia Woolf's portrait of Rhoda in *The Waves*—let me quote a deeply moving and ironic passage from Emily Dickinson, in which the desire to live frustrates itself, creates an overestimation, a sense of panic that distances passion from fulfillment in the same way that the Parousia of divine presence is deferred in Christianity:

> I cannot live with You—
> It would be Life—
> And Life is over there—
> Behind the Shelf
> The Sexton keeps the Key to—[4]

Yet pride of place in my symptomatic anthology must go to Hegel's *Phenomenology of Mind*. Hegel accompanies a description of this dissociated or abstracted state, this feeling that life is a phantom, or elsewhere, or haunted by something other than what we see, with an acknowledgment that only an odyssey, as he says, a close to interminable historical and dialectical process, can fill the void. Hegel's epic history of humanity will (1) make us aware of all "the forms of unreal consciousness," (2) show that "the exposition of untrue consciousness in its untruth is not a merely negative progress" (this should inhibit the charge of negativism or nihilism), (3) disclose that it is in the character of conscious life, as distinguished from "a life of nature," to suffer a "violence at its own hands in progressing beyond the determinate," to *alienate* itself in order to go forward and be fulfilled. Even the Here and the Now are too abstract in their immediacy: when we try to hold them fast in writing, they are unmasked as empty or labile impressions. Our wishful endowment of objects of sense with being, and our disappointment in them as they become, inevitably, mere symbols, as they betray their self-insufficiency, is a lesson that even the animals can teach us. They know instinctively the religious skepticism taught by the Eleusinian mysteries, as Hegel tells us in a passage that is itself quite wonderful: "[Animals] do not stand stock still before things of sense as if these were things *per se*, with being in themselves: they despair of this reality altogether, and in complete assurance of the nothingness of things they fall-to without more ado and eat them up. And all nature proclaims, as animals do, these open secrets, these mysteries revealed to all, which teach what the truth of things of sense is."[5]

My announced subject is culture, not a primordial feeling. But I have a good if daunting precedent in Freud, whose *Civilization and its Discontents (Das Unbehagen in der Kultur)*[6] also begins by speculating on a feeling, although one that is eudaemonic rather than daemonic and so perhaps the obverse of what I have described. I would prefer, of course, to keep some suspense as to how I will get from ghostliness to culture, but since there will be enough shoals and indirections to negotiate, let me state my argument at this point. "Culture" at present—I mean the ring and function of the word, its emotional and conceptual resonance—even when it is abusively applied, keeps hope in *embodiment* alive. Consciousness, as ghostly as ever, cannot renounce that hope in a living and fulfilling milieu. "We live in a place that is not our own," Stevens writes; such honesty, however, is a torment. He continues, therefore: "And hard it is in spite of blazoned days."[7]

I need not emphasize that the strongest imaginative needs are also those most likely to be trivialized, even deliberately "wasted." Whenever a novel, biography, news story or new historical essay begins in the manner of "It was a cold and foggy evening . . . ,"[8] this is a repetition of a venerable technique, called "composition of place," that continues to stir us deeply and tritely. It is also a fact that with the advent of television a new kind of communal memory is created, promoting false embodiments, charged images that are the equivalent of fixed ideas. Artists must work with these as well as against them. Yet historically each superrealism proves to be a phantom. Ideologies of culture, which are as dangerous and effective as the art they inspire, also exploit our reality hunger by proposing "a cure of the ground" (Stevens, "The Rock").[9]

That phrase, "a cure of the ground," remembers culture as cultivation. But in Stevens it is also a euphemism for death. Nothing, he implies, can relieve us of imagination except imagination itself, even as that faculty conceives, ironically, its own demise and so approaches both the "plain sense of things" and an absence of the imagining self close to death. I take that to be the meaning of "a cure of ourselves, that is equal to a cure / Of the ground, a cure beyond forgetfulness." The rock—from which Stevens's poem derives its title—exists, but not as a foundation; it is, necessarily, the motive for metaphor. A restless imagination localizes itself by a pseudospecification that is not unlike love's fantasia. This rock, or "the gray particular of man's life," is transformed, humanized; its barrenness becomes, through poetry, "a thousand things." The spirit seeks, that is, the local, not the literal: indeed, to advocate that cure of the ground as a literal "blood and soil" doctrine would curse the ground.

Yet we should not ignore the political backdrop of this distinction between local and literal. The cosmopolitan ideal of "civilization"—the Enlightenment picture of the world citizen—has proved to be too vague, has not engaged our full imaginative and symbolic powers. "If we are dreaming of a 'national culture' today," Van Wyck Brooks writes in 1918, "it is because our inherited culture has so utterly failed to meet the exigencies of our life, to seize and fertilize its roots." And, he adds sarcastically, "that is why we are so terribly at ease in the Zion of world culture."[10] Indeed, intellectual history teaches us that "culture" achieves its pathos as a counterconcept to "civilization," especially in Germany. Consider Max Weber's famous definition: "Culture is something finite, excerpted by human thought from a senseless and boundless world history, and invested with sense and meaning."[11]

In such definitions the feeling of nonpresence I have described seeps back and infects the very ideas intended to exorcise it. We continue to sense an incipient nihilism. This nihilism can turn against culture as well as nature, renounce all hope in secular incarnation, and become near-apocalyptic.[12] Theology and metaphysics have always engaged with a desire that is distinct from mere need in that it cannot be assuaged. The relation between idealism and skepticism, as in Plato, or of spiritualism and the anxiety of being perpetually excluded from true knowledge, as perhaps in Descartes, also points to a phantomization that lies just beneath the proud architectonics of philosophy, religion, and art and leads to the Pandemonium of political theologies.[13] Moreover, sociology has recently suggested that the dominant class creates and sustains itself by a principle of "aesthetic" distinction that limits both use and exchange value, a principle I interpret as a way of pursuing embodiment through a continually reinforced self-inclusion.[14] By a systematic, continuous, and institutionalized closure, we remain insiders. No wonder Bourdieu writes: "There is no way out of the game of culture."

So, after documenting the modern explosion of "culture" as word and idea, I want to ask: are not images of embodiment that haunt us and feelings of abstractness or nonembodiment that tell us we are not real enough, or that we inhabit the wrong body, the postreligious source of ideologies whose explanatory and remedial strictures increase rather than lessen abstraction and too often incite a cannibalistic violence far greater than that of Hegel's animals?

It is here, also, with this kind of question, that one encounters Marx's strength as an imaginative and consequent thinker. He would claim that I have described the "ghostly objectivity" of reified life, "Monsieur Le Capital and Madame La Terre ghost-walking," but divorced it from its foundation in the socioeconomic realities of capitalism by depicting the ghost feeling as independent and permanent, "as the timeless model of human relations in general."[15] Like Hegel, I have stood matters on their head and not understood that my suspicion of postreligious ideologies is itself deeply ideological. Marx's vivid sense of alienated labor and damaged life brings a specific formula for reform and so for hope; unfortunately, all attempts to embody that reform by revolutionary change, to remove the false mystique of reified gods or human goods, have so far not exorcised the ghost feeling but continue to water it with blood.

Culture speech is an aspect of our culture: everything now tends to be seen in culture terms. "Culture" has become our most prevalent "complex word," to use Empson's striking phrase.[16] There is no mystery about its linguistic development, starting with Cicero's metaphor "cultura animi": culture of the soul, rather than of earth or deities associated with agriculture. (The transferred meaning, as Hannah Arendt points out, fortifies the intuition that the soul needs a human habitation, a dwelling place that does not simply subject nature to man.[17]) The well-known ambiguity of the genitive allows the construction "the culture of" to go in two semantic directions. One is the dynamic or functional meaning, as when we construe Rémy de Gourmont's "culture of ideas" to mean "cultivating the ideas," developing, understanding them better; the dynamic meaning is also aptly caught by John Stuart Mill, when he praises the "culture of the feelings" transmitted by Wordsworth's poetry. The other direction of the genitive focuses on the formal product, the "culture" produced by this activity. When a police department claims that it is "the culture of the agency" to undertake certain procedures, the second kind of meaning has taken over, though the first persists.[18]

A world in which a Paris street still bears the name "La culture de Sainte Cathérine" and that advertises a book *Beyond Beef: The Rise and Fall of the Cattle Culture* remains unified in the sense that we catch the connection between cult and agriculture;[19] at the same time the gap between provincial and global, between the church as a toponymic institution (however universal its hopes) and mass technology, can jar us into a sense of nostalgia about local attachments. The same is true when writers try to suggest a link between place and spirit, as if "culture" were continuous with soil and climate: "the peculiar flavor," we read, "of that old New England culture, so dry, so crisp, so dogmatic, so irritating."[20] Even if such expressions as "mass culture," "popular culture," "working-class culture," and "inmate culture" (Erving Goffman) make a certain sense—because they point to a sizable group, a quantitative spread, and because they are often applied in a provocative or questioning way (is *this* what or where culture is today?)—surely the quantitative factor is not defining, except as an undertone of anxiety, in such offshoots as camera culture, gun culture, service culture, museum culture, deaf culture, football culture, bruising culture (boxing, and all who follow the sport), the "insistently oral culture of Washington" (i.e., gossip and slander), the culture of dependency, the culture of pain, the culture of amnesia, etc.[21] Why has this word taken over, like a linguistic weed? Let me add some examples of its proliferation.

An average day. In the New York Times, *after the Jefferson High School killings, there is mention of a "culture of hidden weaponry." My* London Review of Books, *just out, describes a new theory speculating that the origin of culture was in a "sex strike," during which the females, in order to defeat the "alpha male," a macho type capable of inseminating many of them one after the other, devised a way of hiding their ovulation. This so-called strike gave the averagely sexed male a chance and increased female control of the entire matter. Here culture does not mean lifestyle but the control of nature.*

But what does "Adjusting to Japan's Car Culture" mean, a headline on the first page of the next day's business section? Does it refer to the role cars play in the life of the Japanese, with a suggestion that cars run them (an inversion of culture managing nature)? The article actually describes the "corporate culture" of Japanese industry and the difficulty American executives have fitting in. (Headlines are the one place in a newspaper where condensation permits striking and even malicious ambiguities. Perhaps we should talk of a "headline culture.") "Culture," in the cases just cited, generally takes on the meaning of a habitual way of doing things that claims to express a basic national or group trait, as if it were "the nonhereditary memory of the community."[22] But principally the word serves as a means to age a modern practice instantly, to give a product—obviously of our making—traditional status.

This is problematic, of course. The anthropological meaning of "culture" as a traditional way of life[23] is now extended to cover what is merely a lifestyle, whose legitimacy does not derive from tradition but precisely from what challenges tradition: modern technology. It is ironic that a word that Nietzsche had defined as "a unity of artistic style manifest in all the vital activities [*Lebensäusserungen*] of a people"[24] and that for the greater part of its semantic career in English denotes "the harmonious development of the whole person" (Raymond Williams), a development compensating for scientific and industrial specialization, now presents that specialization itself as the basis of a way of life.[25]

While one is tempted to see this antithetical extension of meaning as parody rather than paradox, it could not have prevailed without something attractive in the very notion of cultural history. What is suggested, beginning with Vico, is a view of history (he says "civil society" and "the world of nations") as human creation, a history, therefore, that we can understand, reinvent, and even control. The diversity of historical event, as well as the creative energy of a historical writing that changes nature from indifferent background to cultural milieu, raises the hope that Stevens will be proved wrong in his rearguard action on behalf of the universe: "It is the human that is the alien, / The human that has no cousin in the moon." Yet has our knowledge of history and nature as it leads to power over them worked to our benefit? This is the great post-Enlightenment issue, which confronts us daily.[26]

For this entrepreneurial vision of human development could be an illusion fostered by advanced capitalism; it is not, moreover, entirely absent from Marxism.[27] Whereas "culture" used to point to the way we organized our leisure time (the culture page of the newspaper, which sees no difference between culture and entertainment, reflects and abets that meaning), a not-so-subtle reversal has recently taken place. It makes "changing the culture" shorthand for an alteration in habits of work rather than of leisure, an alteration, for example, that might benefit the national economy or industrial policy.[28] Thus it includes the recognition that we now have greater powers to shape the environment but also that habits of the workplace carry over into our free or leisure time. As a result, the concept of leisure as the realm of freedom (freedom from governmental or social interference as well as from toil) weakens, even though our power to alter nature or society has significantly increased. Culture, I read, "is imagined as a plastic medium which politically powerful social elites may rework and remould at will"; indeed, when such "reworking" is shorn of its exclusively economic goal, such as improvement of productivity in the workplace, then "culture" moves very close to the sense it has in contemporary culture studies.

> Culture is thought of as directly bound up with work and its organization; with the relations of power and gender in the workplace and the home; with the pleasures and the pressures of consumption; with the complex relations of class and kith and kin through which a sense of self is formed; and with the fantasies and desires through which social relations are carried and actively shaped. . . . It is not a detached domain for playing games of social distinction and "good" taste. It is a network of representations—texts, images, talk, codes of behaviour, and the narrative structures organizing these—which shapes every aspect of social life.[29]

That same day, entering Phelps Gateway at Yale, I see a metal coat hanger with the inscription: "This is not a medical instrument." I think: to understand a symbol like this requires some knowledge of a specific cultural context. Damn it, culture again, in the cultural studies aspect of a "network of representations" that shapes social life. What has to be recalled is, first, the abortion debates of fin-de-siècle America. Then, to savor the exhibit fully, Magritte's well-known picture of a pipe with the motto: "This is not a pipe." For something like the metal hanger is, alas, too often used as a medical instrument. The hanger is not a clever symbol drawing attention to the difference between art and reality but an object highlighting an underground practice that society denies or refuses to take responsibility for. The negative ("This is not . . .") serves to affirm the existence of the practice.

Here "cultural context" points not only to a specific social situation but also to a scandalous mode of representation that made toilets into works of art and generally disrespected boundaries, especially those between private and public, popular and sophisticated, marginal and established. (Picasso's Venus de Gaz, *a burner framed as a fetish, mocks our own art fetishism.) But this mode—related to Murray Krieger's "fall of the elite object"[30]—cannot entirely control the meaning of the symbols it creates: their transgressive character transcends any assigned, stable significance, so that the cheap wire hook that stands for the endangering and demeaning of women forced into back-alley abortions may also evoke a violence intrinsic to all acts of abortion, whatever the instrument. The pro-choice symbol becomes ominous when it links up with an unlimited claim to control nature, with the idea that culture reinvents nature and could desanctify or instrumentalize life.*

Now science enters, as Bacon's improvement of nature, implicit even in such common phrases as "cell culture,"[31] but also as it tends to challenge, by alternatives, long-established social patterns. A pro-choice fantasy, a feminist tract as visionary as Erasmus Darwin's Love of the Plants, *is entitled* Simians, Cyborgs, and Women: The Reinvention of Nature.[32] *It describes a potential liberation of the body more radical than N. O. Brown's* Life against Death *or* Love's Body *by treating physical intercourse as an evolutionary stage, with the present state of affairs as stodgy as the nuclear family. For literary readers Donna Haraway writes a form of science fiction based, like Ferenczi's* Thalassa, *on biological (now sociobiological) data. But where Ferenczi was interested in the genealogy of sexual feelings and drives, in how our evolutionary past has influenced present comminglings, Haraway is resolutely future-oriented and therefore ends with the conviction: "Science is culture." Not a culture, mind you, as in C. P. Snow's* The Two Cultures, *which deplored that the specialization endemic to modern society had divorced scientists and humanists.[33]*

Of course, not all uses of "culture" converge. But whatever the word touches receives at present a sort of credibility. One hears of a smokers' culture, of [Australia's] beach culture: do such things really exist? The point is that the term bestows, like rights language

run amok, a certain dignity, one that is based not so much on numbers as on a sense that *a meaningful nucleus of life, a form of social
existence, has emerged or is emerging*. And we pay attention to it, I
suggest, because social fragmentation means two things that together amount to a disabling paradox: the general culture seems too distant or alien, while the hope for some unity of being—which I call
embodiment—can migrate to groupings often held together by
parochial, sectarian, self-serving, and even antisocial interests.[34]

These interests range from the folklore of indigenous or immigrant cultures, or the practices of a religious cult that has broken with
a mainstream denomination, to the lifestyle of gay people or the
agenda of political, commercial, and even criminal organizations (a
TV report on the Bank of Credit and Commerce International talked
as easily of "BCCI's criminal culture" as of a "Washington culture").
So abusive is the extension of the word, so strong and vulgar its pathos, that I begin to understand an Africanist claim about the West.
It is alleged that an ingrained Cartesianism has *ghosted* the colonizers, abstracted them from life, so that "culture" becomes a dream for
what is missing, a phantom or proxy comforting the "white-man-
who-has-problems-believing-in-his-own-existence."[35]

Yet, to repeat, not all uses of "culture" converge. In fact, the proliferation of the word in the sense I have singled out is only part of
the picture, if a part that seems to have taken over. The *other* major
sense of the word, as in "high culture" or "a cultured person" or
Arnold's *Culture and Anarchy*, has almost an antithetical resonance. Often an elegiac aura surrounds it. "To say, 'Here we no
longer use citation' means the end of our culture, in the West, as
we have known it, more or less, since the PreSocratic thinkers."[36]
This threatened "culture" is, so to say, less culture-bound; a distinct
cosmopolitan perspective enters. *Bildung* (liberal education leading to self-development) rather than *Erziehung* (systematic or specialized training) is emphasized, while an aesthetic element or
prestigious "je ne sais quoi" is tolerated. So a French philosopher,
writing for a general audience, fudges elegantly when he says that
his book presupposes "une certaine culture, un certain acquis phil-
osophique." You acquire this culture actively, as a modification of

some natural traits; at the same time, you make it seem natural, as if breeding and background had predisposed you to receive it. Sainte-Beuve claims that it pervades, because of the classical tradition, French literary life, which "consists in a certain principle of reason and culture [*un certain principe de raison et culture*] that has over time penetrated, and modified, the very character of this gallic nation."[37] The word still suggests an integrated way of life, although what is integrated is understood to be artificial, even consciously highbrow ("kulcha").[38]

Culture in this older sense goes together with affluence or social climbing, for it is freedom from ordinary conditions of a material, parochial, or ideologically exigent kind that invests the word with promise.[39] The relation between being cultured and being free is one of the great commonplaces of humanistic (or "liberal") education. (Kant, in an especially subtle move, claims that the real end of culture is freedom rather than happiness and that it promotes the former by instilling an affection for thoughtfulness.)[40] Yet despite culture's "free play of ideas," a respect for embodiment continues to prevail, and nation or religion or ethnic identity is often viewed as a necessary form of local attachment. Toward the end of his life Coleridge wrote in his notebook that "the self is in and by itself a Phantom"; nonetheless, it was "capable of receiving true entity by *reflection* from the *Nation*." Both the self and mankind were, as graspable, psychological notions, too abstract. The nation, however, was "something real to the imagination of the citizen" and became distinct "in relation to the personalities of other nations."[41] The *other* idea of culture, then, while stressing the play of ideas and its effectiveness in modifying or even (as Matthew Arnold hoped) gradually doing away with the class structure, was not free of a tension between culture and nation, or culture and society (which gives Raymond Williams's crucial study of the word its title).[42]

The creation of a cultural sphere within society or nation-state, a sort of free zone for the market of ideas, can be traced back to the *honnête homme* concept, promoted by the salons of Parisian society in the eighteenth century. They were themselves a development of courtesy ideals that emanated, as the word suggests, from the court. In the seventeenth century, culture moves closer to urbanity, the culture of cities. The new decorum joins courtiers and significant personalities from the bourgeoisie to create an ideal public of court and town ("la cour et la ville").[43] Within that charmed circle of sociability, and within it alone, people of different ranks and professions mingled and talked freely, affirming values characterized as "honnête," that is, *unaffected*, in the twofold sense of unpretentious and independent of vested interests. A premium was placed on an intelligence that could see matters from a broad perspective and did not specialize itself in turn: that remained conversational and not excessively ostentatious.

That this ideal degenerated into a new "culture of wit" was inevitable; and Rousseau's attack on its far-from-simple "honesty" as another form of hypocrisy revealed the problem. Still, in this ideal of the *honnête homme*, which Erich Auerbach already associates with Montaigne the self-reflective essayist, who is more interested in being a writer than a gentleman—an ideal infiltrating the citified and robuster café society of *The Tatler, The Spectator*, and the beginnings of English literary journalism—we catch a glimpse of Matthew Arnold's understanding of how culture promotes a wholeness of being that might overcome the divisiveness and parochialism of the class structure. Also adumbrated is Karl Mannheim's definition of intellectuals as an interclass stratum. Though from a socially stratified and class-conscious point of view intellectuals appear to be deracinated airheads (*Luftmenschen*), they alone may be in a position to demystify the conversion of special interests into universals.

To define these two major senses of culture—the one denoting *a* culture, that is, a specific form of embodiment or solidarity;[44] the other pointing to a general ideal, held despite class, profession, or broader allegiance (religion, race, collectivity, nation) and positing a shared human heritage, a second or accrued nature[45]—is to differentiate contrasting and perhaps contradictory concepts. We can spot this contrast as early as Moses Mendelssohn's "On the Question: What Does Enlightenment Mean?" (1784),[46] written at a time when "culture," as well as "enlightenment" and "formation" (*Bildung*)—

three words Mendelssohn tries to clarify by a veritable intellectual minuet—are so new that he calls them bookish and barely intelligible to the common reader.

Compared to "enlightenment," Mendelssohn says, "culture" is a practical and sociable virtue, an embodied quality, "just as a piece of land [*Grundstück*]"—falling back on the agricultural analogy—"is said to be cultured and developed the more it is made capable of producing things useful to mankind by human industriousness."[47] In what is a most interesting distinction for our purpose he also claims that as human beings we need enlightenment more than culture, which suggests that "culture" is indeed a word emphasizing practical over universal. Our way of life as citizens (*Bürger*) rather than human beings (*Menschen*) is determined by class and profession, and the impression given by the philosopher's phrasing is that he advocates qualities of culture and polish for each differentiated segment of society while hoping that this will affect the entire nation. "The more the latter [*Kultur und Politur*] harmonize [*übereinstimmen*] throughout the classes and their professions, that is, [harmonize] with the latters' respective destiny [*Bestimmung*] as members of society [literally, *Glieder*, body parts], the more a nation has culture." Mendelssohn, then, describes both a "culture" that permeates the entire nation and "a culture" appropriate to each class and profession in a society that will soon become even more specialized and segmented because of industrialization. This tension between national (general) culture and class-bound culture anticipates a later debate, reaching its height in the 1930s, as to whether there can be a proletarian culture; that is, whether a single class in a divided society can produce a more authentic, less "abstract" mode of life than the despised bourgeoisie.[48] Mendelssohn seems to suggest that a national culture can be built, not on the repression of the productive power of the working (or any other) class, but on the corporate integration of all *Glieder*.

My purpose in examining the resonances of "culture" is critical as well as historical. There are, no doubt, other sexy words around—"community" or "identity"—that exude a similar promise.[49] But the historical semantics of "culture" clarify what we are experiencing in literary studies at this time. The conversion of literary into cultural studies arises, certainly, from an urgent and growing concern with social justice and what may be called *species thinking* (now that we know so much of our history, what does it tell us about the human species?). Yet it also arises from an imaginative need that operates at all levels of life, private as well as public. Our hope that culture can provide an embodiment to satisfy a ghostly hunger, as devouring as a vampire, persists despite an impasse. The intimacy of the small or homogeneous group, of an extended family that promises to transmit and foster a tradition, runs up against other such formations and requires, in order to prevent a perpetual war between communities, a larger and transpolitical perspective, a universal culture. This other "culture" has the mission to make what seems intransitive transitive again. The very effort, however, leads to a further contradiction, perhaps because it takes place primarily in another relatively small group, an international elite or universities that are never the communiversity we hope for. As we debate the issues, a highly specialized discourse is produced, a *Fach* that sins by its technical diction and aggressive bearing against the very qualities that "culture" as a historical and progressive movement is meant to achieve: qualities of accessibility and participatory momentum.[50]

The critical yield of these reflections affects two areas. The first is our understanding of the relation, or rather contest, among art, religion, and politics. The ghostly feeling I have evoked has been traditionally honored and regulated by an established church. But poetry often strikes us as a wild religion—indeed, as a city of refuge for suppressed or exiled spirits (the "parting Genius" of Milton's *Nativity Ode*, the nymphs and satyrs displaced by "faery broods," exorcised in turn by the vacuum of a stricter doctrine). These spirits are not as innocent as they appear to be. They always represent a defeated religion or worldview, some archaic power, often more explosive because of time spent underground. John Edgar Wideman's story "Damballah," about the survival of a voodoo god who brings death to a slave, is an example. The imagination refuses to be emptied out: it strikes back by aggressively developing its prior inheritance, one that seems indissociable from a visionary or figurative language indebted to either Christian or heterodox sources. Smart, Blake, Shelley, and Yeats are obvious instances of modern poetry becoming more rather than less ghostly. The imagination is seen as religion's birth mother and in that role rescues the religious sensibility from religion.

T. S. Eliot, after the Second World War, in an address entitled "The Unity of European Culture" (which he eventually appended to his *Notes Towards the Definition of Culture*), asserts that he cannot conceive of culture without a religious foundation. I would agree that, despite upheavals in church history, the ghostly feeling has been at once delimited and preserved by traditionary ceremonies and symbols that form a national way of life, whatever the degree of religious conviction. Spectral speech, the detritus of past beliefs, haunts cultural memory: in Eliot's *The Waste Land* it figures as an incurable wound. Yet Eliot neglects the fact that culture often turns into culture politics because the pressure for a particular form of embodiment is felt to be salvational. It is possible to revise his insight about "the common tradition of Christianity which has made Europe what it is" and suggest that the only religions that count are political religions.[51]

But these will try to suppress, or at the very least regulate, the "wild" symbolism of art, and indeed all unlicensed images. Eliot's statement, in the same essay, that "our common responsibility is to preserve our common culture uncontaminated by political influences" is laudable.[52] However, his divorce of Christianity from the political sphere and his failure to acknowledge the drive for embodiment that the pathos of the titular word "unity" and his pleonastic repetition of "common" still convey make an otherwise sane and sophisticated essay as evasive a gesture after the Second World War as "Tradition and the Individual Talent" was after the first.

The conflict between art and religion (almost always a state religion, or the state as a religion) opens a breach between the notion of "a culture" as a distinctive and unified whole and "culture" as an ethos that guarantees the free play of ideas and the individual exercise of imagination in the context of tradition. Indeed, a turning point is reached early in formal cultural historiography when Jacob Burckhardt gives up the belief that "a culture" is a synchronic entity, unified by the zeitgeist and so embracing all aspects of society. That basically Hegelian conception (though less dialectical) had inspired Burkhardt's famous *Civilization [Kultur] of the Renaissance in Italy*. Only a decade later, in "The Study of History" and as he is planning lectures on Greek culture, Burckhardt's concern with decadence leads him to a more nuanced view of the great but fragile civilization of Greece. He now stresses, perhaps under Nietzsche's influence, the agonistic relation among culture, religion, and politics. I quote Felix Gilbert's summary of Burckhardt's point of view: "Whereas state and religion claim universal validity and feel justified to enforce their claim by coercion, the existence of culture depends on the possibility of individuals' moving freely in different directions, of spontaneity. . . . The particular character of a culture is determined by the extent to which state and religion allow or restrict a free development. The Greek culture and the modern world exemplify that, at least for a time, culture can escape the embrace of state and religion and develop freely."[53]

Religions must be taken seriously, then, though I feel foolish making so obvious a statement. Religions (including the state presenting itself as a religion) are political in urging as total an embodiment as possible; they are not just the source of a cultural sedimentation that provides continuity and an option. In countries where a de facto or a constitutional separation of church and state has occurred, religions cannot enforce their totalizing way of life. But they continue to flourish there and will do so until every ghost is laid, until, in Blake's words, "All Human Forms [are] Identified" by a political revolution or apocalyptic reincarnation. A society, therefore, that claims to be secular or even antireligious will continue to foster pledges of allegiance and what has been called "civil religion."[54] Even if diversity is nominally cultivated by this society, the religions it has exorcised, or any residual, unbound spirituality, is feared; consequently, it too may seek a total commitment and insist on political correctness, even in art.

Today there are those who see the "general culture" as hege-
monic. If we acknowledge, however, the antinomy between "a culture" and "culture," then the right conclusion would be that it is "a
culture" that tends toward hegemony, while "culture," understood
as the development of a public sphere, a "republic of letters" in
which ideas can be freely exchanged, is what is fragile.[55] In this
area, things are very complex. On the one hand, the general culture can deceptively claim to be on the side of breadth and gen-
erosity, while it is actually imperious or imperialistic. On the other
hand, "a culture" can be deeply conformist and seek to limit individual rights, which it may even denounce as a *culte du moi*, as
excessive individualism. So Maurice Barrès plays on the organicist
and agricultural analogy to express his belief in the necessity of a
culture grounded in French soil: "J'ai besoin qu'on garde à mon
arbre la culture qui lui permet de me porter si haut, moi faible
petite feuille" (I need culture to conserve my tree and to allow it to
carry me, a feeble, small leaf, upward).[56]

With Burckhardt and Nietzsche the historical image of Greece
begins to change, and "culture" is now seen as a precarious, even
heroic, achievement against great odds, a sort of tragic *agon* always threatened by decadence. It does not solve anything, therefore, to denounce "culture" as "high culture," that is, as elitist and
obsolete. Herbert Marcuse called this move a "repressive desubli-
mation," and he insisted on the importance of "aesthetic incompatibility." Although the main target of his attack was mass culture, his words on the "flattening out of the antagonism between
culture and social reality through the obliteration of the oppositional, alien, and transcendent elements in the higher culture"
remain cogent.[57]

Perhaps Václav Havel is a better guide here than either Marcuse
or T. S. Eliot. Coming from the republic of letters to politics, he insists that "civility," or what he renames "the culture of everything,"
must penetrate the political sphere as well. The notion of a high or
autonomous sphere of culture is neither conceptually protected
nor attacked by him: his argument is that manners must become
moeurs, a second nature or tradition, if everyday life in post-Marxist

society is not to be ravaged once more by regressive nationalisms or an all-usurping economic imperative.[58] The question that remains, however, is whether Havel's ideal can accrue enough imaginative force to displace the appeal of political religions and their uncompromising, spiritualistic demand for total devotion, sacrifice, embodiment. Civility, as Havel uses it, comes close to what Hannah Arendt called "classic virtues of civic behavior" that distinguish "a responsible member of society, interested in all public affairs" from a bourgeois, "concerned only with his private existence" and who becomes too easily a "functionary" of the state.[59] Nationalism, in Arendt's view, is not genuine patriotism at all but eliminates open public discussion in favor of a propagandized mass ideology. My provisional conclusion about Havel's civic ideal is pessimistic. Once the nation-state or a faith community has appropriated what might be called the superego ideal of culture by promising embodiment and exacting collective obedience, civility is often viewed as a minor virtue to be sacrificed on the altar of a higher destiny.

The antinomy between "a culture" and "culture" leads to a second critical observation. I have mentioned my concern that ideological strictures, intended as social remedies, may increase rather than lessen abstraction; certainly, the exponential growth of cultural studies has produced a highly specialized and sometimes cultic discourse. What Henry James called, at the beginning of this century, when immigration was making its impact, "The Question of Our Speech," must now be posed in every generation of *professionals*. One form this question takes at present is whether the culture speech of the last fifty years has achieved anything more than that of the last two hundred.

While this anticipates my next chapter, a few bridging remarks may be appropriate. I am not concerned, as in *Minor Prophecies*, at least not primarily, with the culture wars that pit the public intellectual against professors and their jargon. Yes, cultural critique can be countercultural in diction and spirit; it is still fighting gentility, civility, middle-class hypocrisy, etc. But there is nothing intrinsically wrong with a technical vocabulary that is inventive, that renews tired analytic terms by an energetic mixture of the vernacular or the exotic (*vide* Frye, Burke, Bloom, all of them *bricoleurs*, as well as Barthes, at his essayistic rather than schematic best). The question of our speech, the contemporary question, asks how long critical discourse must remain critical: that is, questioning; that is, in a negative mode. Can an affirmation emerge from all this splendid—cerebral, demystifying, deconstructive—"labor of the negative"?

Sometimes, in the midst of reading our strongest readers—Derrida, for example—I begin to think we have simply expanded the linguistic sway of periphrasis and praeteritio. How not to speak ("Comment ne pas parler"), when our humanity is deeply offended, our social agony aroused daily, our profession in disarray; yet also how to speak in a scrupulously negative way ("Comment ne pas parler"), avoiding ideas of reference, the seductive promissory melody in every gesture of voice and the tricks and errors of cultural prophesy with its "présent futur"?[60] Are we caught between two extremes: on the one hand, artful structures of avoidance that turn us into philosophical *précieuses ridicules*; on the other, a diction with more pathos than ever, as embodiment, empowerment, fulfillment, identity rise from undersong to theme song?

This question of our speech is also the question of "our" speech. Two related kinds of integrity are involved: that of language under modern conditions, and that of the critic's—the language bearer's—relation to a particular community, to "a culture" as well as to "culture." These are difficult issues to raise in conclusion. On the critic's relation to a community, let me recall Trilling's preface to *Beyond Culture* (1965), where he sticks up for his right to say "we" though he admits to representing a rather narrow class, that of New York intellectuals. In short, his concern in 1965 is more with the "we" than the "me" generation, because of the "tendency toward homogeneity in modern culture." Despite claims of difference, he argues, despite contemporary attempts to liberate us from the tyranny of middle-class values ("the free creative spirit at war with the bourgeoisie"), despite the advocacy of new experience and new knowledges, even the "adversary culture" is forming a class:

> There has formed what I have called a class. If I am right in identifying it in this way, then we can say of it, as we say of any other class, that it has developed characteristic habitual responses to the stimuli of its environment. It is not without power, and we can say of it, as we can say of any other class with a degree of power, that it seeks to aggrandize and perpetuate itself. And, as with any other class, the relation it has to the autonomy of its members makes a relevant question. . . . There is reason to believe that the relation is ambiguous.[61]

Here the definition of "class" is almost as broad as "culture" is coming to be and understates the social struggle. Indeed, Trilling uses this convergence of terms to emphasize a well-known mechanism of progress: "How else are civilizations ever formed," he asks, "save by syntheses that can be read as paradoxes?" Yet if that is so, if syntheses can be read as paradoxes (or vice versa), language does not have integrity in the sense that we ascribe it to *character*.

The vista opened by Trilling's urbane question is disconcerting. Language is either very manipulable, or contemporary language has become so. Among the most relentless and influential statements concerning our language condition are those of Adorno and Horkheimer, and—more specifically focused on the weakening of social bonds—of Henri Lefebvre.

The founders of Critical Theory see a collapse of bourgeois civilization, a movement toward uniformity and pseudoclarity that they describe as an Enlightenment ethos bound for self-destruction. As the public sphere and modern economic forces take over, thought is commodified and speech pervaded by promotional purposes. This tendency has gone so far that we glimpse an impasse: social critique, even their own, becomes impossible because its words are involuntarily co-opted by the forces of rationalization. Deprived of an effective oppositional language, critique turns into affirmation. In this incurable condition, "the most honest reformer, who urges renewal in current terms of speech, because he adopts a smooth, adaptable cat-

egory machine and with it the supporting structure of a bad philosophy, reinforces the established power he seeks to demolish."[62]

Sadly, the effectiveness of words may now stand in inverse relation to their truth. Lefebvre takes up the other side of this false yet
coercive "we" denounced by Critical Theory: its shallow, even hypocritical nature. He argues that today every "we" is weak and has to
be reinforced by a special rhetoric "packed with allusions, stuffed
with icons . . . with images and chants that celebrate an ill-defined
cohesion and tries to consolidate it." The object of Lefebvre's critique is not, or not primarily, the pseudocommunitarian bias of
post-Marxist rhetoric, as that becomes an aggressive, even counter-
cultural means of identity formation. He does not target a shocking
outcome of the Enlightenment but focuses on the deterioration of
language as it adjusts to the technological networks of postindustri-
al society and dissipates a referentiality that, according to him, had
preferred clarity and closure over a polysemic float in the linking of
signified and signifier.[63]

One does not have to accept this account of the decline and fall
of referentials to appreciate Lefebvre's analysis of the increasing
slippage of keywords.[64] Nor does one have to accept Adorno and
Horkheimer's view of the consequences of the Enlightenment to be
concerned with the question of our speech, and in particular with
how to maintain a critical language that is not co-opted by the very
fact of communicating successfully. For in literary studies the relation of paradox to synthesis or of ambiguity to the creation of meaning has been the single most important topic of poetics since
Richards and Empson. The recurrent concept of a second fall of
language, in modern or postmodern times, leads by reaction to new
efforts that would limit language doubt, our skepticism about the
truth of words. These efforts are many and intriguing; they make up
the bulk of what we call literary theory, which has allied itself to an
intense and ongoing scrutiny of language and its communicative
powers. If the culture of words cannot contribute adequately to
truth, what can?

A decorum is often suggested that seems distinctively though not
dogmatically moral. Both Trilling's "authenticity" and Heidegger's

"Eigentlichkeit" not only revise previous criteria of sincerity or *honnêteté* but endow speech with a tacit dimension, a quality that, though fully verbal, cannot be reduced to either intentionality or phenomenality and so approaches silence. This intelligible silence, more primordial than speech, is "embodied" as writing. The impotence of words, and of culture generally, both before and after such disasters as two world wars and the Holocaust, intensifies the dilemma. "To keep the silence, that is what unknowingly we all wish for, as we write," observed Maurice Blanchot in *Disaster Writing*.[65] We are back to "Comment ne pas parler." This development I will discuss more fully in the chapters that follow.

NOTES

1. "Mont Blanc," ll. 52–57.

2. "Adonais," LV.

3. See, e.g., Jean Baudrillard, *La Guerre du Golfe n'a pas eu lieu* (Paris: Galilée, 1991). Andreas Huyssen in *Twilight Memories: Marking Time in a Culture of Amnesia* (New York: Routledge, 1995) explores the impact of postmodern derealization on our principal cultural institutions.

4. *The Complete Poems of Emily Dickinson*, ed. Thomas H. Johnson (Boston: Little, Brown, 1960), poem 640.

5. *The Phenomenology of Mind*, trans. J. B. Baillie (New York: Harper and Row, 1967), 159. "Open secrets" adapts Goethe's view of nature, which is itself based on an earlier commonplace describing nature as the *open* book of God.

6. *Civilization and Its Discontents*, trans. and ed. James Strachey (New York: Norton, 1962).

7. "Notes Toward a Supreme Fiction." Another side of the organic feeling of harmony, "of an indissoluble bond, of being one with the external world as a whole" (*Civilization*, 12), linked by Freud to the experience of the child in the maternal body, is developed by Julia Kristeva and others who seek to understand the role of a pre-Oedipal stage in human development. The oceanic feeling may explain a basic anxiety in the grown child, insofar as it continues to sense a lack of ego boundaries and at once delights in and fears to be engulfed by the "ocean."

8. "One evening in 1919, a short, shy fellow named Irving Caesar [to become Irving Berlin], who was just short of his 25th birthday, sat close to the stage of one of the cavernous theaters on Times Square and took in a performance of the song 'Swanee'"(*New York Times Book Review*, 3 May 1992, 22). " 'It was a fine autumn evening in 1922. I was a notary's clerk in Marommes'" (J.-P. Sartre, on narratable "reality," in his novel *Nausea* [1939]). Even putting the date after the title of a novel reveals a certain nervousness of the same kind, a minimal gesture of emplacement.

9. Embodiment should be, strictly speaking, a "cure of the body," as the erotic imagination always demands, or as the poetic imagination strives for, giving voice a body or not being satisfied with imperfect words. This aspect, neglected here, points to Ovid and the Ovidian tradition in the West. Cf. Lynn Enterline, *Pursuing Daphne: Body and Voice in Ovid and Renaissance Ovidian Poetry* (Stanford: Stanford University Press, 1997). The complex task of sexualizing and gendering embodiment is taken up by Sandor Ferenczi in *Thalassa: A Theory of Genitality*, trans. H. A. Bunker (Albany, N.Y.: Psychoanalytic Quarterly, 1938), and Erich Neumann in *Apuleius: Amor and Psyche, The Labors of the Feminine* (New York: Pantheon, 1965).

10. *Letters and Leadership* (New York: B. W. Huebsch, 1918).

11. "Kultur ist ein vom Standpunkt des Menschen aus mit Sinn und Bedeutung bedachter endlicher Ausschnitt aus der sinnlosen Unendlichkeit des Weltgeschehens" (*Gesammelte Werke zur Wissenschaftslehre*, quoted in Aleida Assmann and Jan Assmann, "Kultur und Konflikt: Aspekte einer Theorie des unkommunikativen Handelns," in *Kultur und Konflikt*, ed. Jan Assmann and Dietrich Harth [Frankfurt-am-Main: Suhrkamp, 1990], 35). My translation. For a short history of the culture/civilization distinction, see appendix 1.

12. Harold Bloom, after a life of studies centering on Shelley, Blake, Yeats, and Stevens, has recently revised his earlier critique (inspired by them) of "Natural Religion." He has identified the primordial feeling of ghostliness, as it becomes a conviction and a religion, with the ancient gnostic heresy that the Nature we know is the work of another power than God, that the Creation is already a Fall, and that we have a spiritual existence apart from any such embodiment, apart from the

secular world. See *The American Religion: The Emergence of the Post-Christian Nation* (New York: Simon and Schuster, 1992).

13. Stanley Cavell has linked philosophy to literature (especially through his readings of Shakespearean tragedy) by disclosing in both an alive and pervasive *skepticism* as the provocative workings of a ghost feeling surely similar to the one I have described. Descartes's philosophical and Shakespeare's tragical method at once acknowledge and avoid a dispossession: the unavailability of our own private world (a skepticism from the fact that we cannot know ourselves intimately enough) and of public reality (a skepticism from the fact that the minds of others, or of whoever orders the world, also may be closed to us). Yet writers like these continue to *dare to know*. I sin against Cavell's patient elaborations with this instant summary and send the reader to, above all, *The Claim of Reason: Wittgenstein, Skepticism, Morality, and Tragedy* (New York: Oxford University Press, 1979).

14. Pierre Bourdieu, *La distinction: Critique sociale du jugement* (Paris: Editions de Minuit, 1979).

15. See Georg Lukács, *History and Class Consciousness: Studies in Marxist Dialectics*, trans. Rodney Livingstone (Cambridge, Mass.: MIT Press, 1971), 95. Lukács supports Marx's attempt to disenchant the "mysticism of commodification." Derrida traces Marx's pervasive recourse to spectral metaphors in the *Specters of Marx*. Lucien Goldmann suggests that Heidegger's concept of *Dasein* responds to Lukács's *Verdinglichung* (reification), itself developed from Marx's basic intuition about the historical rather than permanent status of a world of things, of objects standing against the subjectivity of the worker with a spuriously independent life.

16. Cf. Raymond Williams, *Keywords: A Vocabulary of Culture and Society* (New York: Oxford University Press, 1976), 76: "*Culture* is one of the two or three most complicated words in the English language."

17. See the suggestive survey of the word in Hannah Arendt, "The Crisis in Culture," *Between Past and Future* (New York: Viking, 1961), 211 ff.

18. An early analysis of the historical semantics of the word, with some remarks on its grammatical development, is Joseph Niedermann, *Kultur: Werden und Wandlungen des Begriffs und seiner Ersatz-begriffe*

von Cicero bis Herder (Florence: Libreria Editrice, 1941). It provides an indispensable survey but does not touch sources beyond Herder. For later uses of the word, see A. L. Kroeber and Clyde Kluckhohn, *Culture: A Critical Review of Concepts and Definitions* (New York: Vintage, 1963). A further, but contemporary, linguistic factor favoring the spread of the word promotes all subcultures to cultures by dropping the prefix *sub-*, as if it were infra dig, or a carryover from "subversive." On the culture/civilization antithesis as it coincides with national self-imagining in Germany and France, see Norbert Elias, *The Civilizing Process* (Cambridge: Blackwell, 1994), 3–41, and appendix 1, below.

19. Cf. Jack Goody's *The Culture of Flowers* (New York: Cambridge University Press, 1993), which examines, according to the advertisement, "the secular and religious uses of flowers across a wide range of cultures, from ancient Egypt to modern China."

20. Van Wyck Brooks, *America's Coming-of-Age* (New York: B. W. Huebsch, 1915).

21. Cf. Assmann and Assmann, "Kultur und Konflikt": "Als Suffix kann [Kultur] nahezu jede Konstellation eingehen" (35).

22. Y. M. Lotman and B. A. Uspensky, "On the Semiotic Mechanism of Culture" (1971), *New Literary History* 9 (winter 1978): 211–32.

23. "By 'culture', then, I mean first of all what the anthropologists mean: the way of life of a particular people living together in one place. That culture is made visible in their arts, in their social system, in their habits and customs, in their religion" (T. S. Eliot, *Notes Towards the Definition of Culture* [London: Faber and Faber, 1948], 122). We see here how infectious the anthropological meaning is: we have slipped from "tradition" (as in his well-known essay "Tradition and the Individual Talent") to "traditional way of life" to "culture." Eliot does not specifically argue that culture, in this sense, is the only way of conferring identity; that stage, with its "determination to respect art only within the ground rules of culture" and stemming "from a prior definition of culture that ties it to the social or anthropological group, rather than individual taste or judgment" is attacked by a recent critic as "cultural idolatry." See David Bromwich, *Politics by Other Means: Higher Education and Group Thinking* (New Haven: Yale University Press, 1992), 12 ff.

24. See the first of his "Untimely Observations" of 1873.

25. While in the modern era complaints about the "machinery" of living increase (see n. 42 below), there is evidence that specialization can also simplify the multicultural demands of traditional societies. As Ganash N. Devi has pointed out, "The English term 'culture' is not sufficiently large to cover the semantic scope" of India's cultural situation, where people live "within a bilingual and even multilingual cultural idiom" and have to switch their culture codes according to the needs of their social situations ("The Multicultural Context of Indian Literature in English," in *Crisis and Creativity in the New Literatures in English*, ed. Geoffrey Davis and Hena Maes-Jelinek [Amsterdam: Rodopi, 1990]). Multiculturalism, which represents subcultures as cultures, tries to restore a complexity that was removed by modern political and scientific streamlining. For how these complexities turn into perplexities when a modern national culture tries to control a traditional multicultural situation, see Clifford Geertz, "Thick Description: Towards an Interpretive Theory of Culture," *The Interpretation of Culture* (New York: Basic Books, 1973), 3–30.

26. Both Michel Foucault and Michel de Certeau are of importance here. See, especially, Certeau's remarks on "l'articulation natureculture" in *L'écriture de l'histoire* (Paris: Gallimard, 1975), 82 ff. Certeau emphasizes how history, as a discipline, actively moves "natural" elements into the "cultural" domain, making them more available, for instance, for a literary transformation into symbols: "Of waste materials, of papers, of vegetables, even glaciers and 'eternal snows,' the historian makes *something else*: he makes history out of them. . . . He participates in the work which changes nature into environment and modifies in this way man's nature." Ernst Cassirer, in his *Logic of the Humanities [Kulturwissenschaften]*, trans. C. S. Howe (New Haven: Yale University Press, 1961), credits Vico (followed by Herder) with a "logic" that "dared to break through the circle of objective knowledge, the circle of mathematics and natural science, and dared instead to constitute itself as the logic of the humanities—as the logic of language, poetry, and history" (54).

27. If we adduce Althusser's concept of "Ideological State Apparatuses," or the way the dominant class reproduces through superstruc-

tural organizations such as schools and churches, opinions favorable to its control of the modes of production, then such proliferating talk about "corporate culture," the "culture of the agency," etc., could be seen as spreading a deceptive idea of human creativity yet favoring the actual "State Apparatus": business, police, and so forth. (Marxism has its own, competitive understanding of how human creativity, as a means to mastery over nature, is to be developed.) In *L'état culturel: Essai sur une religion moderne* (Paris: Fallois, 1991), Marc Fumaroli describes a similar technique of control. He documents the "elephantine" growth and spread of the word "culture" in contemporary France and charges that it has become the name of a state religion, permitting "the flattering illusion that administrative and political activity applied to the arts is in itself of artistic and genial quality." The "creative" *dirigisme* of the state in cultural matters reduces culture to client status: it is the extension, the Frankfurt School might say, of administrative reason and celebrates a state apparatus rather than the liberal arts. "Abstract and sterile, the Culture of cultural politics is the insinuating mask of power, and the mirror in which it wishes to take pleasure [*jouir*] in itself" (my translation). See chapter 3, "La Culture: Mot-valise, mot-écran."

28. During the pope's visit to the United States in October 1995, I heard in the media that his speeches aimed at "changing the culture," which now meant the moral culture, worldwide. And consider the following, from Meaghan Morris's *Ecstasy and Economics: American Essays for John Forbes* (Sidney: EMPress, 1992): "During the 1980s, the word 'culture' began to be used in a rather peculiar sense. In 1990, a week after the worst company crashes in Australian history had ended a decade of financial mismanagement and 'de-regulated' corporate crime, a groveling TV current affairs show host asked Rupert Murdoch (back home to shut down a couple of newspapers) what 'we' could do to save 'our' economy. The mighty multinationalist replied, 'Oh you know—change the culture.' . . . What Murdoch 'meant' was a cliché: a 1980s media commonplace that Australia's biggest problem is the lazy, hedonist, uncompetitive, beach-bound, lotus-eating ethos of the ordinary people" (124). Morris's entire essay "On the Beach" should be of great interest to cultural studies.

29. From the introduction to John Frow and Meaghan Morris, eds., *Australian Culture Studies* (St. Leonards, New South Wales: Allen and Unwin, 1993). Cf. Morris's *Ecstasy and Economics*, 124 ff. A *New Yorker* portrait of Colin Powell, which contrasts him with Jesse Jackson, shows both leaders using the "culture" word in a similar way. Powell, Jackson says, is "flowing with the culture. . . . He's created a comfort zone among the guardians of the culture." Powell is reported to say that "As a culture, the Airforce. . . ." Jackson, though oppositional, "counter-cultural" to "the dominant culture," must still express himself in culture terms. See Henry Louis Gates Jr., "Powell and the Black Elite," *New Yorker* 71 (September 25, 1995): 64–80.

30. Murray Krieger, *Arts on the Level: The Fall of the Elite Object* (Knoxville: University of Tennessee Press, 1981).

31. A December 1992 article in the *New York Times* on the popularity of vampire movies is headlined "Blood Culture" (Frank Rich, "The New Blood Culture," *New York Times*, 6 December 1992, sec. 9, 1). This brings together the scientific connotation with the ordinary sense of art-as-culture but also, wittily and ominously, with the claim that, because of AIDS, an entire subculture is being created of people united by their concern with that disease.

32. Donna J. Haraway (London: Free Association Books, 1991).

33. Further signs of the times: I receive a reader's catalog from the University of Chicago Press. It lists the following titles or subtitles: *Cultural Misunderstandings; Cultural Aesthetics; Culture and Anomie; Re-envisioning Past Musical Cultures; Women's Culture, Occultism, Witchcraft, and Cultural Fashions; Symbolic Action and Cultural Studies; The Culture of Politics and the Politics of Culture in American Life; The Cultural Politics of Race and Nation; Science as Practice and Culture; Women, Achievement, and College Culture; Culture Wars*. Or consider this, from a 16 July 1994 *New York Times* op-ed piece on a city kid by Barbara Nevins Taylor: "He didn't bother with his homework and fell behind. The culture of the housing projects and the hormones of adolescence collided with the culture of the school" (21).

34. A theory recently put forward is that we have become a *Kultur-gesellschaft*, the German word demonstrating the symptom that it seeks to describe. It defines "a society in which cultural activity functions in-

creasingly as a socializing agency comparable to and even often against the grain of nation, family profession, state" (quoted in Huyssen, *Twilight Memories*, 31 ff).

35. Wole Soyinka, *Myth, Literature and the African World* (Cambridge: Cambridge University Press, 1976), 138–39. Yet "culture" appeals just as strongly to Africanists; it stands for an original cohesion, an organic community, that the colonizers are said to have destroyed. A fuller discussion would begin with Frantz Fanon's "On National Culture" in *Les damnés de la terre* (Paris: François Maspero, 1961; published in English as *The Wretched of the Earth*, trans. Constance Farrington [London: MacGibbon and Kee, 1965]), which delineates in compelling detail the situation of the "colonized intellectual" who participates in the project of decolonization. Here I wish only to note the abundance of body or embodiment metaphors in Fanon's essay. Commenting, for instance, on the style of the conflicted intellectual who is freeing himself from the colonial culture but has not integrated with ("faire corps, c'est à dire, à changer de corps, avec") European civilization, Fanon writes: "Style nerveux animé de rythmes, de part en part habité par une vie éruptive. . . . Ce style, qui a en son temps étonné les occidentaux, n'est point comme on a bien voulu le dire un caractère racial mais traduit avant tout un corps à corps, révèle la nécessité dans laquelle s'est trouvé cet homme de se faire mal, de saigner réellement de sang rouge, de se libérer d'une partie de son être qui déjà renfermait des germes de pourriture. Combat douloureux, rapide où immanquablement le muscle devait se substituer au concept."

36. George Steiner, in Pierre Boutang and George Steiner, *Dialogues: Sur le mythe d'Antigone/sur le sacrifice d'Abraham* (Paris: Lattès, 1994), 154. My translation.

37. "De la tradition en littérature, et dans quel sens il la faut entendre," *Causeries du Lundi*, vol. 15 (Paris: Garnier Frères, 1857–62). My translation.

38. In "The Crisis of Culture," Hannah Arendt adopts Herbert Marcuse's famous attack on the "affirmative culture" of a bourgeoisie that reduced Schiller's "aesthetic education" to climbing out of the lower regions into "the higher, non-real regions, where beauty and the spirit supposedly were at home." See Arendt, *Between Past and Present*

(New York: Viking, 1961), esp. 201–5. See also Herbert Marcuse, "The Affirmative Character of Culture" (1938), in *Negations: Essays in Critical Theory* (Boston: Beacon, 1968).

39. There is a third meaning of "culture" that lies uneasily between the two I have mentioned. Perry Anderson, in a well-known critique of "National Culture" in 1968, draws up a devastating inventory of what culture amounts to in England at that date. He exempts the hard sciences and the arts from this inventory, which—as he admits in a later statement—belies the "national" in his title or confuses culture with what happens in the academy or gets absorbed through that conduit. Yet Anderson did make the point that the British university had become an inertial system in which innovation came largely from Central European refugees and that even these innovations had been only selectively successful, the criterion of success being whether they could be accommodated to an inertial "Englishness." The inventory meaning of "culture" thus cannot avoid a critical edge: Anderson, like Marcuse, uses non-national cultural achievements to challenge the national status quo, to rouse the national consciousness to equal achievements. Moreover, Anderson's emphasis on *academic* culture as an inertial system promoting "national" values parallels the more scientific and elaborated analyses by Pierre Bourdieu, which show how the French educational establishment reduces culture to style rather than substance, to a "relation to culture" that perpetuates the *honnête homme* ideal of the seventeenth century and reproduces a pattern of social distinction paradoxically based on the attempt of the upper class (the "dominant culture") to make its imposed values seem natural or invisible ("une certaine culture"). See Perry Anderson, "Components of the National Culture," *New Left Review*, no. 50 (July–August 1968): 3–58; and Pierre Bourdieu, "Literate Tradition and Social Conservation" (written with Jean-Claude Passeron), in *Reproduction in Education, Society and Culture* (London: Sage, 1990; original French ed.: Pierre Bourdieu and Jean-Claude Passeron, *La reproduction: Eléments pour une théorie du système d'enseignement* [Paris: Minuit, 1970]).

40. For the ramifications of this, see Cassirer, *Logic of the Humanities*, chapter 5, "The 'Tragedy of Culture,' " and cf. Arendt, "Crisis in Culture," where she brings Cicero and Kant together: "The hu-

manist, because he is not a specialist, exerts a faculty of judgment and taste which is beyond the coercion which each specialty imposes upon us" (225).

41. David P. Callco, *Coleridge and the Idea of the Modern State* (New Haven: Yale University Press, 1966), chapter 5, "The Psychological Basis of the State."

42. *Culture and Society: 1780–1950* (London: Chatto and Windus, 1958). Leonard Woolf, continuing his autobiography under the title *Principia Politica: A Study of Communal Psychology* (London: Hogarth, 1953), suggests that politics, by which he means "constructing the framework or manipulating the machinery of government or society," became more inevitable and preoccupying during his lifetime. "There is something strange in the fact that so much of [my life] has been occupied, not with living, but with the machinery of living. But the strangeness does not end there; it is not limited to my particular experience, for it is part of a general strangeness, a new and fantastic pattern, which has appeared in human life during the last 50 or 100 years. This pattern has been determined by the encroachment of the machinery of life upon living and the art of living" (9–10). The values implied by "culture" seem to offer an antidote to this fact. But Woolf himself, interested in the relation of communal psychology to sociopolitical action, rehabilitates the word "civilization": "What determines whether a society is civilized is its material standard of life, its intellectual and spiritual standards of life, and its contributions to art, science, learning, philosophy, or religion" (53). He refuses to value "culture" (as the fine arts) and its products higher than the other civilized standards.

43. My account is primarily indebted to Erich Auerbach, "La cour et la ville," now in *Scenes from the Drama of European Literature* (Minneapolis: University of Minnesota Press, 1984), 133–82. See also Elias, *The Civilizing Process*, 32: "The *homme civilisé* was nothing other than a somewhat extended version of that human type which represented the true ideal of court society, the *honnête homme*." Hannah Arendt concurs in interesting and sardonic remarks on the origin of "good society": *Between Past and Future*, 199–200. Rémy de Gourmont is characterized as an *encyclopédiste honnête homme* in the introduction to essays translated from his *La culture des idées*: see

Decadence and Other Essays on the Culture of Ideas (New York: Harcourt, Brace, 1921).

44. "Solidarity" is the word Raymond Williams uses as a near-equivalent of what I call "embodiment": I introduce it deliberately here. See, e.g., *Culture and Society*, 332: "The feeling of solidarity is, although necessary, a primitive feeling."

45. While I cannot accept Arendt's sharp dichotomizing—assigning culture to objects and the world and separating it from entertainment that relates to people and consumable life—she makes a charge that still needs answering: "Culture is being threatened when all worldly objects and things, produced by the present and the past, are treated as mere functions for the life process of society, as though they are there only to fulfill some need" (*Between Past and Present*, 208). Her intuition that cultural objects have a "thingness" and can only be evaluated by their permanence (to which she says life is indifferent), while it saves culture from the philistine or from consumer society generally, points once more to the desire for embodiment, one that is associated with durability rather than reification. What the "function" of this desire may be or that of art objects "which every civilization leaves behind as the quintessence and lasting testimony of the spirit which animated it" (201), is not clarified by her.

46. My translation. My text for Mendelssohn's *Über die Frage: Was heisß Aufklären?* is taken from Immanuel Kant, *Was ist Aufklärung? Aufsätze zur Geschichte und Philosophie*, ed. Jürgen Zehbe (Göttingen: Vandenhoeck and Ruprecht, 1967), 129–33. Kant's essay also appeared in 1784.

47. There exists an external form of culture he names polish (*Politur*), but it is said to be, ideally, the outer splendor of culture and enlightenment working from within. Whereas speech achieves enlightenment through scientific knowledge, it achieves culture through sociability, poetry, and rhetoric. Together these fashion a well-formed (*gebildete*) language. Mendelssohn translated Rousseau's Second Discourse and perhaps used *Politur* on the analogy of that author's *politesse*—a synonym for *civilisé*—which is not used.

48. See, e.g., Marcel Martinet, *Culture prolétarienne* (Paris: Librairie du Travail, 1935). Martinet complains at the very threshold of

his book about the word "culture," "which I am forced to repeat so often [and which] is so displeasing. It is abstract, obscure, pretentious and has a pronounced aftertaste of conformism, self-satisfaction and treachery." But, he goes on, "The question is to learn if this disagreeable word points all the same to a reality, if the working class can renounce the intellectual life and possession of this reality without abandoning itself."

49. For "identity" as a "plastic word," see Lutz Niethammer, "Konjunkturen und Konkurrenzen kollektiver Identität. Ideologie, Infrastruktur und Gedächtnis in der Zeitgeschichte," *PROKLA: Zeitschrift für kritische Sozialwissenschaft* 96 (1994): 377–99.

50. Not only the study of culture but culture itself as a separate and quasi-autonomous sphere is subject to this paradox pointedly expressed by Guy Debord in *La société du spectacle* (Paris: Buchet/Chastel, 1967): "La culture est le lieu de la recherche de l'unité perdue. Dans cette recherche de l'unité, la culture comme sphère séparée est obligée de se nier elle-même" (149). See also chapter 1, above.

51. Eliot, *Notes Toward the Definition of Culture*, 122.

52. Ibid., 123.

53. *History: Politics or Culture? Reflections on Ranke and Burckhardt* (Princeton: Princeton University Press, 1990), 71.

54. For the concept, see Robert N. Bellah, *The Broken Covenant: American Civil Religion in a Time of Trial* (Chicago: Chicago University Press, 1992).

55. A good historical treatment of the concept of a "republic of letters" is found in Michael Warner, *The Letters of the Republic: Publication and the Public Sphere in Eighteenth-Century America* (Cambridge: Harvard University Press, 1990). For contemporary thought, the strongest development of the idea is Hannah Arendt's notion of "world" as a public sphere in which political action can be freely debated and a communal sense (Kant's *Gemeinsinn*) is made manifest, "a faculty of judgment which, in its reflection, takes account . . . of the mode of representation of all others" (*Critique of Judgment*, trans. Werner S. Pluhar [Indianapolis: Hackett, 1987], 294; translation modified). See Kant, *Critique of Judgment*, paragraph 40. I comment on Arendt's "republic of letters" in "Art and Consensus in the Era of

Progressive Politics," *Yale Review* 80 (1992): 50–61. Habermas's magisterial treatise on *Öffentlichkeit* is well known.

56. Cited by Alain Finkielkraut, *La défaite de la pensée* (Paris: Gallimard, 1987), 61. My translation.

57. Herbert Marcuse, *One-Dimensional Man: Studies in the Ideology of Advanced Industrial Society* (Boston: Beacon, 1964), chapter 3. Cf. Frederic Jameson's *Postmodernism; or, The Cultural Logic of Late Capitalism* (Durham, N.C.: Duke University Press, 1991), which expresses Marcuse's complaint in terms of a new and disorienting cultural space that requires our mapping. After noting what he calls the "dissolution of an autonomous sphere of culture" in the form of an "explosion," that is, a "prodigious expansion of culture throughout the social realm, to the point at which everything in our social life—from economic value and state power to practices and the very structure of the psyche itself—can be said to have become 'cultural,' " he admits that no leftist theory of cultural politics has been able to do without "a certain minimal aesthetic distance, of the possibility of the positioning of the cultural act outside the massive Being of capital." But he then goes beyond these theories (and beyond Adorno) in asserting that "distance in general (including 'critical distance') has very precisely been abolished in the new space of postmodernism" and that the task of theory is to find out the historical reality of that new global space. Jameson seems to position himself at once as a scientist observing an objective phenomenon and an explorer charting unknown seas of thought—for purposes of *disalienation*, or "the practical reconquest of a sense of place" (47–51).

58. " 'The Culture of Everything,' " *New York Review of Books* 34, no. 10 (28 May 1992): 30.

59. Arendt's distinction is already put into play in "Organized Guilt and Universal Responsibility," a discussion of "real political conditions which underlie the charge of collective guilt of the German people," published in 1945. See Hannah Arendt, *Essays in Understanding, 1930–1945*, ed. Jerome Kohn (New York: Harcourt Brace, 1994), especially 128–32.

60. I am referring mainly, of course, to Derrida's essay in *Psyché: Inventions de l'autre* (Paris: Galilée, 1987), translated as "How to Avoid

Speaking: Denials," in *Languages of the Unsayable,* ed. Sanford Budik and Wolfgang Iser (New York: Columbia University Press, 1989), 3–69.

61. *Beyond Culture: Essays on Literature and Learning* (New York: Viking, 1965), xv–xvi.

62. Max Horkheimer and Theodor W. Adorno, preface, *Dialektik der Aufklärung: Philosophische Fragmente* (Amsterdam: Querido, 1947). My translation.

63. *Le langage et la société* (Paris: Gallimard, 1966). Recently this question of the "we" has been raised again by Jacques Derrida and linked to the issue of "culture" in its identitarian and nonidentitarian aspects. See "The Other Heading: Memories, Responses, and Responsibilities," *PMLA* 108 (1993): 89–93. But compare, already, the (more) Hegelian "nous" in the opening line of his *Glas* (1974).

64. Raymond Williams chronicles a similar experience, after the Second World War, in the introduction to *Keywords* (New York: Oxford University Press, 1976), and Paul Fussell suggests over and over again, both in his important *The Great War and Modern Memory* (New York: Oxford University Press, 1976) and *Wartime: Understanding and Behavior in the Second World War* (New York: Oxford University Press, 1989), that the euphemistic and propagandistic use of words left a mark on writers that contributed to the irony of modernism and language skepticism generally.

65. *L'écriture du désastre* (Paris: Gallimard, 1980).

chapter three

The Question of Our Speech

The true Man is the source, he being the Poetic Genius

—WILLIAM BLAKE

It is important to bring poetry, or literature generally, into the fold of cultural discourse. Not only does poetry often express the same themes, but it can also challenge the quality of that kind of talk. At one level, of course, poetry has no bearing on cultural critique. It cannot confirm or disconfirm specific remedies concerning social and political reorganization that may be drawn from theories about our imperfect transition from feudal and rural conditions to an industrial society. It may take sides, of course, through passionate impersonation; what it does most convincingly, however, with its famous "concreteness" or illustrative energy, is to provide counterexamples to disembodied thought and unearned abstraction.

I bring literature (and the literary sense of language) directly into the debate for other reasons as well. Comparing Schiller's *Letters on Aesthetic Education* with Raymond Williams's *Culture and Society*, a difference of style appears that should be meaningful. But has there been progress, or is that too crude a notion for changes between 1795 and 1958? One admires "The Development of a Common Culture," Williams's conclusion to *Culture and Society*, for its careful stopping at keywords, its verbal massage, its pragmatic probing that understands how stiff our mental habits are, and a historical semantics that broadens cultural memory. Yet at the end of *Culture and Society* do we not feel—despite our assent to these good words and our relief that dogmatism and prophecy have been displaced—that the underlying situation may not have changed? Is not Williams's question, for example, of whether there can be a "compatability of increasing specialization with a genuinely common culture" as urgent and insoluble as ever, despite his addendum that the question is "only soluble in a context of material community and by the full democratic process"?[1]

The adjective-noun compounds in the above sentence are as distinctive and obscurely affecting as "poetic diction" was in the eighteenth century or sublime-sounding hypostases were in Schiller. A High Church vocabulary has been exchanged for a Low or Broad Church one, altar has become table, but otherwise there remains a muffled drumbeat, an insistence, in these last subdued yet eloquent pages of Williams's book, on something close to a jargon of commonality. This may be preferable to the "jargon of authenticity" Adorno charges Heidegger with, but it nonetheless raises a rhetorical issue beyond that. What will persuade us that it is all right to live within our means, to quicken our response to low-profile words rather than wishing to be moved by thaumaturgic ones? *Mundus vult decipi*: because there is a biological play instinct; because the imagination, which partakes of it, does not really want a puritanical commonwealth; because, as Blake said, "One Law for the Lion and the Ox is Oppression," what should we do with our surplus imagination, its *uncommon* culture, which is playful, extravagant, dangerous, often both sublime and a bit crazy?

This problem does not lessen my appreciation of the plain or middle style, but it makes a place for another more high-flown or high-tech, which has its own historical and continuing achievement and is part of "the common need." There is, however, what Williams has named a "Long Revolution," whereby industry and democracy, helped by this emphasis on culture, successfully shift away from a "dominative mood," marked by "the theory and practice of man's mastering and controlling his natural environment." "We are still rephrasing this," Williams adds, using an odd metaphor, "as we learn the folly of exploiting any part of this environment in isolation . . . learning, slowly, to attend to our environment as a whole, and to draw our values from that whole." This is an unexceptionable thought, because the feeling that a totality has been lost, that the individual has shrunk into specialization or sectarian folly—become, to quote Blake, a "Human Abstract"—does indeed determine both Schiller's restorative concept of culture and that of the English critics to whom Williams's book is devoted. Exceptional, however, is that odd metaphor of "rephrasing," which tells us that Williams considers words as part of the harmed environment. So this is where literature comes back, finds its value: the ability to "rephrase," to think experience and words in tandem, to experience words as well as to word experience. His penultimate sentences say too much but say it slowly. "The evident problems of our civilization are too close and too serious for anyone to suppose that an emphasis is a solution. . . . Yet we are coming increasingly to realize that our vocabulary, the language we use to inquire into and negotiate our actions, is no secondary factor, but a practical and radical element in itself."[2] Despite their more forceful theorizing and historicizing and their skepticism about progress, Adorno and Horkheimer would be in general agreement.

A further reason to keep literature in mind is that while cultural theory has a clear focus, it is often tendentious, as sure as the doctrine of original sin of the nature of humanity's fall. Literature, however, captures such elegiac themes as the loss of the organic community, or the loss of totality, or the mutilation and reification of human relations in modern (capitalistic, industrial, modern, postmodern) society in a way that is not predetermined by a casuistic ideology or causal system. Art is neither didactic nor pedagogical, except by fits and starts. Whatever its purposes may be—and they do not exclude the expression of strong beliefs—it does not strive for a univocal solution, catechism, or definitive means-end relation. And though Williams thinks of culture instrumentally, as a very special means of social education and progress, the difference between the tradition he carries forward and overt authoritarian *dirigisme* is found in his sense of culture as a "tending of natural growth" that reforms society and the state by means of a "Long Revolution." Culture never loses for him either the agricultural or process-oriented— *cultura/culturans*—meaning.[3] This chapter, then, will not be devoted to the Henry Jamesian question of how, if at all, immigrant speech or emergent vernaculars might be integrated into an existing culture; James had always feared that America had no culture at all, in the Arnoldian sense, and his essay of 1905, responding to the influx of East European Jews after the Russian pogroms of the 1880s, only restates that fear acutely.[4] My concern is to advance a point of view that would see literature itself as cultural discourse, in that way getting beyond lip service or a purely abstract esteem for art. This aim involves showing precisely the relation between literary instance and cultural crisis.

Art, like cultural theory, wishes to liberate the "Human Abstract." In Blake, art fights the system: it discloses how ideologies manacle the mind and distort everything creative: modes of thinking, imagining, writing. The question of our speech arises because poems like "The Tyger" are spoken from *within* the system, from within a totalizing and forceful ideology that has corrupted the very idea of creation. Blake's depiction of a self-induced and paralyzing astonishment before the sublimity of that mind-boggling creature is at once seductive and demystifying:

Tyger, Tyger, burning bright
In the forests of the night,
What immortal hand or eye
Dare frame thy fearful symmetry?

The questioner, as this apparently orthodox praise of creation proceeds, becomes increasingly dizzy:

What the hammer? what the chain
In what furnace was thy brain . . .
What the anvil? What dread grasp . . .

The seeming inadequacy of terms derived from human and especially manual labor (hands, feet, and tools) is used satirically to project the tiger as a sublime and mystical thing, *as if there were no analogy possible between divine creation and human labor*. The end of such rapturous exclamation is the worship of established power or a submissive silence like Job's, after God has spoken from the whirlwind and reprimanded him ("Where wast thou when the world was created . . . ?"). Yet Blake, because he wishes to save rather than deflate visionary perception, rejects a merely ironic or satirical stance. His fantasy is polemical *and* defamiliarizing, "unlike," as Stevens might say:

It must be that in time
The real will from its crude compoundings come,
Seeming, at first, a beast disgorged, unlike,
Warmed by a desperate milk.[5]

The project of overcoming the Human Abstract, and placing our kind (the human species) once more into its larger "organic" community, embraces "Animal Forms of Wisdom" like the Tyger; and it is with them that Blake's hero, the Man, converses at the end of *Four Zoas*. In Blake's wondrous and sprawling epic about the four "creatures" the biblical Book of Revelation had developed out of the prophecies of Ezekiel, the poet expresses astonishment at things created but undoes (how many times!) the rapt paralysis that befalls his "dizzy questioner." These "compoundings," Blake's cosmic fabliaux, are as sophisticated as the return to the ballad in Coleridge and Wordsworth.

Coleridge's "Rime of the Ancient Mariner," for example, which literary taxonomists classify as a supernatural ballad, is basically a story about *phantomization*, about the way the human in us is emptied out. The poem's plot first separates the protagonist from society and then restores him to it via a larger, communitarian consciousness of "man and bird and beast." Tradition tells us that when the soul leaves the body, or genius its natural element, a sound of lamentation is heard. So poetry, in this pivotal period of romanticism, is the sound of a disembodied spirit trying to come back, to redeem imagination from abstraction.[6]

The case of Christopher Smart, however, the greatest if also most idiosyncratic poet to offer a visionary representation of the restored human link with the *res creatae* (animal, vegetable, or mineral) and who wrote around 1760 the strange and long-neglected lines published only in 1939 as *Jubilate Agno*, shows that a strict literary-historical periodization is deceptive. Yet Wordsworth's nature poetry is particularly intriguing as a new rhetoric of community, or as an attempt to repair—in a style very different from that of Smart—the breach between nature and culture.[7]

Romanticism, Walter Pater observed, added strangeness to (classical) beauty. This strangeness comes at first through a predilection for the Gothic, a style that the romantics refined. They used the spectral as a device, a technique to disclose psychic states that required interpretation rather than dismissal. They heeded the internal weather of ominous feelings and imagistic flashes that induced prognostic and even prophetic intimations about the disturbed relation between nature and mankind. The spectral was often a shadow cast over ecology, over nature as man's home. In terms of conventional classicist representation the question became: Will nature outlast the physical or mental ravages of War, Industry, and City? Would the genius loci of woods, rivers, sky, and field depart forever into utopian memory? Wordsworth fought a tremendous rearguard action against the bad signs. Why should Paradise, the Elysian Groves, the Fortunate Fields, he asks in a famous passage, be "A history only of departed things, / Or a mere fiction of what never was?"[8] *Lyrical Ballads*, Wordsworth and Coleridge's early and most famous collection, was, among other things, a project to keep the genius from parting by accommodating supernatural intimations, especially the aura of particular places. To compare Wordsworth's "Hart-Leap Well" with both Coleridge's "Ancient Mariner" and Bürger's "The Wild Huntsman" is to understand the continuing appeal of Gothic incident and the way different poetics merge it with place, landscape, nature, cosmos. In Wordsworth the notion of a threatened (sometimes threatening) spirit of place assumes a central role: from juvenilia, in which it is a gothicized cliché, to his autobiographical *Prelude*, where its more subtle presence is linked to the themes of personal identity, poetic election, and growth. But in all the poets I have mentioned (and Milton would have to be added) the venerable topos of a sympathetic Nature—a Nature with feelings—is fading.

Wordsworth still tries to keep it alive, even if he rejects anthro-pomorphic personification and resorts to scrupulously negative for-mulations. He writes of the hunted creature in "Hart-Leap Well," "This beast not unobserv'd by Nature fell, / His death was mourn'd by sympathy divine." An animistic superstition that had supported many poetical conceptions in the past becomes as threatened as the Rainbow is according to Keats; its vanishing is an "Enlightenment" that foreshadows a further and final flight of Milton's "parting genius." Yet paradoxically this is the time when an *imagination* in-creasingly tagged as "sympathetic" makes its appearance and refus-es to accept nature's total disenchantment.

Only now does the imagination tolerate the real world as the only source for its representations. The great and conscious pro-posers of this change are Wordsworth and George Eliot. A new complexity enters, however, since the traditional myths and vision-ary forms lose their hold just when, in terms of fears about nature, they are most needed. Do they really disappear from both the world and poetry?

Surely the crisis poem after Wordsworth still tries to "simplify the ghost" of nature, to meet it in some startling, adventurous form. Failing that, poets represent its loss as the basis of a new quest ro-mance: even as the supernatural ballad dies out, both poetry and the novella find new ways of throwing the lights and shadows of the un-canny over the realism now filling the pages of fiction. A concern prevails that if the common aspects of life in nature are not cultivat-ed by imaginative rather than instrumental reason, nature will cease to be an object of vital interest and eventually render us homeless. "The sun strengthens us no more, neither does the moon," is D. H. Lawrence's lament. By cultivating nature through the feelings—it is this quality in Wordsworth that relieved John Stuart Mill's intellec-tual crisis—we are bonded to "the world, which is the very world / Of all of us."[9] Lacking this "culture of the feelings," however, our imag-inative energies face increasing alienation, to the point of becoming spectral, even apocalyptic, as when Wordsworth encounters imagi-nation after crossing the Alps, and the disembodied power is com-pared to a sudden mountain mist, an "unfathered vapour."[10]

What is impressive here, and in romanticism generally, is not the discovery of a new truth (it isn't new) but a greater honesty and force in representing it. This also holds for traditional forms like the ballad. Revived less as a naive than as a native genre, the ballad now expresses the experience of phantomization as a modern and intelligible fact. In many ballads and folktales a ghost too vengeful or desirous enters. Cold by nature, this ghost needs human warmth and seeks to combine with, to rape if necessary—so I understand Goethe's "Erl-King"—a human companion. In Goethe's "Bride of Corinth," a female ghost, denied fulfillment in life because of religious repression, demands that life back and becomes a vampire.

Though it is faddish to discourse on vampires, let me stay with a more general Halloween, a sort of low-grade, permanent spookiness. The most formal reaction to the sense that nature and imagination are falling away from each other, that the link of nature has weakened, is a fetishistic and extreme cathexis named by Ruskin the "pathetic fallacy." It leads far beyond Tennyson's "cruel, crawling foam." If beauty, at least classical beauty, is marked by balance and correspondence, a perfect matching of subjective and objective, of shape and spirit, then the "pathetic," that is, sympathetic, fallacy breaks the mold or shows a crack in this ideal. Visionary or hyperbolic forms, of course, had always sinned against that ideal: Milton's *Lycidas* and Donne's *Anatomy* are sustained pathetic fallacies. But when the sympathetic imagination acts up yet is deprived of traditional visionary symbols, then a new tension emerges between hyperbolic pathos and realistic narrative, most noticeably in the shorter fictional forms.

Consider the way Virginia Woolf, for example, pans in her short story "Solid Objects" from "one small black spot" in the distance, which turns out to be a boat on the water, to her main character, John, who gives up a political career after finding a lump of green glass, a discovery that leads to his endless fascination with the beauty and solidity of found objects. This panning is a complex defense against empathizing too much, against moving into the secrets of matter or mind in order to compensate for the consumerism and insubstantiality of ordinary social life.[11]

It happens that one of the starting points of Wordsworth's earliest
mature poem, "The Ruined Cottage," is a speck of glass:

> I crossed this dreary moor
> In the clear moonlight, when I reached the hut
> I looked within but all was still & dark
> Only within the ruin, I beheld
> At a small distance on the dusky ground
> A broken pane which glitter'd to the moon
> And seemed akin to life.[12]

Wordsworth circumvents the pathetic fallacy, though not pathos,
by scrupulous phrasing. He draws from this fragment the entire
story of "The Ruined Cottage," a tale of broken sympathies leading
to the mutual abandonment of man and nature and so to the destruction of the very notion of *milieu*. The artistic problem raised
by this ghostly moment is not only how to resist extreme pathos or
spectral symbolism in order to prevent narrative space collapsing
but also how to express, here as elsewhere, the relation of "mute, insensate things" (including, crazily, that speck of glittering glass) to
the sympathetic imagination.

"The Ruined Cottage" is the site of the tale of Margaret, aban-
doned by a husband who cannot bear to see his family starve and
so sells himself into the army during the Napoleonic Wars, leaving
her to waste away silently in hope of his return. The story is con-
jured up from that site by a wandering Pedlar and told to the Poet
(Wordsworth himself) who has met him there. The speech situation, then, becomes quite complex: at the center is a silent ruin, a
symbol of inarticulate suffering that resists, even as it redemptively
elicits, the fluency of moral reflection:

> And never for each other shall we feel
> As we may feel[,] till we have sympathy
> With nature in her forms inanimate[,]
> With objects such as have no power to hold
> Articulate language. In all forms of things
> There is a mind.[13]

On one level, Wordsworth succeeds: the story of Margaret becomes a vivid reminder of how human sympathies develop. Nature, he implies, serves as a transitional object; eventually her "gentle agency" turns us from love of the rural to love of humanity, even to the passion of Margaret. However, at the level of language itself, there is much less clarity. What remains untheorized in Wordsworth's argument is argument itself: the "power to hold / Articulate language." How does language enter the developmental process? How do we pass from "mute dialogues" with the mother (1850 *Prelude* 2.269), and then with nature, to articulate language, especially poetic expression? Wordsworth assumes (and Coleridge will challenge the assumption) that rural speech embodies a special quality, a counterurbanity that reflects nature's influence on human development.

As a philosopher—a role Coleridge imposed—Wordsworth remains obscure.[14] Yet his moral position is quite clear: poetry articulates a silent sympathy and prevents language from becoming a "counter-spirit." So the Pedlar's decorum of disclosure, his respect for the muteness of things, for their opaque and quietistic mode of being, limits the audistic pleasure we take in hearing about suffering and catastrophe. The result is a displacement from tale (vicarious adventure, vicariously experienced suffering) to teller, from narrative action to narrator: the slowness of the story, its retardations, are antitheatrical devices serving to reduce voyeurism and to make us thoughtful about the character of poet or storyteller, their attraction to the heart of darkness.

At any point, so Wordsworth would like us to believe, the story could lapse, become silent, merge back into a reticence of nature from which the Pedlar's watchful ear and eye have drawn it. This turning toward nature has struck some critics as a turning away from human suffering, but it is, after all, the poet who uncovers the story, who rescues it from nature's "oblivious tendencies." The creation, moreover, of a narrative space is also the virtual creation of a community: storyteller and listener—Pedlar and Poet, and then the poet and those who receive his poetry—form a special bond. They bring an understanding of how "mute, insensate things" affect imagination and convey "the still, sad music of humanity." A common destiny of nature and mankind is affirmed. Within this frame the Pedlar, as the poet's mentor, transmits an ethos, a consistent, integrated, exemplary way of conducting one's life.

The thought of such a legacy—passing from Pedlar to Poet—is important to Wordsworth. The Pedlar is similar to the Peasant in "Hart-Leap Well" or to the poet himself in "Michael." Wordsworth enters the prologue to that poem in his own person: he negotiates a threatened breach between rural and modern by becoming, as it were, Michael's heir. He reacts to the changes in rural England, which are seen as deceptively slow and immensely sad. Another great work of time is being ruined: English nature itself.

Wordsworth always means by nature an entire complex of feelings and perceptions: precisely what we would now call a culture. But the changes in that culture, as the enclosure movement gains momentum and industrialization transforms country into city, do not signal something new that has its own integrity. Instead they prompt the fear that nature as a whole will fade from the human imagination, that an immemorial compact between mind and world, nature and imagination, is in danger of being dissolved. This compact, deeper than any religion, involves what for the Enlightenment is a superstition: the idea that nature has feelings, even "passions," as Wordsworth will say, using a favorite word ("The sounding cataract / Haunted me like a passion").[15]

Readers who demystify his focus on nature and charge that it hides an antisocial streak, a deeply troubling solipsism, mistake the task he has set himself, or the immensity of the shift in sensibility that is occurring as Wordsworth constructs a new vision of community. It may be true that he is as solipsistic as any of us. But his subject, the growth of a poet's mind, cannot be reduced to the psychological and compensatory trick of someone who has trouble growing up, who cannot turn his imagination to social life and politics. If Wordsworth has survived such criticism, from Matthew Arnold, who accused him of averting his eyes from "half of human fate" (in "Stanzas in Memory of the Author of 'Oberman'" [1849]), to certain New Historicists, it is because he is the only writer to carry forward a *pastoral culture* as a fully modern poet. Humble as it may seem, this feat, if successful, would amount to a *translatio studii*: the significant transmission of a culture into a new era.[16] The modernizing impetus of other English romantic poets is not a *translatio*: they are either forthrightly urbane (like Byron and, to an extent, Shelley), or creatively nostalgic (evoking, like Keats, "Flora and Old Pan" while seeking to go beyond the fairy way of writing), or deliberately local and provincial (like John Clare). Wordsworth alone rescues for a modern sensibility what can—or in his view, must—be saved.

No doubt his effort too is retrospective; it is, in Schiller's sense, sentimental rather than naive. In *A Guide through the District of the Lakes*, mainly written in 1810, Wordsworth claims to have given a faithful description of "a perfect Republic of Shepherds and Agriculturalists," indeed an "almost visionary mountain republic" as it existed for centuries, "until within the last sixty years." What I have called a pastoral culture is a construct, but that does not mean it has no basis in fact.[17] Wordsworth's well-known letter to Charles James Fox, sent with the second edition of *Lyrical Ballads* and inviting the politician to pay special attention to "Michael" and "The Brothers," expresses forcefully his admiration for the independent farmers called "statesmen," as well as for the "sacred property" of the poor. It is "sacred" because property, especially landed property, is essential to "the feelings of inheritance, home, and personal and family independence."[18] At this point Wordsworth does not identify with a specific social class; he represents a more general ethos and claims for the poet an independent privilege, a "Power like one of Nature's" (1850 *Prelude* 13.307–311).[19]

Such portents as Goldsmith's *The Deserted Village*, published in 1770 (the year of Wordsworth's birth), which describes the depopulation of the English countryside as the enclosure movement creates more itinerants and industry draws workers into the cities, and daily evidence around Wordsworth that "even in the most sequestered places, by manufactures, traffic, religion, law, interchange of inhabitants, etc., distinctions are done away which would otherwise have been strong and obvious"[20] do not seem to affect Wordsworth's faith in a trustworthy rural imagination. *It is my view that the failure to carry this imagination into a modern form, the failure to translate into a modern idiom a sensibility nurtured by country life, creates—less in England, because of Wordsworth, than in continental Europe—an unprogressive, overidealized, image of what is lost, and thus a deeply anti-urban sentiment.* After 1815, when the worst aspects of capitalistic farming and the industrial revolution begin to be felt, Wordsworth's influence increases but can also be used for reactionary purposes. It is on the continent, however, that pastoralism eventually distorts cultural thinking and leads to serious political consequences.[21] I would like to give an impression of the virulence of this utopian and unintegrated ideal and how it has affected the issue of the "inexpressive" or "silent" in poetic language.

There is—let me begin by admitting this—something absurd in seeing the Pedlar or Michael or other protagonists of Wordsworth's "Pastoral" as culture bearers. A faint absurdity like that hovers over *Lyrical Ballads* as a whole. Applying the concept of tradition in its strong form of a *translatio studii* is a way of characterizing at once Wordsworth's originality and his incongruity. His *translatio* is not based on a complete pass-through of an older culture or on a Renaissance-type of modernization, of making illustrious a dialect or vein of folklore by an expertise derived from the classics (a pattern sometimes described as new wine in old bottles). Nor—and this is a more serious matter—does Wordsworth infuse the city, the urban landscape, with any kind of splendor, however intermittent.[22] A vision of the culture of cities is not within his reach. Instead, Wordsworth's culture bearing tries to cut across the nature/culture divide by conveying the still unmediated, accessible, and integral—yet barely so—presence of a half-perceived and half-created mode of life, one that is rapidly disappearing as a "culture" with more authenticity than most.

It was Lionel Trilling who introduced the idea of authenticity in order to characterize the inexpressiveness of Michael. His touchstone, like Arnold's, is the verse that describes how the shepherd would sit an entire day by the sheepfold "and never lifted up a single stone":

Michael says nothing; he *expresses* nothing. It is not the case with him as it is with Hamlet that he has "that within which passeth show." There is no within and without: he and his grief are one. We may not, then, speak of sincerity. But our sense of Michael's being, of—so to speak—his being-in-grief, comes to us as a surprise, as if it were exceptional in its actuality, and valuable. And we are impelled to use some word which denotes the nature of this being and which accounts for the high value we put on it. The word we employ for this purpose is "authenticity."[23]

Sincerity involves the test of speech: it is because speech can be hypocritical or ambiguous and because it is always for show—even when not explicitly audience-directed and rhetorical—that the issue of the character behind the speech arises, and even a question of whether speech, distinct from the unfathomable person, can ever be sincere. A suspicion may also be voiced that speech is always impersonation, that someone else (the "ghost" I have previously introduced) is speaking us or in us. Plato's attempt to distinguish oral from written by attributing a sincerity he names truth to the oral mode cannot be sustained. The idea of authenticity moves the issue away from speech toward other evidences, such as character, though these evidences too are not truly silent or self-evidential but continue to depend on report. There is a regress of evidence until we reach a religious or mystical stratum: authenticity suggests a mode of being so self-coincident, so integral, that it signals the absence of internal division, or of the intellectual consciousness we associate with such division. Authenticity means living only in the eye of God or Nature.[24]

In overflow passages to "Michael" Wordsworth struggles with the issue of both the shepherd's language and nature's language. The language of nature was, of course, a topos of long standing: nature is said to "speak" to us by signatures or symbols. God has given us this second "Book" (of Nature), which expands the truth of Scripture to all eyes. The religious background of the authenticity concept surfaces here. That something of Bible or liturgy may

affect the diction of "Michael" only strengthens its own authenticity. Yet when Wordsworth, in an alternate beginning to the poem,
tries to convey this language of nature, he fails, because intention
demands articulacy and what he shows remains subarticulate:

> There is a shapeless crowd of unhewn stones
> That lie together, some in heaps, and some
> In lines, that seem to keep themselves alive
> In the last dotage of a dying form.
> At least so seems it to a man who stands
> In such a lonely place.

This fragment may have been discarded because the image of a
mysterious intention arising directly from nature (an appearance of
mystery resolved later in the poem), or the image of an obscure
feeling *in* the stones, is just too close to a crazy empathy, to an extreme form of the "pathetic fallacy."[25] Other fragments refer to the
shepherd's attempts to express himself, to the peculiar integrity of
his language. Yet Wordsworth has to admit a residual silence or
even idiotism:

> No doubt if you in terms direct had ask'd
> Whether he lov'd the mountains, true it is
> That with blunt repetition of your words
> He might have stared at you, and said that they
> Were fearful to behold, but had you then
> Discours'd with him in some particular sort
> Of his own business, and the goings on
> Of earth and sky, then truly had you seen
> That in his thoughts there were obscurities,
> Wonders and admirations, things that wrought
> Not less than a religion in his heart.[26]

The near-muteness of Leech-gatherer and Idiot Boy comes to mind.
Can we really talk of a *culture*, or what should sustain it, when its
language is so sparse ("simple and unelaborated") and has to be
purified of "all lasting and rational causes of dislike and disgust"? I
am now quoting, of course, from the 1800 preface to *Lyrical Bal-*

lads, which introduces the topic of a more natural language for poetry, one that is taken from "low and rustic life." Coleridge will quarrel with his friend's formulation of the matter in chapter 17 of the *Biographia Literaria*.

There is no need to interrogate that quarrel. Coleridge's response is strong and correct, yet not entirely to the point. Wordsworth's attempt to justify the diction of poetry in mimetic terms— by claiming, in the preface, that he wishes to introduce "the real language of men"—may indeed be inept, for he is advocating a quality not based primarily on speech. It is clearly not language as such but rather an ethos or a culture the poet wishes to save. That culture, while it is peculiarly English, has not yet *emerged* into poetry; speech, therefore, can become a "counter-spirit" to it. Hence Wordsworth is compelled to use mimetic terms in such an equivocating manner. If he were asked bluntly what characterizes that culture, which is relatively mute and very near subsistence level, the answer would have to fall back on the "authenticity" of passions and affections[27] that center on "nature": on landed property, rural homestead, or patrimony as the minimum gage for freedom of spirit and family independence.[28]

At this point what I have called a pastoral culture, which *fades into memory before it has emerged into maturity, like the twilight presence of Lucy*, seems to unmask itself as a cultural politics defending property rights. Such emphasis on property is not new in English political thought. Yet Wordsworth's concept of property qualification is quite different from the standard use of it to justify restricted voting rights or citizenship, though he opposed the Reform Bill of 1832 "as giving a grace to an industrial, propertyless society."[29] It is true that property, in both Wordsworth's and the standard philosophy, is thought to foster a reality relation and individual dignity. A man without property becomes too easily a man without properties (qualities, *Eigenschaften*): deracinated, lacking local attachments, abstract in his thinking—a space cadet, we would now say. But Wordsworth's focus on the rural scene and on the modest or the poor is not ipso facto a defense of larger holdings. Property has no value for him except as a need of the soul, close to the need for roots. It is not fungible in the ordinary sense; it must remain *in na-ture*, merging with it, tied to an imaginative community of beings, to a living, interactive nature culture. To achieve a spiritual home requires associative links to a specific place and a sensitivity to "gra-dations" that cannot occur without a material homestead. As a poet Wordsworth does not presuppose this fact on the basis of received ideas: he creates or recreates it as the "cultured Vale" we find in his nature poetry.[30]

The sense that we exist in *this* world, that we are not ghosts and strangers on earth, doomed to wander about in exile, is called by both Rousseau and Wordsworth the "sentiment of being," and Tril-ling, in associating it with authenticity, names it an "unassailable intuition." It is assailed, of course, all the time. Yet such "moments of being" are attested by imaginative residues in our speech. The word "be" itself, Trilling adds, is used by Wordsworth as if he were conscious that it enters the name of God ("I am that I am"). Such simple words, carrying a reservoir of silence, though not less capa-ble of betrayal than complex words, raise the issue of whether we can ever fuse being and meaning through language. Heidegger looks in that direction; he is always "on the way to language" (*unter-wegs zur Sprache*). Yet we know how vulnerable he was to a political doctrine that stressed the organic community and the possibility that it could be recovered by a decisive historical act. Is Heidegger's lan-guage, so close to poetic paranomasia, an advance over Words-worth's as cultural discourse?

In the conclusion to the *Letter on Humanism*, written for a French admirer soon after the Second World War, Heidegger links future thought to an ending (the end of metaphysics) and a beginning (a "more originary" thinking). But he seems careful about prospecting the future. Cultural prophesy—including his own brand of deci-sionist rhetoric that for a time credited the Nazi *Aufbruch* as expos-ing the neediness and inauthenticity of his era—had hastened rather than prevented catastrophe, and his emphasis now reverts to the relation of thought and language. Still, the style of the con-cluding paragraph remains promissory:

Das künftige Denken ist nicht mehr Philosophie, weil es ursprünglicher denkt als die Metaphysik, welcher Name das gleiche sagt. Das künftige Denken kann aber auch nicht mehr, wie Hegel verlangte, den Namen der "Liebe zur Weisheit" ablegen und die Weisheit selbst in der Gestalt des absoluten Wissens geworden sein. Das Denken ist auf dem Abstieg in die Armut seines vorläufigen Wesens. Das Denken sammelt die Sprache in das einfache Sagen. Die Sprache ist so die Sprache des Seins, wie die Wolken die Wolken des Himmels sind. Das Denken legt mit seinem Sagen unscheinbare Furchen in die Sprache. Sie sind noch unscheinbarer als die Furchen, die der Landmann langsamen Schrittes durch das Feld zieht.[31]

(Future thought is no longer philosophy, because it thinks more originally than metaphysics, whose name means the same. Yet future thought also cannot any longer, as Hegel demanded, lay aside its name of "Love for Wisdom" and become wisdom itself in the form of absolute knowledge. Thought is descending into the poverty of its temporary mode of being. Thought gathers language into simple speech. Language is the language of being as clouds are the clouds of heaven. Thought places with its speech unapparent furrows in language. They are even more unapparent than the furrows made in the field by the slowly striding peasant.)

The apparent simplicity and pastoralism of this prose are not accidental. The war is over, including a very real culture war between Germany and France that I have not had the time to describe except to indicate (in chapter 2) that it focused on the *Kultur/civilisation* antithesis.[32] That this war is still going on, however, despite Heidegger's much-subdued style (there is pathos in this paragraph, but not *pathos* in the oratorical sense, that is, the heroic-pathetic vein of some Heidegger writings in the Nazi period), is suggested by the fact that he continues to shun words derived from the Latin or Romance stratum. But at least he does not indulge in the violent punning whereby he used to furrow words, claiming to recover a more original meaning. The tone has changed, for the time being, and the only etymological move is a very old one, which derives the idea of linear writing from the pattern of the furrow.[33] When we think, however, of Vico's magnificent interpretation of Roman law—that "severe poem," as he called it—or E. R. Curtius's defense of *romanitas* in the magisterial *European Literature and the Latin Middle Ages*—written during the Nazi period and demonstrating the immense Latin heritage that Goethe transmitted to modern German literature—one can only wonder at Heidegger's provincialism.

Heidegger's rejection of Latinity is, nevertheless, a philosophically complex act. It preceded the political change in Germany and was based on his judgment that the language of philosophy was not the language of thought and that both had become inauthentic. The abstraction that has invaded modern life is denounced as an occultation of Being. The history of our thinking about Being, enmeshed in categories supplied by language, requires therefore an aggressive mode of analysis (*Destruktion*) that must alter the diction of philosophy and thought as a whole. Heidegger rejects, in short, not the classical heritage as such but its faulty mediation of more radical Greek intuitions. He returns to the possibility of a direct German-Greek axis of linkage. In a strange parallel to Wordsworth, there is the hope in a new *translatio*, an original and originative thinking that will restore language to simplicity and human life to its unalienated place in nature, so that "humanism," with its secularist, antisacred pretensions, becomes superfluous. Heidegger's "Thought gathers language into simple speech," together with the final image of the philosopher-peasant cultivating a speech with unapparent furrows, has a relation to Wordsworth's own cure of language.

Unfortunately, as I have suggested, the very absence on the continent of a Wordsworth or a Wordsworth reception removed what might have moderated a cultural and political antimodernism vulnerable to vicious dichotomies. Political thought, especially in Germany, pitted the archaic *numen* of *Kultur* against the superficial classicism and cosmopolitanism of *civilisation* and exaggerated the organic relation of man to nature (also, mysteriously, to nation) in country life, in order to set that pastoral culture against urban deracination.[34] It is not possible to read Heidegger's final evocation of the peasant without thinking of the polemic in fascist thought against *bodenloses Denken* or "groundless thought." This overdetermined phrase is applied by Heidegger to "metaphysics" as the wrong kind of unworldiness but also, more generally, to deracinated and deracinating speculation. The paragraph is an example of what Lyotard has called Heidegger's *impensé paysan*.

"Groundless thought," interpreted as the mentality of the person without property or who does not feel he has a hereditary national stake, motivates from the late nineteenth century on the intersecting discourses of anti-intellectualism and anti-Semitism. It would be easy to cite a masterpiece of *ressentiment* like Maurice Barrès's *Les Déracinés* (The uprooted) to illustrate the exploitation of a regionalistic and rural nostalgia. Or to examine how Nazi ideology played on the suffering of the peasantry and attracted that group by promises of equality with other professions or estates (*Stände*) in the new *Volksgemeinschaft*. Or to show how Edouard Drumont, the arch anti-Semite, linked finance capitalism and a corrupting city life to deracinated immigrant Jews, accused of dispossessing native citizens and turning the good old country (*le vieux pays* or *la France d'alors*) into *la France juive*. Even when Jews are praised, it is for their ability to deal with abstractions, a talent that is said to derive from their having been excluded throughout Christian history from work on the land and other "productive" professions and therefore having to turn to the handling of "abstract money" and the institutions associated with it.[35]

Nor is it difficult to cite less prejudiced texts haunted by the Human Abstract. Count Keyserling declares roundly in 1926: " 'Abstract Man' was the invention of the eighteenth century."[36] F. R. Leavis quotes "Rilke on Vacuity," protesting American commodification: "Now there come crowding over from America empty, indifferent things, pseudo-things, dummy-life. . . . A house, in the American sense, an American apple or wine, has nothing in common with the house, the fruit, the grape into which the hope and pensiveness of our forefathers would enter. . . . The animated, experienced things that share our lives are coming to an end. . . . We are perhaps the last to have still known such things." Rilke wishes to preserve "their human and Laral worth."[37] The ancient authorities guiding our morals were blended, according to Walter Lippmann, "with the ancient landmarks, with fields and vineyards and patriarchal trees, with ancient houses and chests full of heirlooms, with churchyards near at hand and their ancestral graves." But modern man is an "emigrant who lives in a revolutionary society," who can find no fixed point outside his conscience and does not "really believe there is such a point, because he has moved about too fast to fix any point long enough in his mind."[38] Commenting on the modern intellectual, Trilling adds: "It is a characteristic of the intellectual life of our culture that it fosters a form of assent which does not involve actual credence."[39]

The painter R. B. Kitaj, born in Ohio and now living in London, makes an identity out of all this. He calls himself a Diasporist. "I've come to make myself a tradition in that Diaspora . . . as a real American rootless Jew, riddled with assimilationist secularism and Anglophiliac-Europist art mania, besieged by modernisms and their skeptical overflow, fearful at the prospect and state of Wandering, un-at-homeness, yet unable to give myself to Ohio or God or Israel or London or California."[40] But in most cases, when fear of modern life, of an exponential growth of this identitarian nonidentity, combines with the charged themes of emigrant, Jew, and intellectual, an explosive situation is created.

No one needs to be reminded how much greater the panic about refugees is today than even between the world wars. The chief propagandist of Le Pen's National Front, an "unassuming, baby-faced technocrat," according to a report in the *Wall Street Journal*, can suddenly change and bark out a doctrine of racial venom, asserting "a world-wide 'cosmopolitan' conspiracy that seeks to abolish national identity and infect the world with the AIDS virus. He says that racial integration has corrupted the U.S. He mocks those in French politics with Jewish-sounding names—pronouncing the names in an exaggerated way."[41]

Yet the most inflammatory element in this rhetoric that seeks to halt the reign of *bodenloses Denken* or universalist abstraction is the memory of a rural culture. Maurice Bardèche even sees its loss *legislated* by the Nuremberg Tribunal, which recognized a "humanity" above and beyond the national state. The nation, the patria, the patrimonial culture (whether of country or town) is devalued, Bardèche claims, in favor of a general *Personne Humaine*. He gives the gist of the new law in the following extraordinary peroration:

> You will be a *citizen of the world,* you too will be packaged and dehydrated, you will cease to hear the rustling of the trees and the voice of the clocktowers, but you will learn to listen to the voice of the universal conscience: shake the earth from your shoes, peasant, that earth is worth nothing any more, it is dirt, it is embarrassing, it prevents the making of pretty packages. Modern Times have come. Listen to the voice of Modern Times. The Polish handyman who changes employ a dozen times each year is as much a man as you are; the Jewish Old Clothes dealer who has just come from Korotcha or Jitomir is as much a man as you are; they have the same rights as you in the country [*sur la terre*] or the town; respect the negro, o peasant. They have the same rights as you and you will make place for them at your table and they will enter into council with you and teach you what the universal conscience is saying, which you do not hear as well as you should. And their sons will be *messieurs* and will be appointed judges over your sons, they will govern your town and buy your field, for the universal conscience gives them expressly all these rights. As for you, peasant, if you consult your friends and if you regret the time you only saw boys from the canton at village festivals, know that you are murmuring against the universal conscience and that the law does not protect you from the same.[42]

In a similar spirit, but focusing on what he calls postwar aesthetic taboos, Hans Jürgen Syberberg, creator of *Hitler: A Film from Germany*, sees Nazi "Blut und Boden" propaganda as a distortive populist incarnation of a premodern rural culture (*ländliche Kultur*) that had been aristocratic (Blut = blood = lineage; Boden = landed property). He suggests that, because of the postwar taboos, we have repressed rather than come to terms with a still valuable aesthetics. "Heidegger," he asserts, "to the day of his death, was in all his judgments on poets from Hölderlin to Rilke, and in all his philosophic discoursing, a man of this culture that drew its nourishment from the soil."[43]

The countryside, the silent universe of ill-hap . . .
—*I, Pierre Rivière . . . A Case of Parricide in the Nineteenth Century*

Let Tola bless with the Toad, which is the good creature of God, tho' his virtue is in the secret, and his mention is not made.
— CHRISTOPHER SMART

There are three correlative issues that any analysis of the language of cultural criticism must take up. One is its authenticity, meaning by that the quality Trilling ascribes to Michael, Wordsworth's near-silent peasant and "statesman." Cultural rhetoric is noisy and explicit; its very aim is often to give voice to the voiceless, representation to those who are anonymous and marginalized. Wordsworth talks of "mute, insensate things" whose influence on thought and emotion he wishes to evoke, but people like Michael, or those still more humble or oppressed, are mute and *sensate*, and the visionary poetry of the romantic period focuses on the animal creation, which is equally subjected, and not always, as Scripture has it, "in hope" (Romans 8:19–23). From this point of view Wordsworth's "Hart-Leap Well" and *The White Doe of Rylstone* are as central to his oeuvre as "Michael," "The Pedlar," or *The Prelude*. What is *quietly* conveyed in Wordsworth's poetry, too quietly for some, is the misery of the rural poor in the countryside or those displaced into the cities; part of this misery is that, being treated no better than animals, and sometimes worse, they are also deprived of the very pleasures Wordsworth depicts: a freely exercised and excursive imagination, a sense for both animal and meanest flower, sympathy for "Nature."

There were differences between the condition of English peasants and those in the rest of Europe. Every country had its own specific problems, especially as capitalistic farming developed.[44] The scholars assembled by Foucault to understand Pierre Rivière's butchery of his mother and two siblings at Aunay-sur-Odon in 1835 move from that crime and Pierre's bleak though articulate testimony to a frightening picture of rural life, in some ways worsened when peasants became full citizens after the Revolution. The kind of bloody particulars printed up in contemporary French broadsheets are very unlike the incidents described and reflected on in Wordsworth's ballads, though by calling them "lyrical" he signaled that their content would differ from the usual sensational contents of the popular ballad. Reporting ominous symptoms of Rivière's "silent universe of ill-hap," the authors of a note in Foucault's volume headed "Blood and Cry" put a question that barely arises when reading Wordsworth: the "acts [of murderers like Pierre] were discourses; but what were they saying and why did they speak this terrifying language of crime?"[45]

It proved difficult, clearly, for these authors to find the right voice—the right rhetorical emphasis—for their own discourse. They are concerned, beyond saving from oblivion the historical facts and a significant text, with creating testimony of their own. They do not want to leave the scene "without an echo" by simply adding particulars to particulars or writing a becalmed social history. They too, one senses from their style throughout, want a "terrifying language."

It remains to be determined, as I have said, how different the situation of the rural poor was in the France in the 1830s from that in the Lake District during the Napoleonic Wars. But surely there was great suffering in both places; as to silence, both good and bad, there might have been more in England, given that the exemplary incident recovered by Foucault was aggravated by endless quarrels in the Rivière family over contractual property rights.[46] Wordsworth's poetry, if culturally significant, cannot be spared a juxtaposition with Pierre's "blood and cry," yet to compare them does not displace his (or my) understanding of how to preserve a reticence that, close to nature's own in the poet's depiction, might prevent language from becoming a "counter-spirit."

A second question affecting cultural discourse is the difficulty of forging progressive words that would not simply reverse the signs ("devil" and "angel" in Blake's *The Marriage of Heaven and Hell*; "culture" as cosmopolitan and "culture" as racist in National Socialist Germany). To work the system against itself is to risk that sooner or later one's own revision will appear as merely a variant of the system. Blake attempted to make a virtue of this difficulty; he refused to abandon corrupted or trivialized visionary categories, instead compounding them into a new "system" by creating a super-sublimity and often a wicked inversion of traditional dichotomies. Raymond Williams's prose, I have suggested, remains in the verbal orbit of idealism, despite his improved understanding of the "material community." Another interesting case is Walter Benjamin's avoidance of such terms as "creative" and "genius" in "The Work of Art in the Era of Mechanical Reproduction," because they were bourgeois clichés appropriated by Nazi rhetoric. Yet Benjamin has not escaped a fierce critical debate on whether his language betrays a materialistic or a mystical orientation.

The deception of hoping to be objective about one's culture through criticizing it is raised by Adorno: "By such exclusivity [*Vornehmheit*] the cultural critic assumes a privileged position and establishes his legitimacy, even while contributing to that culture as its salaried and honored gadfly."[47] In his *Aesthetic Theory*, Adorno holds that art can stand in opposition to modern society only by identification with that against which it rebels. He falls back on a homeopathic view of art's effect, mentioning its "admixture of poison" and recalling the ancient topos of the spear of Achilles, which alone can heal the wound it inflicts.[48]

Recently Derrida, also fascinated by the "gift" (*pharmakon*) of speech, has explored the "polysemic mobility" and "all [the] sources for reversal" in an early Benjamin text and has even suggested that there was a complicity—"specularity" is the better word—between the best and worst cultural discourses in the Nazi era, as they engage with German nationalism.[49] Let me also cite Leo Spitzer's comment regarding a fellow scholar of Romance literature, Karl Vossler. In 1936 Vossler, receiving an honorary degree in Madrid, gave a speech in which he declared that his study of Spanish culture was founded on an aversion to materialistic and positivistic theses. But a London paper reporting the event pointed out that antimaterialism and antipositivism were Nazi slogans. "So ambiguous," remarks Spitzer, "had humanistic studies become in Germany."[50]

This question of "our" language is further bedeviled by the fact that every social and political philosophy of modern times makes the same virtuous claim: it seeks the reconstruction or recovery of community, culture, nation-state. Yet at the same time the question of what *rhetorical* devices become necessary to cohere people of some diversity, to encourage them to agree or even sacrifice to that common purpose, tends to be suppressed in liberal-democratic thought. Isn't it clear enough from elections we have gone through that either the words of candidates for office are discounted, and some other criterion such as "character" or "charisma" tends to prevail, or the most manipulative slogans are greeted with applause and roars of approval? We uphold the fiction of the thoughtful voter while always doubting the honesty of the candidate seeking that vote. In this strange rhetorical situation, all the frankness, as Wyndham Lewis observed, is on one side, "and that is not on the side of the West, of democracy. All the traditional obliquity and subterranean methods of the Orient are, in this duel, exhibited by the westerner and the democratic regime. It is *we* who are the Machiavels, compared to the sovietist or the fascist, who makes no disguise of his forcible intentions, whose *power* is not wrapped up in parliamentary humbug, who is not eternally engaged in pretences of benefaction."[51]

The last problem is the expanding and overdetermined nature of the word "culture" itself. We have seen it become a talisman against the abstract life, against a feeling of increasing and encroaching unreality, all the more so when an available doctrine links that condition causally to a social or political condition. The rhetoric of culture is then associated with a corrective politics and may become revanchist. An intrinsic utopianism often surfaces: the memory of a *temps perdu*, of a pastoral moment in personal or collective history. However delusive, this belief in a vanished and more unified mode of life that once graced a homeland, a place that is our own, a prior ecological innocence, conspires with ideologies that seek a cure of the ground and wish to sacralize a community in its land. The archaic and allegorical forces of the genius loci may then be appealed to, as blood (race) and soil (nation, patrimony) become identifying slogans.

The cultural situation in the United States is not quite as dangerous. There is a constitution that spells out an ideal: it would safeguard, for each of us, life, liberty, and the pursuit of happiness. Still, happiness—a substitute, in the preamble, for the more traditional "property"—was always the most questionable of the triad. We pursue something that would bind gently and invisibly, tie us to, into, a community, without tying anyone down. Property, humanely defined as home, subsistence, family ties, fortified by guarantees of freedom of association and expression, as well as equality before the law, is indeed essential to life. The problem arises when cultural ideas become a property substitute, compensating those who have too little yet need to embody and define themselves.[52]

For the plight of the poor is not a transcendental but a real homelessness. Foucault's recovery of Pierre Rivière's testimony proves doubly relevant: it explodes rural idealism and demonstrates what may happen when those in nature, yet little more than chattel, revolt against "enduring the unlivable, day in day out." "The enclosed horizon of the hedgerows was from time immemorial a profusion of lives devoid of all future, deprived of all prospects. . . . For the mute horror of the daily round, for the predicament of dumb beast and dupe, [Pierre] has substituted a more flagrant horror, protest by hecatomb. And he thereby assumes the right to break the silence and speak at last. To speak the heart of the matter like one returned from the dead."[53] Deprived of a vital milieu even while alive, it is no wonder that so many of the poor felt trapped in an unreal reality. Because they have never fully lived in the world, they may become, like the undead, vengeful spirits.

NOTES

1. Raymond Williams, *Culture and Society, 1780–1950* (London: Chatto and Windus, 1958), 333. The complaint against specialization can be found as early as Socrates, of course. But in a political rather than philosophical context an early locus is Rousseau's "Discours sur les sciences et les arts" (1750): "Nous avons des Physiciens, des Géometres, des Chymistes, des Astronomes, des Poètes, des Musiciens, des Peintres; nous n'avons plus des citoyens; ou s'il nous en reste encore, dispersés dans nos campagnes abandonnées, ils s'y périssent indigens et méprisés." I should add that in the 1960s and 1970s Williams got to know continental Marxist thinkers more thoroughly and that he goes much further in specifying what he calls "material community" by refusing to consider cultural history (intellectual life and the arts) as merely secondary or superstructural. See the introduction to his *Marxism and Literature* (New York: Oxford University Press, 1977).

2. Williams, *Culture and Society*, 336–38.

3. For a forthright critique of an instrumental view of culture, see Hannah Arendt, "The Crisis in Culture," in *Between Past and Future: Eight Exercises in Political Thought* (New York: Penguin, 1977), 197–226.

4. "The Question of Our Speech," in *The Question of Our Speech; The Lesson of Balzac: Two Lectures* (Boston: Houghton, Mifflin, 1905), 3–52.

5. "Notes Toward a Supreme Fiction," *It must give Pleasure*, VII.

6. The expression is from Yeats, describing the effect of Chaucer on him. The role of Chaucer during the romantic period, his significance compared to that of Spenser and Milton, deserves fuller treatment. In the quest, moreover, for an imagined (and lost) community, which underwrites the many stirrings of nationalism at this time, the genius loci figure appeals for its archaism rather than its neoclassical elegance. It is gothicized, as in Walter Scott's *Waverley*.

7. "No poet is more emphatically the poet of community. A great part of his verse . . . is dedicated to the affections of home and neighborhood and country, and to that soul of joy and love which links together all Nature's children, and 'steals from earth to man, from man to earth' " (A. C. Bradley, "Wordsworth," in *Oxford Lectures on Poetry* [London: Macmillan, 1909], 143–44).

8. Prospectus to *The Excursion* (1814)

9. 1850 *Prelude* 11.142–3.

10. 1850 *Prelude* 6.595.

11. Cf. Douglas Mao's analysis of the episode in *Modernism and the Question of the Object* (Ann Arbor: UMI, 1994), 17–20.

12. *The Ruined Cottage and The Pedlar* (The Cornell Wordsworth), ed. James Butler (Ithaca: Cornell University Press, 1979), 87.

13. From the Alfoxden manuscript, quoted in *The Ruined Cottage*, 15.

14. There is no sustained consideration in Wordsworth on the origin of language, as in Rousseau's essay or Herder's. The latter was written for the Berlin Academy's contest of 1770: "Are men, left to their natural faculties, in a position to invent language . . . ?" Interesting remarks in John P. Klancher's *The Making of English Reading Audiences, 1790–1832* (Madison: University of Wisconsin Press, 1994) bring a sociological perspective to the problematics of language and cultural transmission in Wordsworth. Klancher explores what the poet meant by tasking himself with "creating" the public taste by which he would be appreciated. But Klancher's conclusions, very different from mine, are that Wordsworth found his nineteenth-century audience only by displacing "the real cultural and historical conflicts of the early nineteenth century with an essentialized 'Romanticism' [Klancher essentially repeats here Jerome McGann's charge that there was, and still is, a "Romantic ideology"] and Wordsworth, among others, successfully established the terms for that subliming of the historical in the ideal" (150). Klancher does add that Wordsworth "did not do so without great pain." Klancher's remarks on the romantic mystification of ideal (virtual) reader and audience (5) can be compared with Gary Harrison's more specific analysis of middle-class appropriations of Wordsworth's poetry in his "Postscript" to *Wordsworth's Vagrant Muse: Poetry, Poverty, and Power* (Detroit: Wayne State University Press, 1994), 173–93. There is, obviously, a methodological problem as well as a moral issue here: not only, do we hold an author accountable for misuses or partial uses of his text? but also, do these (ideologized) uses really represent the accumulative force of his poetry on readers and the way it opens a problematic that others then attempt to control or close?

15. From his poem "Tintern Abbey" (1798). A quasi-human sensi-

tivity, according to this ancient idea, animates the entire cosmos. The mechanical fancy might put a genie in the waterfall, but this trivializes the belief. By Wordsworth's time such neoclassical machinery has clogged the arteries of an imagination that must work harder than ever to keep the idea of a sympathetic nature alive. Nor can the poet revert to an older, explicitly visionary mode of figuration, because that is just as injurious to nature's integrity.

16. A literary-sensitive description of the *translatio studii* idea is found in Frank Kermode, *The Classic: Literary Images of Permanence and Change* (New York: Viking, 1975). The relation of a predominantly rural culture to the form of literary transmission, in particular to an "artisanal form of communication" like that between Pedlar and Poet, is described by Walter Benjamin in "The Storyteller"; see *Illuminations: Essays and Reflections*, ed. Hannah Arendt, trans. Harry Zohn (New York: Schocken, 1968), 91. Yet Wordsworth's *translatio* is best understood as a fidelity to the "immemorial compact" previously mentioned: it resembles the feudal *homage* applied to the relation between man and nature. The poet becomes, so to say, nature's "man." On the feudal *homage*, see Marc Bloch, *La société feudale* (1939; rev. ed., Paris: Albin Michel, 1942), 223–37. Needless to say, this analogy is only approximate: the dedicated poet feels liberated by his discovery of a bond with nature, which had been made "for him" and to which he rededicates himself.

17. The complexity of this construct, related to the linked fortunes of pastoral and georgic as literary genres, is delineated by John Murdoch, "The Landscape of Labor: Transformations of the Georgic," in *Romantic Revolutions: Criticism and Theory*, ed. Kenneth R. Johnston, Gilbert Caitin, Karen Hanson, and Herbert Marks (Bloomington: Indiana University Press, 1990). Murdoch spins a fascinating *political* tale by combining social history and the history of pictorial representation, arguing that "the absorption of the Georgic into the collective cultural consciousness, into a region almost *beyond* consciousness"— which assimilated, in effect, the georgic to the pastoral—was a deliberate concealment of the ethos of "hard, unremitting labor" as well as cultural propaganda for the progressive state that had given up the golden age and "primal otium." The "landscape of Labor," he con-

91

cludcs, "is being transformed into the landscape of Nature" (190, 184, 192). Yet Murdoch does not consider Wordsworth and does not discuss the imaginative truth of such "constructs," only their presumed *realpolitik* origins. Michael H. Friedman's *The Making of a Tory Humanist: William Wordsworth and the Idea of Community* (New York: Columbia University Press, 1979), especially chapter 5, is a more judicious consideration of the changes and forces against which Wordsworth conducts what Friedman considers a rearguard politics that weakens him as a poet. The classic and relatively neglected work of Kenneth MacLean, *Agrarian Age: A Background for Wordsworth* (New Haven: Yale University Press, 1950), delineates very carefully the poet's relation to a declining peasantry and the agricultural changes in England. Wordsworth, according to MacLean, does not simply maintain a "ruralism classical in spirit" but remains "faithful throughout to the ideal of an agrarian society of small proprietors," while deploring the suffering caused to domestic cottage industry by the disappearance of home spinning (see in general chapter 3). One should compare with Murdoch's ideology critique the following assertions of MacLean as an alternate point of view: "Poetry is not men's trades and tackle and gear. Poetry is the science of feeling. The georgic element in Wordsworth's peasant poetry was only incidental. His first duty as a poet was to interpret the emotional character of peasant life" (96). The real change, as Raymond Williams has shown, has to do with the notion of pastoral itself as a literary genre affecting perception and ideology. In *The Country and the City* (New York: Oxford University Press, 1973), especially chaps. 2 and 3, he shows what must be demystified and what can be salvaged of this perspective. For a balanced survey of rural myths and value, see Christiana Payne, *Toil and Plenty: Images of the Agricultural Landscape in England, 1780–1890* (New Haven: Yale University Press, 1993), chapter 2; and Harrison, "The Discourse on Poverty and the Agrarian Idyll in Late Eighteenth-Century England," in *Wordsworth's Vagrant Muse*, 27–55.

18. See *Wordsworth's Literary Criticism*, ed. W. J. B. Owen (Boston: Routledge and Kegan Paul, 1974), 99–102. For this "ruralism classical in spirit," as MacLean calls it, Walter Scott is also important. There are important affinities between Wordsworth and Scott in this linking of

rural and national character. See especially Katie Trumpener's "National Character, Nationalist Plots: National Tale and Historical Novel in the Age of Waverley, 1806–1830," *ELH* 60 (1993): 685–731, and her *Bardic Nationalism: The Romantic Novel and the British Empire* (Princeton: Princeton University Press, 1997).

19. He understands, moreover, that the competition is not primarily with a sublime and resilient classicism, as was the case in Germany and later in France. For him, the georgic and pastoral style of Virgil, itself a recreation marked by urbanity, points to a vision partially realized by the mixed rural and urban culture of British life, now endangered.

20. Letter to John Wilson, 7 June 1802.

21. There is nothing in continental Europe to compare with Raymond Williams's *The Country and the City* for a careful, engaged, and at the same time politically conscious description of country life and its fatal alteration. Cf. also John Barrell's more narrowly construed but powerfully focused books, such as *The Idea of Landscape and the Sense of Place, 1730–1840: An Approach to the Poetry of John Clare* (Cambridge: Cambridge University Press, 1972). Yet there is, between the wars, Marc Bloch's great study of rural France in feudal times (useful to Barrell); see *Feudal Society* (Chicago: University of Chicago Press, 1963). There is also Foucault's remarkable edition of Pierre Rivière's memoir that recalls the suffering and annulled humanity of French peasants, both before and after the Revolution. (Their abject status and universal poverty, however, were not primarily the result of industrialization.) Recently, moreover, the attempt to understand the rise of fascism has focused on the fact that the movement gained its strongest hold in places where industrialization threatened the greatest loss of the past or where preindustrial traditions resisted modernization. Consult, e.g., H. Stuart Hughes, *The Sea Change: The Migration of Social Thought, 1930–1965* (New York: Harper and Row, 1975), 130–32. I should also remark that Germany and France industrialized (and became *functioning* nation-states) later than England. On this matter, see especially Gregory Jusdanys, *Belated Modernity and Aesthetic Culture: Inventing National Literature* (Minneapolis: University of Minnesota Press, 1991); and Eugen Weber, *Peasants into Frenchmen: The Mod-*

ernization of Rural France, 1870–1914 (Stanford: Stanford University Press, 1976).

22. There are exceptional moments, such as the Westminster Bridge sonnet. See Geoffrey Hartman, *The Unremarkable Wordsworth* (Minneapolis: University of Minnesota Press, 1987), 211.

23. Lionel Trilling, *Sincerity and Authenticity* (Cambridge: Harvard University Press, 1972), 93.

24. Cf. the conclusion of Wordsworth's "The Old Cumberland Beggar": "As in the eye of Nature he has lived, / So in the eye of Nature let him die!" The fundamentalism of the late Tolstoy in such tracts as "What is Art?" is another (I think unfortunate) response to the nature/ culture divide on the Continent that over-idealizes the ethos of the peasant.

25. The passage, nevertheless, is not all that removed from the affect of the famous dejection scene that opens Keats's *Hyperion*. In Wordsworth, however, there is no classical machinery.

26. The two passages are found in E. de Selincourt, *The Poetical Works of William Wordsworth* (Clarendon: Oxford University Press, 1940–49), 2:482. On "rural idiocy" and romantic localism generally, see the fine pages in David Simpson, *The Academic Postmodern and the Rule of Literature: A Report on Half-Knowledge* (Chicago: University of Chicago Press, 1995), chapter 6, especially 139–41, on William Cobbett.

27. The word "passion" often connotes in Wordsworth a strong affection trying to express itself in words.

28. Susan Eilenberg, in *Strange Power of Speech: Wordsworth, Coleridge and Literary Possession* (Oxford: Oxford University Press, 1992), successfully combines economic issues of property, sociopsychological ones of identity or propriety, and literary ones of speech, diction, and genre. She links, for example, Wordsworthian matter-of-factness and propriety as an element of style to "the epitaphic coincidence of property and identity at the spot (*topos*) at which the earth is not only *where* it is but also *what* it is" (29).

29. MacLean, *Agrarian Age*, 102.

30. J. G. A. Pocock has emphasized the survival of republicanism and its rhetoric of civic virtue in the eighteenth century. A major conflict arose between it and the ideology of commerce; as Robert Griffin

has pointed out, what was at stake was not "a division of property between the haves and the have-nots" but a "dispute between two types of property." He quotes from Pocock's "The Mobility of Property" (*Virtue, Commerce and History* [Cambridge: Cambridge University Press, 1985]): "We are contrasting a conception of property which stresses possession and civic virtue with one that stresses exchange and the civilization of the passions" (115). See Robert J. Griffin, *Wordsworth's Pope: A Study in Literary Historiography* (Cambridge: Cambridge University Press, 1996), 12. It seems clear that Wordsworth attempted to merge civic virtue and rural virtue and that the "cultured Vale" was more civilizing for him than the city as the encroaching hub of commerce.

31. Heidegger, *Brief über den Humanismus* (Frankfurt-am-Main: Klostermann, 1946), 47. My translation.

32. See also appendix 1.

33. I have previously discussed this Heidegger passage in *Minor Prophecies: The Literary Essay in the Culture Wars* (Cambridge: Harvard University Press, 1991), 9–10.

34. "Wordsworth" stands here as a metonymy for a complex development, somewhat less divisive and bloody in England than elsewhere. The issue of the peasantry in modernity remains vital and difficult today, especially in South Africa, if we listen to the Ugandan political theorist Mahmood Mandani, as quoted by Breyten Breytenbach: "If we are to arrive at a political agenda that can energize and draw together various social forces in the highly fragmented social reality that is contemporary Africa, we need to devise an agenda that will appeal to both civil society and peasant communities, that will incorporate both the electoral choice that civil society movements seek and the quest for community rights that has been the consistent objective of peasant-based movements" (*New York Review of Books*, 26 May 1994, 4).

35. See, e.g., the Marxist comment by David Rousset—his *L'univers concentrationnaire* (Paris: Pavois, 1946), a description of the structure of Nazi concentration camps in which he was himself a political prisoner, is a classic—who understands the fate of the Jews through the prism of their forced role as "magicians of abstract money": "With a truly remarkable sureness of reaction, the vast majority of this people [the

Jews], formed and maintained in its originality [!] by its traditional historical practice of merchant and usurer, awkward in acting directly on things but skillful in recognizing their abstract relations, will engage in the complex maze of worldwide commerce, will find its vocation in speculations on modern law," etc. (preface to F. J. Armorin, *Des juifs quittent l'Europe* [Paris: La Jeune Parque, 1948], 9, 10–11; my translation). For an ambitious speculation of how the Jew becomes, for Nazism, the personification of the principle of abstraction behind the evil of capitalism and rapid industrialization, see Moishe Postone, "Nationalsozialismus und Antisemitismus: Ein theoretischer Versuch," in *Zivilisationsbruch: Denken nach Auschwitz*, ed. Dan Diner (Frankfurt-am-Main: Fischer, 1988), 242–54.

36. Hermann Keyserling, in his preface to his *Menschen als Sinnbilder* (Darmstadt: Reichl, 1926), 9. Cf. Wyndham Lewis's far more interesting remarks throughout *The Art of Being Ruled* (London: Chatto and Windus, 1926), e.g., "Our minds are still haunted by that Abstract Man, that enlightened abstraction of a common humanity, which had its greatest advertisement in the eighteenth century. That No Man in a No Man's Land, that phantom of democratic 'enlightenment,' is what has to be disposed for good" (375).

37. R. M. Rilke to Rudolf Bodlander, 23 March 1922, quoted by J. B. Leishman in his introduction to *New Poems*, ed. J. B. Leishman (New York: New Directions, 1964), 18.

38. Walter Lippmann, *A Preface to Morals* (New York: Macmillan, 1929), 59.

39. *Sincerity and Authenticity*, 171.

40. R. B. Kitaj, *First Diasporist Manifesto* (London: Thames and Hudson, 1989), 115.

41. *Wall Street Journal Europe*, 23 March 1992, 1.

42. Maurice Bardèche, *Nuremberg; ou, La terre promise* (Paris: Les Septs Couleurs, 1948), 246–47; my translation. The intellectual roots of this attack go back to the critique of the *Declaration of the Rights of Man* by conservative or counterrevolutionary political thinkers, who claim that the "l'homme en soi" assumed by the *Declaration* is purely abstract, a metaphysical entity. See chapter 6, below, and cf. Lewis, *The Art of Being Ruled*. In France, the rural culture to which Bardèche

appeals was indeed slow in being displaced by an urban mentality, but it was hardly the peaceable realm he evokes. For a description of peasant life in France, its resistance to administrative measures of the central state, and its gradual change and assimilation to such nationalization, see Weber, *Peasants into Frenchmen*.

43. H. J. Syberberg, *Vom Unglück und Glück der Kunst in Deutschland nach dem letzten Kriege* (Munich: Matthes and Seitz, 1990).

44. See, e.g., Max Weber's review of West European communities, and especially Germany, in "The Relations of the Rural Community to Other Branches of Social Science," as translated in *Congress of Arts and Science, Universal Exposition, St. Louis* (Boston: Houghton-Mifflin, 1906), 8:725–46.

45. *I, Pierre Rivière . . . A Case of Parricide in the Nineteenth Century*, ed. Michel Foucault, trans. Frank Jellinek (Lincoln: University of Nebraska Press, 1982; original French edition, 1973), 183. Wordsworth's early "Salisbury Plain," however, written but not published in 1793, moves in the same direction.

46. The condition of the French peasant around the time of the French Revolution, in terms of landholding, almost complete freedom from serfdom, yet oppressively heavy taxes and punitive legal discrimination, is described by Alexis de Toqueville in *The Old Regime and the French Revolution* (1856), pt. 2, chaps. 1 and 12. See also Georges Lefebvre, *The Coming of the French Revolution*, trans. R. R. Palmer (1939; reprint, New York: Vintage, n.d.), pt. 4, "The Peasant Revolution."

47. "Kulturkritik und Gesellschaft" (1949), collected in *Prismen* (Berlin: Suhrkamp, 1955). My translation. *Vornehmheit* could also be translated as "distinction," in Bourdieu's sense of the word.

48. *Ästhetische Theorie* (Frankfurt-am-Main: Suhrkamp, 1970), 201–2. His main examples are Baudelaire and Poe, but an earlier example of this purposeful contamination could be Blake.

49. Jacques Derrida, "Force of Law: 'The Mystical Foundation of Authority,' " *Cardozo Law Review* 11 (July/August 1990): 919–1047. I will take up Derrida's relation to the "Question of Our Speech" in chapter 4.

50. Leo Spitzer, "Das Eigene und das Fremde: Über Philologie und Nationalismus," *Die Wandlung* 1 (1945–46): 576–595.

51. Lewis, *The Art of Being Ruled* (1926), ed. R. W. Dasenbrock (Santa Rosa: Black Sparrow, 1989), 74–75.

52. A problem of the Republican Party in the 1992 presidential elections, most starkly exhibited at the party's August convention in Houston, was defining these so-called noneconomic values designated as "family values" and as "cultural." Most notoriously, figures like Pat Buchanan proclaimed a "cultural" and even "religious" war to affirm those values. The economic issue was almost entirely sidestepped. Interestingly enough, through the proclamational rhetoric that marks conventions, the term "value" began to move toward open and flamboyant statement, toward credolike assertion, shedding the sense of something quietly and unassumingly active.

53. Jean-Pierre Peter and Jeanne Favret, "The Animal, the Madman, and Death," in *I, Pierre Rivière*, 176–177 (trans. slightly modified). The irony in this case is that the misery of Rivière's family does not come primarily from poverty but from quarrels about property between wife and husband and the dignity available to them through contract legalisms. "[Pierre's father] identified himself with the being of the Contract, alienated himself in it, and lost himself in it" (180).

chapter four

Language and Culture
After the Holocaust

Our clock strikes when there is a change from hour to hour; but no hammer in the Horologe of Time peals through the universe, when there is a change from Era to Era. — CARLYLE, *"On History"*

In matters of historical change we often give priority to a reference point drawn from revolutions, wars, disasters: from that kind of eventful history. In rare cases, such as Freud or German culture's infatuation with classical Greece (what E. M. Butler called "the tyranny of Greece over Germany"), we include a crucial system of thought that has widely influenced terms of discourse or sensibility. When we periodize by concentrating in this way on a catastrophic or epochal event, are we simply dramatizing historical change, enlarging it as it were, or are we actually seeking to explain that change?[1]

The assumption that a field of knowledge or the culture itself alters because of a macrohistorical event underlies most periodization. What is also evident, however, is a wishful quest for certainty, even the certainty of loss. With a death certificate, we can hope that a new era will commence. We declare one epoch over, that another has begun, and that the calendar itself should undergo a revision, at least in our internal reckonings. Thus 1997 could be redated as 52 After Auschwitz, or 55 After the Coordination of the Final Solution at the Wannsee Conference.[2] Let me consider further what is involved in proposing that the Holocaust's impact is strong enough to have created, in effect, a before and after.[3]

Auschwitz has certainly opened our eyes to atrocities in the gu-
lag and, nearer to the present, in Cambodia, Guatemala, Bosnia,
and Rwanda. Through its dark light we also look back at the callous
waste of life that characterized the First World War and imperialist
ventures before that. And we focus more sharply on a distant past
that Steven Katz is depicting in a multivolume project on the history of genocide.[4]

It may be, then, a psychological shift that makes Auschwitz a
date of absolute significance. Its comparability, in fact, and the tear-
ing away of a veil go together: a half-suppressed segment of human
history enters consciousness as never before. If we absorb what happened and follow the injunction "Never Forget" religiously, then,
as Maurice Blanchot remarks, "what took up again from this end
(Israel, all of us) is marked by this end, from which we cannot
come to the end of waking again."[5] Mankind, a devoted part of it,
a kind of priesthood, would have to forsake sleep and engage in a
"ceaseless vigil."

This pattern, however, is familiar: it discloses once more a well-
known structuring of history. A catastrophe and a salvational event,
usually paired, are separated off as sacred time; everything else is
diminished as "profane time," though it may be granted the potentiality of reversal. The event, by falling outside of or terminating
time, by being identified as the "end of history, close of a period,
turning point, crisis,"[6] constitutes a *tremendum*, with ourselves, or a
great poet like Hölderlin or Celan, its "Last Witness." Yet to see a
contemporary crisis event as a definitive wake-up call is only as
strong as the opposite temptation: to normalize and historicize, to
diminish the event's exclusive importance or sacralization by view-
ing it as part of a sad vista, part of a repeated, historical series. Given
this tension, how should we understand, today, Freud's "On Transience" (1915), which reveals that a sense of irremediable loss also
accompanied the First World War? The war of 1914, Freud declared
with unusual pathos, "robbed the world of its beauties. It destroyed
not only the beauty of the country-sides through which it passed
and the works of art it met with on its path but it also shattered our
pride in the achievements of our civilization, our admiration for

many philosophers and artists and our hopes of a final triumph over the differences between nations and races."[7]

The idea of a history without either progress or regress (not circular): it is no more able than any other concept or affirmation to escape the multiple demands whose pressure is inscribed in the form of an *era*. To write in ignorance of the philosophical horizon—or refusing to acknowledge the punctuation, the groupings and separations determined by the words that mark this horizon—is necessarily to write with facile complacency.
— MAURICE BLANCHOT, *The Writing of the Disaster*

The act of writing is a temporal punctuation within the pressure of "era-tic" events. Freud's "On Transience" discloses, from today's perspective, a double and antithetical truth. On the one hand, time, or this particular sense of an ending, opens up again, as if time took refuge in time instead of withdrawing once and for all.[8] Unpredictable incidents supplement the significance of prior events. Whether or not we consider the Holocaust unique, it leads us to review a past that is far from inert, in the sense that we rediscover it, having forgotten or repressed too much. Time is homogeneous only insofar as it is always "out of joint."[9] On the other hand, *predictable* national and cultural differences, real or imagined, harden and stand out, as Freud observed.[10] This second effect is amplified as modern propaganda multiplies in quantity and force, using first the press, then radio and television.

A potent instrumentality shapes the present, a means of information production that can pass into the control of the state or its elites.[11] Even discounting that danger in strong democracies, the way a present reality and a past history are communicated influences our reception of them. If our inner life is affected by memory traces that take the form of images (magnified in dreams, fainter in ordinary consciousness), then the second-order yet superclear images of the new media, which so often focus on traumatic events, must cause some change, even disruption, in how we stay in touch with ourselves or use symbols to that end.[12]

This inclusion of communicative technology into the problem

of cultural change is banal, yet it coincides with the insights of Raul Hilberg (and the Frankfurt School before him) on the expansion of administered life in the contemporary era. Propaganda techniques, increasingly sophisticated and effective, intensify the burden on speech and visual discrimination. The cynical role played by Nazi terminology and the coordinated press,[13] their instrumentalizing of word and image, turned communication into a treacherous megaphone for collectivized meanings. How to speak, or how not to speak, becomes an acute and self-conscious decision.[14] Since we cannot get outside of language, how do we resist imposed forms of discourse without being contaminated by them? Under such conditions, can we speak at all, or without equivocating?

The situation becomes more critical because of two complicating factors. First, the burden on speech and perception does not derive only from instrumentalized mass media. There is also an independently dangerous media effect, dangerous not because it is in the service of a specific ideology but because it surrounds us with invasive simulacra of time present, especially real-time news. These immediacies demand consent to a worldliness for which there seems to be no alternative. It is as if time itself had become a commodity in Marx's sense, an abstraction with a fetishized and spooky life.

The second complicating factor is, if anything, more grave. Language in the camps had to be refused, partly because certain words, insofar as they evoked the normal world, especially consolations of natural beauty, might weaken the prisoner's resolve. Talking about "sea," "water," "sun," one risked, according to Robert Antelme, "losing the will for moving on or getting up." But speech was also affected by a more radical discipline. "The tortured person," writes Blanchot in reference to Antelme's *L'espèce humaine*, "refuses to talk in order not to enter, through the extorted words, into the antagonist's power play but also to preserve true speech, which merges for that moment, as he knows only too well, with its silent presence." No force can destroy that presence which becomes, according to Antelme, "the ultimate feeling of belonging to the human race."[15]

After the camps, then, the survivors not only testify, that is, describe the terror undergone, but *speak*: they testify to speech itself as an act of which they had been deprived and that enters once again into normal human intercourse. There is a rebirth of language out of the spirit of powerless utterance, out of what could not manifest itself in the camps. No wonder the silent speech of writing, the near-mystical solitude of concentrated reading, the affecting complexities of literature, and the layeredness of semantic fields enter theoretical reflection.

An *aesthetic* protest restoring the relative opaqueness of word and image arises at the very moment that the aesthetic is attacked as elitist or escapist. It is neither of these, of course, but an "uncommunicative" provocation.[16] Alexander Kluge, German writer and filmmaker, will not allow the "forces of the present," in the form of a programmatic realism, "to do away with the past and put limits on the future." Silence, Blanchot remarks, "is linked to the cry, the voiceless cry, which breaks with all utterances, which is addressed to no one and which no one receives, the cry that lapses and decries. Like writing . . . the cry tends to exceed all language, even if it lends itself to recuperation as language effect."[17]

This simultaneous turn toward and against language suggests how difficult it is to attain maturity of voice. Though forms of silence are not a politically adequate response—both Arendt and Habermas see politics as an expansion of the public sphere through deliberative speech—they challenge the optimism of a project whose clearest formulation dates from Kant's essay of 1784: "An Answer to the Question: What Is Enlightenment?" Kant's answer, "Enlightenment is humanity delivered from its self-inflicted lack of a mature voice [*Unmündigkeit*]," includes language, if only through a figure of speech for "coming of age." Kant defines *Mündigkeit*, mouth maturity, as independent thought: "dare to know." Once we attain our majority we have no excuse to remain dependent on the words of others.

At this very point, however, the philosopher himself resorts to slogans, and these, while capturing our attention, are too easily repeated. So I could play with Kant's formula and frame the admonition: dare to know . . . the Holocaust. But what if such knowledge does not lead to enlightenment but rather to the "thousand darknesses" Paul Celan perceived in language after the genocide? What does "After Auschwitz" involve? What kind of language use, what kind of education, culture, or hope for a "coming to terms"?[18]

deine Stunde / hat keine Schwestern (your hour has no sisters)
— PAUL CELAN

Our questioning is not made easier by the fact that in continental philosophy from the 1930s to the present a single and problematic figure blocks the way. Despite Levinas, Jaspers, Adorno, Lacan, Arendt, Sartre, Blanchot, Lyotard, Derrida, and Habermas, it is harder to analyze philosophy's response as such because its path leads through the seeming *nonresponse* of Heidegger. That is, if Heidegger's is a work of philosophy that stands for greatness in its field, and Heidegger ignores the Shoah, what can be concluded about philosophy? Derrida is entirely aware of this when he opens his book on Heidegger with a declaration:

Je parlerai du revenant, de la flamme et des cendres.
Et de ce que, pour Heidegger, *éviter* veut dire.

(I shall speak of what [or: of the one who] comes back, of flame and cinders. And what, for Heidegger, *to avoid* may mean.)[19]

Despite the declarative "I shall speak" and the suggestiveness of "cinders," the Holocaust is not mentioned in Derrida's book, which is wholly devoted to a clarification of the word "*Geist*" (*esprit*) in its principal Heideggerian uses. Derrida's commentary, importing as context an interconnected family of contemporary discourses (including Husserl and Valéry), is very different from Heidegger's in its extraction of meaning from words. After Mallarmé, Derrida finds his own way to "cede the initiative to words," enhancing their presence by exploiting the fugacity of semantic or the complexity of referential meanings. He fashions a philosophic style that flirts with surrealism and in which words are traces rather than roots, traces irreducible to one (prestigious) locus or origin. What holds words together, what makes them meaningful, is a promise related to identity ("I shall

speak"), a promise fulfilled, if at all, through the operation of a spirit
(Geist) that is a phantom (revenant) or "synthesis as a phantom."[20]
The imperative, egotonic summoning of a future in "I shall speak"
deceives: the new sound remains an amalgam of old sounds.

Deconstruction, then, is not—or not just—mimesis in the shadow of the Shoah. Yet style seems to have become a moral as well as
cognitive issue, even in philosophy; indeed, one can hardly avoid it
when considering Heidegger. The question Derrida puts to him is
the question of our speech, its "ground" or possibility. For despite
Heidegger's philosophical method of questioning, which taxes our
patience but claims to reach deep into language itself, his assertive
metaphors are sometimes blind—perhaps deliberately so—to their
politically equivocal status.[21]

A different, more truly patient language use launches Derrida's
critique of Heidegger. An absorptive and recapitulative prose en-
joys its vis inertia: it does not seek to be, like Heidegger's, a decisive
purging or breakthrough. Derrida remains within a writing whose
boundaries are elastic, embracing such contrasting figures as Ezra
Pound and Walter Benjamin, who framed their own ruin writing,
or Eliot, whose Waste Land with its montaging of fragments leads
back to the First World War as the nearest historical cause. The
painter R. B. Kitaj, in calling himself a Diasporist, creates a category that includes the Shoah but stretches from Aby Warburg to
Derrida, if not from midrash to Derrida:

> Almost thirty years ago, under the spell of the Diasporists
> like Aby Warburg, Fritz Saxl, Edgar Wind and the Surreal-
> ists, I made a little painting called His Cult of the Fragment.
> I was a fragmented cultist ten years before I discovered Wal-
> ter Benjamin . . . the exemplary and perhaps ultimate Dias-
> porist and his cult of the fragment. It would be fifteen years
> before I ever heard the term Midrash and became transfixed
> by the artful and highly Diasporist history of that very real
> exegetical tradition within Jewish history. Thirty years later,
> I've learned of the Diasporists of the École de Yale and their
> crazed and fascinating Cult of the Fragment (based on their

French Diasporist mentor). . . . I have very little time to study the extra-painting profundity of these comrade Diasporists but, at my own sweet pace, I try; they make me crazier day by day.[22]

These considerations return us to the epochal event: "pressure inscribed in the form of an *era*." We seek to date what is often called a *Zivilisationsbruch*:[23] Nazi criminality viewed as a breach of contract with civilized ideas. We may be in the year XX of the Auschwitz Era, but are we certain that this time cut or caesura occurred with the accession to power of the Nazi regime and definitively with the launching of the Final Solution in the spring of 1941? Or that the German nation as *Kulturvolk*, assisting or at least not resisting the genocide, was as cultured as we like to think? (Nietzsche and Karl Kraus have quite another story to tell.) This is not a question, of course, that targets only Germany: in retrospect, the issue of how fascism could pass itself off as a "spiritual revolution" (a question of how spirit—*Geist*—is defined) comes home to several nations.[24] Among historians, such comparisons or contextualizations have incited the debate that goes under the name of "historicization."

Yet the alignment of Heidegger with National Socialism remains a distinctive and disturbing fact. In Germany *Geist* pitted its flame, its ecstasies, its Wagnerian pathos, against *Zivilisation*, calling it superficial and hollow and choosing to fight it antithetically with the concept of *Kultur* popularized by Spengler.[25] Considering the success of Nazi barbarism, Germany's vaunted *Kultur* may have been a *Scheinkultur*, a pseudoculture rather than a beautiful and necessary illusion (*schöner Schein*). Such an illusion, in Schiller's *Letters on Aesthetic Education*, is an intrinsic aspect of the play instinct that culminates in Huizinga's notion of *homo ludens*, and it sustains the hope for a gradual transition to civil society and political freedom. But Heidegger is always deadly serious: his stress on authenticity and originality, like Ernst Jünger's mockery of museal culture, reflects an anxiety about *Scheinkultur*: *Geist* was more, according to them, than French *esprit* or *civilisation*, and also more than the pedantic education and vaunting complacency of the *Bildungsbürger*. ("The German," writes Jacques Rivière, "is monstrously educable.")[26]

The *Scheinkultur* thesis gained its strongest proponent with Adorno. Auschwitz is the revelation that the Palace of Culture, as Brecht had said, was built of dogshit. "All culture after Auschwitz, including the most penetrating criticism of it, is garbage."[27] Of course, Adorno says more, much more; I cite these crude and bitter words to underline his conviction that Auschwitz was there before Auschwitz. His criticism of Weimar culture, especially the press, was unstinting: he continued the pioneering role of Karl Kraus in holding up the torch of responsible public and—in view of the power of the press—publicitarian speech. "The claim," Adorno writes in *Minima Moralia*, "that Hitler destroyed German culture is nothing but the advertising trick of those who wish to build it up again by placing telephone calls from their desk. What Hitler eradicated in art and thought had long before led a separated and apocryphal life: fascism simply cleaned it out, swept it from its last nook and cranny."[28]

The extermination of the Jews and the existence of death camps where death is manufactured are for history an absolute fact that has interrupted history. One *must* declare this—without, however, being able to add anything. Discourse cannot develop itself starting from that point.

—MAURICE BLANCHOT, *Le pas au delà*

What does it matter, you may wonder, when exactly the evil started or took hold? Why should giving a date be important? Yet this is a major issue in cultural history because it diagnoses an illness or fixes blame. Is the Nazi period an exceptional moment in German history, or is it the outcome of a longer development, starting in 1813, 1848, 1870, or 1914? I borrow these dates from Friedrich Meinecke's *Die Deutsche Erhebung* (The German uprising), essays and speeches by the well-known historian following the outbreak of the First World War. His heightened tone—the word "Erhebung," connected with the uprising against Napoleon in 1813, recalls the sublime, "das Erhabene"—is typified by the book's first sentence, which foreshadows a later and more ominous rhetoric (I quote it in German to highlight its ringing rhetoric): "Während wir uns mit unserer ganzen Volks-kraft anstemmen müssen gegen Ost und West und unsere Söhne und Brüder in Not und Tod für uns ringen, hören wir durch alle Schauer des Mitgefühls ein Singen und Klingen in unserem Innern" (While we must gather the entire strength of the nation to resist East and West, and our sons and brothers wrestle for our sake in dire nec-essity and death, we, affected by every trembling of compassion, hear a singing and resonant echoing within our innermost being).[29]

One cannot read this respected scholar (Franz Rosenzweig's mentor, who offered him an academic position despite Rosenzweig's Jewishness) on the relation of culture and state without sensing a continuity between his reaction to "the great days" (the outbreak of the First World War) and that of "Hitler's Professors" to the *Aufbruch* of 1933. It is also difficult not to ask how such words, once spoken, could avoid becoming a deceptive promise (a *Ver-sprechen*) under the external pressure of the war fever and the internal pressure of having to resolve through a speech act the intimate, perhaps unre-solvable, relation between culture and politics. Listen to Meinecke harnessing Kant, Germany's culture hero, to the war effort: "Those of us who dreamt of a culture without a state [he is alluding partic-ularly to the "cosmopolitans"] will now wake up, in the face of the danger confronting our culture. The time of alienation between cul-ture and politics, of which so many signs were seen in the last dec-ades, is over. . . . In a mood of greatness, and with that ethos of auton-omy that Kant preached to us, let culture grasp the hand of the state to become a weapon in that hand."[30]

Comparing 1914 to 1933 complicates the attempt to gain a deci-sive *cultural* dating of a radical change in the character of German life. It becomes harder for us to express what happened in narra-tive form, in the form of a *récit*. We fall into paradox, in the man-ner of Sarah Kofman, who claims Auschwitz as a decisive event in history even as she denies the possibility of narrative after it: "About Auschwitz, and after Auschwitz, no *récit* is possible, if by that one understands: to narrate a history of the events in order to make sense [of them]."[31]

Without narrative form, however, and its gift of meaning, it is much harder to keep the events in mind. The urgent command to remember could be jeopardized. We glimpse once more the bind that Maurice Blanchot and Derrida, among others, try to loosen by creating new styles of discourse. Fiction too shows a similar trend. Blanchot's novels (more like long short stories) are radically deceptive *récits*, while Aaron Appelfeld and Armando[32] (the first writing mainly of threshold events, the other recreating attitudes after the event) disclose an insidious process of accommodation, an ordinary, pragmatic fatalism. Both show how the very form of everyday life is threatened yet always restores itself. The *Zivilisationsbruch* simply did not affect public norms for many people or took place behind a screen, with words like *Kultur* changing their meaning. That is basic. Other factors contribute: a conviction that cosmopolitanism was a form of internationalism dangerous to the nation-state and that a culture based on it was either superficial or self-subverting. And is there a character continuity, something like Adorno's "Authoritarian Personality," distinctively Germanic, which adjusted itself all too easily to the now overt anti-Semitism and bureaucratic machine of National Socialism? Given the canny (uncanny) way that daily life continues, like parts of a severed worm, it is also possible that we have not thought sufficiently about *dating* as a language.

Dates make us crazy.
— DERRIDA, *Schibboleth*

Dates are a duplicitous construct: on the one hand, a sublime rhetoric that arises from the sense that there exist transformative occasions, epochal events; on the other hand, merely a statistic, a commonplace and even trivial way of organizing the clutter and chaos of history. "Era-tic" and erratic easily change places. This ambiguity surrounding dates, this potentiality they have for lapsing from sublime to trivial, affects verbal terms as well. (Words, that is, also approach the promissory or quasi-performative status of dates.) What the numerical date suggests, in its magic specificity, is a decisive event, a significant happening in a *histoire événementielle*. It is like birth or death, or the dawning of a new era, or even "a date" in the colloquial sense: a rendezvous, though with destiny. Or is it like initiation rituals that actually require a physical mark, one that allows no identity ambiguity?

A date, then, branding the spirit, and though ambiguous in its own structure, potentially places us beyond ambivalence, embarrassment, perplexity, and verbal equivocation. Dates mark the intersection of being and time; while words, shadowed by dates, create a counterecstatic, temporizing temporality. It is not surprising that Derrida's *Schibboleth*, his book on Paul Celan, the poet most closely associated with the Holocaust, should open with: "Une seule fois: la circoncision n'a lieu qu'une fois" ("One time only: circumcision takes place only once"), and that it quickly arrives at the subject of dates: "Je parlerai donc en même temps de la circoncision et de l'unique fois, autrement dit, de ce qui *revient* à se marquer comme l'unique fois: ce que parfois l'on appelle une *date*" (I shall speak then at the same time about circumcision and the one-and-only time, in other words, about what returns to mark itself as unique in time: what is sometimes called a *date*).[33]

By now we are privy to Derrida's style: we have heard that promissory "Je parlerai" before; we note that the phrase "the one-and-only time" is followed by the cliché "in other words," indicating that, as language, nothing is unique, unrepeatable; while "revient" comes back as "revenant" in the inaugural sentence of the later book on Heidegger. Here, moreover, the Holocaust *is* mentioned, quite deliberately, in a context worth quoting:

> You will pardon me if I name here the *holocaust*, that is literally—as I have liked to call it elsewhere—*that which burns everything* [*le brûle-tout*], to express the following: there is certainly today a date for that holocaust we know about, the hell in our memory; but there is a holocaust for each date, and somewhere in the world for each hour. Each hour numbers its holocaust. Each hour is unique, whether it returns and is the wheel that turns itself, or whether [here Derrida begins to allude to a section of Celan's "Engführung": "Geh, deine Stunde / hat keine Schwestern"], being the last hour, it

does not return any more than the sister does, his own, the same, his other that comes back [*revenant*].[34]

Dating subverts narrative time, even while making it possible. The result is an interlacing play with terms and texts that could be seen as an insidious universalizing of the Shoah, removing, that is, all historically specific coordinates, though not the agony. "Each hour numbers its holocaust." Derrida's title, *Schibboleth*, seems to announce an essay on particularism, or what defines national or racial identity, indeed *any* assumed or constructed—and potentially fatal—difference between self and other, nation and nation. Yet Derrida rarely proceeds by choosing one thematized focus; we cannot be sure that "Jewishness" is central to the eccentric path of this discourse. What is clear is that he gives to Celan's "unbestattete Worte" ("unburialed words"), by means of their own sparseness and his wordy dissemination, more than "a grave in the air": he gives them a universal, or at least repeatable presence. "The poem raises its voice beyond the individualizing wound" ("Le poème porte sa voix au-delà de l'entaille singulière").[35]

Though Walter Benjamin is not named, the question of reproducibility, or whether the numinous quality of art he calls its aura can preserve itself in a technological and media-mediated age, joins this meditation from the outset. Emphasis shifts from the uniqueness ("Une seule fois . . .") of the historical Holocaust, or of Celan's elliptical testimony, to the analogous and familiar quest of bringing back—from the dead, from the past—what cannot be brought back and associating this orphic pursuit of the irrevocable ("Nach / dem Unwiederholbaren") with the fact that memories can only perpetuate themselves by entering a figurative space, an invented present different from the "anterior present" they evoke. Because of the impossibility of "presenting the present" and the paradox in "representing the present," there is always a virtual space—Maurice Blanchot identifies it with literature itself—in which such representation "takes place." Writing, in seeking to recapture the unique, or to image what is absent, hardens it, so that we are left with the consciousness of language as incorporating a void ("Ungeschriebenes, zu / Sprache verhärtet").[36] That void is at once very personal and quite impersonal: the loss of a sister, but also what language, as a condition of its possibility, passes over or sublimates (in Hegel's sense of *Aufhebung*). Thus literary space is marked by ellipsis, by conscious or unconscious "avoidance," even by lightness;[37] and the "nothing" of this ellipsis makes discourse, despite its referential or memorial function, as spectral as the old moon holding the new in its arms.

The enigmatic opening of *De l'esprit* (the book on Heidegger) points to this at once numinous and ghostly status of writing, caught between *relève* (*Aufhebung*) and *revenant*. "Je parlerai du revenant, de la flamme et des cendres" is close to a praeterition (cf. "Comment ne pas parler")[38] in the form of its obverse: mock-epic invocation and enumeration. For Derrida's follow-up sentence, "Et de ce que, pour Heidegger, *éviter* veut dire," evokes not what is included but what is avoided or the meaning of that avoidance. Derrida's promissory opening turns on a periphrasis built around the voided/avoided referent "holocaust"—which becomes, here, Derrida's avoidance too, not only Heidegger's.[39]

Yet does "holocaust," as the (a)voided word, resolve the periphrasis? The situation is more complex. Derrida is playing with fire, as he does explicitly in *Cinders* (*Feu la cendre*).[40] The word Heidegger would like to avoid, and uses only too often, turns out to be *Geist*, or "spirit," not "holocaust." Derrida, it is true, describes "spirit" as "cerné par le feu," encircled by fire. He may be thinking implicitly about holocaustal fire, but explicitly he refers to all crimes committed in the name of the spirit and most literally to the book burning that was decreed for Helvetius's eighteenth-century book *L'esprit* or the larger, more vicious conflagration of May 1933 in Nazi Germany, shortly after Heidegger lauded a new order in his inaugural speech as rector of Freiburg.

In *Cinders*, Derrida takes up the problematic at the heart of Hegel's wager to make the truth of history, the truth in history, visible. If life is more than life (or death), more than a self-consuming, ever-renewed bonfire, if it is endowed with progressive "historical" meaning, or at least with a meaningful residue, how does it break with spirit as flagrant, pure immediacy? From ancient oriental religions of fire and light, from their pyres, must emerge the dialectical phoenix of construction, mediation, civilization.

"Cinders," therefore, is a symbol for something that, residual and dynamic, survives time and flares up in Derrida's astonishingly poetical prose. The spirit of the word "*Geist*" is an unstable, flammable essence, at once inspiring and subverting the ziggurats, pyramids, palaces, tombs, systems of philosophy; there is an *Abbau* (dismantling) of philosophy as architecture and also of historical discourse as ecstasy datings of the spirit by a historicizing *Geistesgeschichte*. Derrida understands Heidegger's avoidance (or embarrassed usage) of "spirit" as the equivocal act of a thinker wary of the word's aggressive past, its vitalistic claim ("the letter kills, the spirit gives life"), one that can turn murderous and nihilistic. Yet precisely what Heidegger seems *unable* to avoid at this time, writing in the glaring shadow of a political chimera, is the act of proclamation itself. In his *Rektoratsrede* and concomitant pronouncements he often uses the language of philosophy to imply that there has been a decisive spiritual revelation (*geistig* rather than *geistlich*), one with a more than imaginary, indeed with a potentially immemorial, claim on history. Heidegger's methodical "*Destruktion*" of the old—so-called Western—ontotheology collaborates with the new order in the name of that revelation-revolution, whether it took place "then and there" (in a quondam Greece) or is upon us "here and now" (in the Nazi era).

With Derrida, however, *Destruktion* undergoes a change: it becomes "deconstruction" and is said to coincide with writing itself. In this reversal, *letter* is spirit and reclaims a non-nihilistic revelation. Everything turns on the signifying force of a writing that is generically no more (and no less) than the independent trace of an originating, inspiring *feu*. It is a former fire, a *feu* (from Latin "functus" or "fatutus") *feu*. Derrida's philosophy celebrates *words that have entered time yet escaped the flames*, that persist despite deadly repetition, on the one hand, and ecstatic vitalism, on the other. From this perspective, writing is the shadow of its own flame and writers the cinder bearers of a "brûle-tout" that "swallows the movement of meaning" (Blanchot), that burns up, without placating, the restless ghost (*revenant*) of such charged words as "holocaust," "spirit," "being."

If Derrida's first words in *De l'esprit* were only a way of skirting Heidegger's moral failure, the entire issue would be trivialized. But the avoidance alluded to is not just an *impensé*: it signals, I have suggested, a preoccupation with Heidegger's basic project of *Destruktion*, the project that also founded deconstruction. Heidegger's "avoidance" subordinates everything to the deconstructive rescue of spirit speech from its unthinking (mechanical or now technological) unconscious and to the reconstruction of a more originary language possibility. This language, restored through a poetic as well as philosophical scrutiny, could recall us, in the words of Levinas, from modernity's mistaken attempt to turn the appropriation of being *by* knowledge (by deadly acts of domination and anaesthetic habits of classification) into something even worse: the identification of being *with* knowledge.

Yet who can ignore, after the event, the fatal convergence of *Geist* and Holocaust, the deep unease we feel that an ideal aspiration, a so-called spiritual revolution, backed up by institutionalized philosophy and cultural discourse, contributed to the tragedy? Derrida does not seek to determine *when* culture went wrong: this would only repeat the "dating" error, which also affected Heidegger and is the residue of a sublime yet standard rhetoric. He lays bare the difficulty of escaping from a contaminating rhetoric. Heidegger, he shows, faces the "Question of German Speech" and devises the linguistic and conceptual hygiene of *Destruktion*.[41]

We do not point here to an incoherence in language or a contradiction in the system. We are asking ourselves about the meaning of a necessity: that of installing oneself in a traditional concept system in order to destroy it.
— DERRIDA

The problem for both Derrida and Heidegger is how to repeal a pseudophilosophical discourse culminating in the Hegelian vision of the West as the home of a greater spirituality: greater because it was attained through the labor pains of historical experience. In Hegel, the West's progressive spiritualization is imaged as an Orient Express in reverse: the fire spirit of *Geist* is the rising sun itself in its first, phenomenal splendor. Yet it lights up rather than extinguishes shadows: the gigantic and oppressive institutions of the ancient Near East. Through an odyssey carefully scripted by Hegel's *Phenomenology*, this fire spirit is brought into the evening land: into a reflective setting, where it rises like a new, more temperate sun upon the evening.[42] In this triumphal westering it is Germany (of course) that is the ultimate culture bearer, receiving and carrying to victory the final torch of the race.

However, while Heidegger anticipates the "end of metaphysics" (this spiritualized imperialism) through an avoidance of Hegelian habits of thought and speech, that very avoidance, Derrida shows, is contaminated by the terms it circumvents, terms that have been given esoteric force: the discourse on German national destiny, of the breakthrough to origins, etc. "Our only choice," Derrida writes, "is between terrifying contaminations. Even if all complicities are not equivalent, they are *irreducible*."[43] At best they are like a *pharmakon*: a poison that is also a cure.

Derrida's own redescriptions consequently write out words in their complex aura (Wittgenstein might have said *Dunst*) of both promise and avoidance. Words are inevitably historical (*Schibboleth*: "une parole est toujours datée") and even wounded or contaminated (Celan: "wundgelesenes"). But Derrida's difficult style conveys a double argument: it is true that time cannot be delivered from history; it is also true that history in the form of *écriture*, of written and "dated" words, returns on time as specters or revenants do, to claim an aborted life, meanings that "history" as a form of ideology had cut off. Thus the weight of these resonant words (of what we name literature) bearing down on words that presently try to maintain themselves, that try to become historical in turn by extending their life beyond the moment—the very load these words must carry threatens any facile construction of meaning, any apparently natural synthesis.

There are no figures on the American or English scene like Derrida or Blanchot, who cross the disciplinary boundaries of philosophy, poetics, and ethics to alter the practice as well as theory of language. Wittgenstein, however influential, remained within the tradition of philosophy; and language experimentation, in the English-speaking world, is almost entirely confined to literature in the generically restricted sense of fiction and poetry. Ordinary language philosophy is a pale shadow of the model, inherited from the Italian and English Renaissance, of expanding the vernacular base of literature, of bringing a spoken idiom, or its equivalents, into a realism without limits. Insofar as discursive writing becomes a focus of attention in our part of the world, or the question of its "style" is raised, only Foucault's analysis of the relation between knowledge and power in discourse systems has much currency. I can see no native attempt as sustained as Derrida's (or Blanchot's) to write the problem through, to acknowledge the inertial force of language also in the discursive realm, and at once to allow for and counter it by deconstructively "installing oneself in a traditional concept system in order to destroy it."[44]

Derrida, however, does not explicitly connect his insight to pressures on language after the Holocaust: to the extreme nature of that event or a crisis in the idea of culture that constitutes an absolute event, one to be dated by that fact. "The circumcision of a word," he writes, "is not dated *in history*" (*Schibboleth*; my emphasis). Where is it dated then? Derrida's reserve includes an awareness that the word "history" itself has become Hegelianized, that it always evokes a master narrative or metahistorical horizon. His refusal to historicize seems to accept one aspect of Heidegger's avoidance: his reluctance to locate the crisis in the epochal events of 1933–1945. He questions, at the same time, Heidegger's archaizing move, the logocentrism that seems to place the origin of the crisis *in illo tempore*, in a mysterious and historically developed schism that befell words long ago.

Derrida focuses on the pervasiveness of an identitarian, nationalistic, and decisionist rhetoric, which the language of philosophy has not escaped. That rhetoric tainted almost all discourse between the world wars and carried to the limit an older antinomy of nation and universality. Yet the full impact of the disaster related to this rhetoric hits consciousness, like a shock wave, only after the Holocaust.

The dilemma of the philosopher is that he cannot accept conditions that negate philosophy and its language, any more than Celan accepted those that negate poetry and his mother tongue. Style, therefore, in both Celan and Derrida, is the negation of a negation. The continuous solecism of Celan in poetry and of Derrida in philosophy gives an unexpected meaning to Adorno's "To write poetry [or philosophy?] after Auschwitz is barbaric." Writing—philosophy, fiction, poetry—is indeed ringed by fire but also by "avoidances" that produce a silent scream. This duality is symptomized by Derrida's—and Genet's—stifled "Je m'éc . . ." on the first page of *Glas*.[45] Poetry and philosophy, even when they carry us beyond the datum, beyond a brute historical reality, remain inscribed—scarred—by it.

The concept of a resurrected culture after Auschwitz is illusory and contradictory, and every construct that still comes into being has to pay a bitter price because of that. But since the world survived its own ruin, art is as necessary to it as the unconscious recording of its history.
—ADORNO, *"Those Nineteen Twenties"*

Even though "art is . . . necessary," to ask what kind of voice (voices) the Holocaust should raise might excite the wrong sort of expectation, as if it hoped for what Ezra Pound called, after the First World War, a sublime "in the old sense." And some monuments, of course, in word or stone, continue to express symbolism of the heroic type.[46] Yet the modernists had already striven for a new sublimity: it is *this* hope that receives through the Shoah a second and fatal blow.

The voice that is raised, the testimonial voice of the survivor or others who wonder what remembrance can do or what reformation of culture might be effective, this voice cannot be sublime or monumental, cannot even risk that association. Adorno's style, therefore, however discursive it may seem to be, is always close to the *Bruchstück*, to aphorism or fragment. "The fragment is the intervention of death in the work. As it destroys, it also takes away the blemish of luminous illusion [*der Makel des Scheins*]."⁴⁷ The choice between styles seems more absolute now: nonsublimity, or silence.

Let me also quote from Lyotard's *Heidegger and "the Jews,"* which follows closely at one point the "After Auschwitz" section of Adorno's *Negative Dialectics* in order to define philosophy's post-Holocaust and postsublime "écriture de survie" (survival writing): "It is what, of thought, survives despite itself, when the philosophic life has become impossible, when there is no longer a beautiful death to hope for and heroism has gone over to the enemy."⁴⁸

This echoes uncannily Oskar Singer writing in 1942 about the agony of Lodz ghetto. "We can no longer die as other people do. We no longer have the possibility of a noble end. Litzmannstadt death is an alien, ugly death."⁴⁹ Jean Améry says in *At the Mind's Limits*: "No bridge led from death in Auschwitz to *Death in Venice*."⁵⁰

Adorno himself does not renounce the sublime. The sublime has antithetical and heterogeneous value. In order to shock and demystify, he accuses high culture of being a lie, even while refusing to tear it down. Culture should resist rather than promote self-deception, should reveal rather than occult human and social misery. Critical Theory enters the scene to deflate every overextension of philosophical thought that peddles ideas of vitalism, as long as "damaged life" is the reality. The aim of the movement is not realism as such; rather, it acts to shame us, like the sublime, or like a redemptive vision that cannot be incorporated into daily existence. As a sinister double of the sublime, the nonintegratability of Auschwitz is part of our present misery.

You cannot get rid of the sublime, yet there is no possibility of a specifically postmodern sublime because of the way spiritual values have, in the past, imbued ideals with violence, or a deadly, authoritarian absoluteness. "No word intoned from high," Adorno writes, "not even a theological one, can be justified, untransformed, after Auschwitz."⁵¹ Commenting on the poisonous effectiveness of ideology, Kaplan writes in his *Warsaw Diary*: "There is war which is nothing but power and worldliness, and there is war whose source is in the spirit—and it is self-evident that this Nazi war is no less than a war whose roots are inspired with spirit."⁵²

I have suggested that even an emphasis on the datable uniqueness of the Holocaust is only a sublimity equivalent. To say "1997 is 52 After Auschwitz" creates a *stigmatic* history. It is necessary to resist encapsulating what is dated here as an embodiment of pure evil: this would only reaffirm a Manichaean worldview, like that of National Socialism, which demanded absolute allegiance and turned out to be the evil it claimed to be fighting to the death. The evil masquerading as a redemptive spiritual force cannot be imprisoned by being bracketed this way: it is a *revenant* to haunt us, to watch out for.

The mania of "spiritual revolutions," therefore, must always be questioned. Nazi exaltation was deeply antihistorical by claiming, like a religion, that history could be totally transformed, vision totally integrated with it. But history is that which remains after all such spiritual or sublime purgations. The flame of *Geist* did not and cannot completely transform or consume it. Derrida calls that (charred) (resistant) remainder *le reste*, and sometimes "cinders."

Today, a renewed theory of culture has become crucially difficult.[53] Culture cannot claim to be, any longer, a definitive triumph of the spirit. Adorno writes, in his contradictory way, that "the integration of physical death into culture is to be gainsaid by theoretical considerations, not to further the idea of death as an ontologically pure essence, but for the sake of what is expressed by the stench of the corpse before it is deceptively laid out as an embalmed body."[54] That stench still comes from the camps: the cadaver is impossible to lay to rest, whatever memorializing or intellectualizing activities we attempt. We are still trapped (to use Van Gennep's famous concepts) in rituals of separation and have not found an adequate ritual of incorporation. Like the sublime, unsublime death (Lodz and Auschwitz death) cannot be integrated into culture. Nor into theory.[55] Even the strongest of interpretive attempts have relied (consider David Rousset or Marxism generally) on ideological closure, on a totalizing method familiar from metaphysical speculation. They promote the affirmative aspect of knowledge—of getting to know and dominate something—over the quintessentially moral moment of being called into question, accused by the place and face of the other. All the more reason, then, to evoke the event's "exteriority":

the impossibility of historicizing the Holocaust or bringing it into an analogical logic of sameness.

The "After Auschwitz" pages of *Negative Dialectics* are Adorno's "unbestattete Worte." Irreconcilable, he becomes there a philosopher in the ancient definition reported by Cicero: *one who studies death*. His rejection of the idea of death as something that can be embraced implies not only a critique of the "Fallen Soldier" ideal that George Mosse has documented[56] but also of Heidegger's "being toward death" and Rilke's intimist vision of mortality as organic and spiritual. All these pretend that, like Dürer's knight in the famous etching, we can outface terror or make friends and transform it in the manner of German Hellenism's seductive and euphemistic representation of death.[57] What Blanchot names "The Great Refusal," a rejection of Hegel's cultural instrumentalizing of death—Hegel associates death both with the beginning of spiritual life and the negativity of the concept in a historically progressive scheme—removes every shred of positivity from that kind of philosophizing.

Now that Lodz and Auschwitz death have caught up with culture, there is an impasse that spirals not into a providential valuing of negativity or a Spenglerian, revitalizing cycle but into a vicious circle, a special circle of hell for the intellectuals that even Dante had failed to invent. "Those who make a plea to preserve a radically guilty and shabby culture set themselves up as coconspirators; while those who deny themselves this culture promote the very barbarity that culture has revealed itself to be."[58] We are still in that place, in that impasse.

[The survivor] is the first of civilized men to live beyond the compulsions of culture; beyond a fear of death which can only be assuaged by insisting that life itself is worthless. The survivor is evidence that men and women are now strong enough, mature enough, awake enough, to face death without mediation, and therefore to embrace life without reserve.
TERRENCE DES PRES, *The Survivor*

How far does Adorno get, and how far can we get after him, in thinking about culture theoretically, if the decay was indeed as pervasive (or bourgeois),[59] as he claimed, and culminated in Nazi criminality and the camps? There is perhaps one opening for us; it is glimpsed at the very point at which Adorno's self-lacerating logic becomes most intense. He asks us to save from the old and discredited world of values an objectivity—even a *coldness*—that helped the survivor to keep living after Auschwitz, yet without which, he says scandalously, Auschwitz would not have been possible.

I probably don't understand him fully, but Adorno presents this coldness, this spectatorial and detached attitude—which can become pathologically callous—as potentially humane as well as inhumane and admits that humanistic ideology rebels against that possibility. The coldness within the capacity for detached, rational, objective thought remains; it cannot be resolved by any reconciling or dialectizing move. Yet even as Adorno saves a "*zuschauerhafte* Haltung" (*spectatorial attitude*) that not only allows but compels us toward an objective assessment of the human condition, a shudder enters through the very word "zu-*schauer*haft" (*shudder* attitude).[60] Despite Critical Theory's exposure of the excessive and self-destructive aspects of post-Enlightenment "objective reason" (anticipated in prescient fashion by Hamann's and Blake's attack on the Enlightenment, specifically its reduction of imagination to "ratio"),[61] there can be no abandonment of either objectivity or reasoning. Adorno is exploring here, like Blanchot, a form of nonconsent that might provide some immunity against the populist ecstasy of demagogic politics. But the crucial question is not where theory comes from or what will maintain it—I grant Adorno the coolth whereof he speaks—it is how we can retain the ability, within such detachment, to feel for others, not just for ourselves against others. This is where Levinas's critique of identity philosophy deepens that of Adorno and revives moral philosophy, or the morality in philosophy.

It is true that in a technological era we require an extra skin, a psychic apparatus (machine for machine) to ward off escalating shocks: that influx of "gross and violent stimulants" Wordsworth had linked two centuries ago to the stimulus flooding of the industrial and urban revolution. This anaesthetic cooling acts to innervate stimuli or dissociate them from affect.[62] But if that is so, what

difference is there between this insensitivity or dissociation endemic to a technological age and classical, premodern coldness: "klas-
sische Dämpfung," as Leo Spitzer once called it, or Yeats's "Cast a
cold eye, on life, on death," or unfeeling racism, or endless praises
of the contemplative life, or a broad acceptance of public torture?
Is not the moral issue always: how does one get through to another
person and . . . to oneself? And *is it not here that art, which generically combines aesthetic distance and emotional participation, finds
its value?*

Leo Löwenthal has said that the leitmotif of Adorno's life and
work was "*Nicht mitmachen*": Don't collaborate, Don't play their
game. This wariness was a deeply reasoned philosophic and social
project that hoped to free the human subject from subjection.
Freud's "Group Psychology" (1923) had laid bare some of the
mechanisms of our dependence on authority and the suspension of
conscious control, the hypnosis, involved in this. What I must
emphasize, leaning on Adorno's extraordinary and impacted "After
Auschwitz" pages, is that how the sympathetic imagination is co-
opted—its vulnerability to being steered by propaganda, despite its
occasional redemptive dissent from social pieties—also played a
role in the subjection that Adorno analyzed and fought. The question comes down to: are compassion and politics reconcilable?[63]
Given our disillusionment with the sublime "in the old sense," is
philanthropy "in the old sense" also a delusion?[64]

Nazi ideology, reinforced by a coordinated culture politics that
amounted to brainwashing, incited an exalted atmosphere, one
that, were it not also alive today, in organized nationalisms or unorganized audiences that respond so totally to extreme performers,[65]
would seem not only inexplicable but as comic as the grimaces of
Mussolini and the boasts and barks of Hitler. This political exaltation, an identity philosophy for the masses based on strong emotional bonding, may have been irrational but seemed entirely rea-
sonable to those caught up within it. It usurped the name of culture
and laid claim to being a spiritual revolution. Adorno confronts us
with the degeneration of the "once reverential concept" of identity
or integration by asserting that "genocide is absolute integration"

and "Auschwitz confirms the philosopheme of pure identity as death."[66]

Surviving is not only the personal problem of the survivor. The long, dark shadow of the Holocaust covers the entire civilization in which it occurred and which must continue to live with the burden and consequences of the event.

IMRE KERTESZ, *"The Holocaust as Culture"*

To talk of a Holocaust culture is impossible. What could it mean? The phrase is ironic, or the worst of oxymorons. Yet in the Germany of 1933 to 1945 the idea of culture became an excuse for the killing or enslaving of millions. What made it into so murderous an ideology, and one that has not entirely disappeared?

When Adorno formulates the striking aphorism that "Genocide is absolute integration," he is evoking the blind side of an eudaemonic ideal: specifically that of the integrated or harmonious ego, in tune not only with itself but also with the world or with superego agencies like church and state. Integration points here to integrity, to unity of purpose and unwoundedness of soul and body. As an ideal, this would seem to be self-evident. Yet it enters modernity through its neoclassical version, derived most explicitly from the age of Schiller and Fichte, which dominated German identity philosophy into the 1930s. It is this version of the ideal that has lost its innocence.[67]

We have learned that what Fichte posited as basic to culture, a drive (*Trieb*) for identity, becomes too readily a demand for political—particularly, national—harmony, one that results in forced conversion, or unity through exclusion, and what is now called ethnic cleansing. Kenneth Burke, writing on *Mein Kampf* in the 1930s, called it "sinister unification." A basic postulate of German idealism, then, may have contributed, in its very idealism, to what happened. It saw as the "ultimate characteristic feature of all rational beings . . . absolute unity, constant self-identity, complete harmony" with oneself. While acknowledging human difference, it posited as the goal of society "the complete unity and unanimity of all of its members." How this formal goal, this counsel of perfection, would be achieved, was not spelled out in detail. Yet despite Fichte's interesting statement that life in the state is not to be considered an absolute aim, that in fact "the state aims at abolishing itself" and "the goal of all government is to make government superfluous,"[68] his theory encouraged an identification of (ideal) person and state and tended to overlook the idolatry of state power and its de facto status as religion. The theory also helped to reinforce the cult of genius, of the supertalented person who "gives laws to nature," or— in Schiller's definition, more in tune with identity philosophy— who approximates an ideal human type. "Each individual human being," we read in Schiller's Fourth Letter on *Aesthetic Education*, "carries within, according to his disposition and destiny, a pure and ideal human type, and to harmonize with the latter's immutable unity, despite the individual's changeable nature, is the great task of his existence. This pure human type, which is more or less distinct, and recognizable in every subject, is represented by the *State*, which is the objective and also canonical form in which the multiplicity of subjects [persons] seeks to be unified."[69]

The nostalgia for representability, balance, and wholeness that the Greeks were assumed to have achieved is unashamedly expressed in Schiller, though its loss, like a fortunate fall, might have been necessary for mankind on its way to achieve personal and political maturity, on its way to realize human creativity more fully, to give laws to nature as well as to itself. Schiller is more convincing, on the whole, on the subject of loss, as when he describes modern fragmentation through his own version of a *musica mundana*. "Forever chained to a single and tiny part of the whole, individual man can only fashion himself as a fragment; hearing forever only the monotonous sound of the wheel that he is turning, he can never develop the harmony of his being, and instead of expressing more fully humanity in its very nature, he becomes a mere imprint of his occupation, of his specialized knowledge."[70]

The *Letters on Aesthetic Education*, nevertheless, suggest—like Hegel's philosophy of history—the "labor, patience, and suffering of the negative." In Schiller there is no time limit to the aesthetic interregnum. He seems to be talking, in any case, about the emergence of a cultural rather than political nation, or about the passage from nature to freedom via the indefinitely extended and self-creative process of *Bildung*.[71]

Friedrich Meinecke, however, in his famous book on the modern nation-state, sees a convergence of the two bases of nationhood, the cultural (not linked, necessarily, to territory) and the political (which makes a territorial claim), a convergence said to constitute "a major turning point" in the development of modern nations. "In this later [i.e., modern] period, if only through the agency of its leaders, the nation becomes aware of itself as a great personality, as a great historical unit, and it now lays claim to self-determination, the mark and privilege of the mature personality." He concludes with a paragraph of extraordinary eloquence:

> Personality means not only the utmost autonomy but also the utmost autarky, a harmonious unity and a cultivation of all inner capacities and potentials. . . . If the full consciousness of a great national community is once awakened and raised to an intense longing for national realization, then this longing is like a flood that pours itself into everything it can fill and is not satisfied until everything is nationalized that is at all capable of nationalization. This process is basically a great extension of the individual personality and its sphere of life. The human being needs the community to sustain him and receive [his] contribution in turn. The more autonomous, the more individualized he himself becomes, the larger the spheres of his receptivity and influence can be. . . . Of all the great spheres of life that a man can enter, there is probably none that speaks so directly to the whole man as the nation, none that carries him so strongly, none that renders so faithfully his entire natural and intellectual being, none that can so readily be or become both macroanthropos and fully realized individual.[72]

To question this ideal of harmonious development, as it expands from individual well-being to the relations between individual and public sphere or nation-state, is not to declare it guilty. It is notoriously difficult to incriminate ideas in the political arena, where they are so easily appropriated and misapplied. I have previously said, and repeat it here, that "the link between the Nazi regime and the Holocaust makes it impossible to see either fascism or anti-Semitism as belonging simply to the history of ideas: they belong to the history of murder."[73] But the history of ideas should not therefore be neglected. There are at least two solid reasons for examining it. The first is that some intellectual responses to fascism, after the war, present themselves as a critique of hellenistic or pseudo-hellenistic residues, especially eudaemonic concepts of harmony.[74] A second reason for not evading Nazi ideas, repulsive and pseudo-scientific as they are, is that the Holocaust was not only a monstrous violation of the norms of human conduct but also an ideologically promoted action, tolerated and even abetted by an astonishing number of intellectuals. National Socialism made euthanasia and genocide normative aspects of state policy.

The war against the Jews left a grim intellectual legacy. Seeking to create a new *Volksgemeinschaft*, a purified and single-minded nation, Nazism encouraged mass murder as a principled, even foundational necessity. Though the genocide was only partially accomplished and eventually discredited by the defeat of the perpetrators, it was carried through with enough vigor and collective participation to raise the possibility that it might have succeeded. Terrence des Pres writes simply and justly: "The Holocaust *happened*. That in itself is the intractable fact we can neither erase nor evade. . . . We dwell in aftermath, and I do not think I exaggerate to say that the Holocaust has forced upon us a radical rethinking of everything we are and do."[75]

The destruction gains, therefore, an unfortunate standing, whatever the opportunistic mélange of ideas—a jumble of Darwin, Gobineau, Chamberlain, and *völkisch* themes—found in Alfred Rosenberg, National Socialist propaganda, and statements by the murderers themselves, who believed they had to kill without mercy in order to "create a better and eternal Germany for our descendants."[76] It is this openly propagated notion of a systematic as well as brutal plan of extermination based on ideology that cannot be reconciled with previous thinking about humanity. Though the Holocaust is sometimes thought of as a crime of political passion—as a temporary insanity—today we continue to hear echoes of the ideology that rationalized it.

Even if intellectual history can be trusted, it will take a finely tuned analysis to trace the murderous turn of German idealism and identity philosophy. All the more so because from the late eighteenth century on a similar ideal of the harmony-restoring function of culture influenced English thought. It found wide acceptance despite significant internal tensions. This ideal, which could go in a cosmopolitan as well as nationalist direction, also sees culture compensating for an alienating sense of abstractness brought on by technology and increasing specialization. Culture is said to keep alive, psychologically and socially, the possibility of a unified mode of being.[77] That so humane an ideal was co-opted by the perverse Nazi concept of *Kultur*, compels us to scrutinize it even in its benign and universalistic form. And that some who criticize what today is labeled "high culture" do it by applying arguments for ethnic solidarity uncomfortably close to *völkisch* notions creates an even more troubling situation.[78]

Contemporary theories, which seek both an identity-reinforcing difference and a nonxenophobic type of solidarity, are still engaged in a bewildering search for a new humanism. The idea of culture continues to protest against a loss attributed to modernity, against the way modern life forces us to split, against the way it compartmentalizes thinking and becomes domain-specific. Yet that same idea of culture encourages specialization at the level of cultures and must always somehow overcome the collective differences it so strenuously maintains. No wonder the notion of a harmonious and organic existence, often associated with a pastoral era, entices the imagination and overwhelms politics. The other side of Auschwitz, as its Nazi architectural history shows, was a dream city, Himmler's rural utopia.[79]

Is enough *mundane* music left to retune the imagination by an effective if harsher accord? I explore in the next chapter a modern poet's effort to expand human sensibility in the direction of compassion. He resists imagination's "prophetic blast of harmony"[80] in favor of a subdued pastoral symphony, of words that reflect a quiet, even nonmusical mode of being.

NOTES

1. This question may parallel something that also puzzles trauma theory: whether the psychic injury must always be referred back to a childhood experience as well as to the trigger event that comes later and is often entirely different in character. In cases of posttraumatic stress, what confronts us is always the massive rather than the subtle point of origination, and even among the various massive causes, though their psychic effects may be comparable, it seems wrong to create an equivalence, as if surviving a car crash were the same as coming out of an ecological disaster or war or genocide.

2. The significance of the second date is not that it marks the beginning of the systematic extermination—which started before, with Hitler's Russian campaign—but that it reveals the all-important role of a bureaucratic machinery of destruction without which the Final Solution could not have taken place. It compels us, therefore, to reflect on the relation of bureaucracy and modernity: it points to an intellectual disclosure.

3. "A new shape of knowing invades the mind," is how Terrence Des Pres puts it in his "Prolog" to *Praises and Dispraises: Poetry and Politics in the Twentieth Century* (New York: Penguin, 1989). "Holocaust literature," writes Alvin Rosenfeld, "is an attempt to express a new order of consciousness, a recognizable shift in being. The human imagination after Auschwitz is simply not the same as it was before" (*A Double Dying: Reflections on Holocaust Literature* [Bloomington: Indiana University Press, 1980], 13).

4. *The Holocaust in Historical Context*, vol. 1, *The Holocaust and Mass Death before the Modern Age* (New York: Oxford University Press, 1993).

5. *The Writing of the Disaster*, trans. Ann Smock (Lincoln: University of Nebraska Press, 1986), 84.

6. Ibid.

7. *The Standard Edition of the Complete Psychological Works of Sigmund Freud*, ed. and trans. James Strachey (London: Hogarth, 1953–

74), 14·307 Compare Freud's sentiments with those of Jacques Maritain in *Primauté du spirituel* (Paris: Plon, 1927): "It is important to understand fully the meaning of the war and the terrifying breach [*coupure*] it signified. The remark of Benedict XV on Europe's suicide resonates more deeply than we thought. Europe has *killed* its past. . . . All gentleness and beauty, forms, values, even images that nourished our ancestors, which made nature seem fraternal and the universe a familiar place and helped to educate us from generation to generation, have suddenly become something distant and apart: perfectly worthy of being admired and respected but frozen in a vanished past" (154–55; my translation). Maritain is chiefly concerned with the effect of this *coupure* on the young, who are in "great disarray." Youth, he adds eloquently, "takes a stroll along its own humanity as in a museum; it sees its heart in those showcases."

8. My formulation is influenced by Emmanuel Levinas, *Sur Maurice Blanchot* (Paris: Fata Morgana, 1975), as well as by Blanchot's own remarks on event (and Heidegger's "Ereignis") in *The Writing of the Disaster*, 98–103. I should caution that Blanchot does not equate the "disaster" with the Holocaust, but that event is certainly the proximate cause of his reflections.

9. Cf. Derrida's Hamletian reflections in the first chapter of *Specters of Marx: The State of the Debt, the Work of Mourning, and the New International* (New York: Routledge, 1994).

10. See, e.g., Ernst Troeltsch's pamphlet, *Deutsche Bildung* (Darmstadt: Reichel, 1919), which starts by recognizing the world war as having been "ein Moral- und Kulturkrieg" and asks for self-criticism and a new constitution for the German concepts of *Geist* and *Bildung*.

11. One thing the Great War made clear is the effect of state-sponsored propaganda, not only how it built up false morale but also how it undermined, eventually, trust in words. "No one can calculate," Fussell writes, "the number of Jews who died in the Second World War because of the ridicule during the twenties and thirties of Allied propaganda about Belgian nuns violated and children sadistically used. In a climate of widespread skepticism about any further atrocity stories, most people refused fully to credit reports of the concentration camps until ocular evidence compelled belief and it was too late" (*The Great*

War and Modern Memory [New York: Oxford University Press, 1976], 316). In everything I will say about language, though I stress Nazism, Stalinism is a parallel and exacerbating factor.

12. Robert Lifton's concept of psychic numbing is usefully distinguished from that of repression (which seeks the forgetting of a mental content), because in the former "the mind is severed from its own psychic forms, there's an impairment in the symbolization process itself." See Cathy Caruth, "Interview with Robert Jay Lifton," *American Imago* 48, no. 1 (1991): 160; and Robert Lifton, *The Broken Connection: On Death and the Continuity of Life* (New York: Simon and Schuster, 1979), especially chapters 13 and 14. Here I am less concerned, however, with death experiences such as Auschwitz or Hiroshima or—at another level—the loss of close friends through AIDS than with the proliferation and dailiness of second-order images of trauma. The impairment, of course, may be similar, yet the numbing could show itself more as an ability to manipulate those images coldly than as a symbolic incapacity or blockage or as Paul Celan's stutter style.

13. Victor Klemperer, whose diaries of 1933 to 1945 have now been published, collected examples of what he abbreviated as LTI (*lingua tertii imperii*). See *Ich will Zeugnis ablegen bis zum letzten: Tagebücher,* vol. 1 1933–1941; vol. 2, 1941–1945, ed. Walter Nowojski (Berlin: Aufbau, 1995). Ernst Cassirer has interesting observations of how, in his time, the "magic word" takes precedence over the "semantic word" and state-sponsored myth (including the myth of the state) gains a multiplier effect through media technology. See the concluding pages of his *Myth of the State* (New Haven: Yale University Press, 1946).

14. An interesting discussion of how even the scholar's speech becomes more self-aware is found in Raul Hilberg and Alfons Söllner, "Das Schweigen zum Sprechen bringen," in *Zivilisationsbruch: Denken nach Auschwitz,* ed. Dan Diner (Frankfurt-am-Main: Fischer, 1988), 192–200.

15. Maurice Blanchot, *L'entretien infini* (Paris: Gallimard), 194–199. My translations.

16. Cf. Aleida Assmann and Jan Assmann, "Kultur und Konflikt: Aspekte einer Theorie des unkommunikativen Handelns," in *Kultur und Konflikt,* ed. Jan Assmann and Dietrich Harth (Frankfurt-am-

Main; Suhrkamp, 1990). It is in this area that the quarrel between Habermas and Lyotard on the importance of "consensus" is being played out.

17. Alexander Kluge, "The Assault of the Present on the Rest of Time," *New German Critique* 49 (1990): 11–23; Blanchot, *The Writing of the Disaster*, 51.

18. Although they do not focus directly on the Holocaust, I see a collection of essays like *Kultur und Konflikt* as exploring this line of thought. The first contribution, by Aleida and Jan Assmann, describes a theory of "uncommunicative action" ("unkommunikatives Handeln") that tries to save Habermas's perspective of "communicative action" by proposing a more complex model of mutuality, one aware of the fact that conflict is generated and exacerbated by the very pressure for consensus and harmony.

19. *De l'esprit: Heidegger et la question* (Paris: Galilée, 1987). All translations are my own.

20. Derrida, *Mémoires pour Paul de Man* (Paris: Galilée, 1988), 64, and the later discussion of Heidegger's notion of thought as *Versammlung*. The phantom synthesis alluded to by Derrida may refer to Kant's critical notion of an "a priori synthesis" and is deconstructed with Heidegger's help in chapter 1 of *Specters of Marx*.

21. Cf. Geoffrey Hartman, "Wordsworth Before Heidegger," in *The Unremarkable Wordsworth* (Minneapolis: University of Minnesota Press, 1987), 197–200.

22. R. B. Kitaj, *The First Diasporist Manifesto* (London: Thames and Hudson, 1989), 59.

23. See, e.g., Dan Diner, ed., *Zivilisationsbruch: Denken nach Auschwitz* (Frankfurt-am-Main: Fischer, 1988).

24. For France, see Zeev Sternhell, *Neither Right nor Left: Fascist Ideology in France*, trans. David Maisel (Berkeley: University of California Press, 1986), especially chapter 7, "Spiritualistic Fascism."

25. Those who do not think semantic signals have much power should read Jacques Rivière's *L'Allemand* (subtitled *Souvenirs et réflections d'un prisonnier de guerre*: "Memories and Reflections of a Prisoner of War") published at the end of the First World War (Paris: Editions de la Nouvelle Révue Française, 1918). The polemic of this future

editor of the *Nouvelle Révue Française* against philosopher Paul Natorp's exaltation of *Kultur, Deutschtum*, and German genius is as eloquent and symptomatic as Thomas Mann's extended quarrel with himself in *Reflections of an Unpolitical Man*, also anno Domini 1918, which not only savages liberal buzzwords but specifically rehearses Romain Rolland's attack on his defense of German *Kultur* against French *civilisation*. Nazism's *Kultur* concept does not coincide entirely with Spengler's, of course: it is racialist as well as pseudoscientific, insisting on Aryan *Artgleichheit*.

26. Rivière, *L'Allemand*, 154.

27. Theodor W. Adorno, *Negative Dialectics*, trans. E. B. Ashton (New York: Continuum, 1992), 367.

28. *Minima Moralia: Reflections from a Damaged Life*, trans. E. F. N. Jephcott (London: Verso, 1974), 57. Translation modified.

29. Friedrich Meinecke, *Die Deutsche Erhebung von 1914: Aufsätze und Vorträge* (Stuttgart: Cotta, 1914), 9.

30. Meinecke, *Die Deutsche Erhebung*, 45. Meinecke seems to have forgotten Nietzsche's critique of German cultural claims after the Franco-Prussian war. See introduction, above. Yet Meinecke retains the hope that nationalism would be moderated, even purified, by German culture joining rather than evading the state. He hopes the war will wake a "vaterländische Liebe" of "hinreissender Gewalt" in "staatsfremden Träumern und Aestheten." See the last essay in *Die Deutsche Erhebung*, written before the war but to which he adds a coda.

31. *Paroles suffoquées* (Paris: Galilée, 1987), 21. My translation.

32. For Armando, much less known than Appelfeld, see his *From Berlin*, trans. Susan Massotti (London: Reaktion, 1996).

33. *Schibboleth: Pour Paul Celan* (Paris: Galilée, 1986), 11, 13. My translation. The book appeared first in an English version, based on a 1984 lecture translated by Joshua Wilner in *Midrash and Literature*, ed. Geoffrey H. Hartman and Sanford Budick (New Haven: Yale University Press, 1986), 307–47. A suggestive remark in Blanchot's *The Writing of the Disaster* anticipates Derrida. Blanchot has just spoken of the concept of "the One" and adds: "Of the whole [*l'ensemble*] which we know only as fully deployed [*déplié*], and in whose retreat the 'one and

only time' [*l'une seule fois*] is hidden away, mortifying itself in the folds of the reserve which safeguards it [*qui s'y supplicie*]." I have kept Smock's translation in *The Writing of the Disaster*, 130. Could *sup(p)li-cier* be rendered as "to torment"; thus "the folds of the reserve which torments itself there"?

34. *Schibboleth*, 83. My translation.

35. Elsewhere Derrida is clearer in suggesting that uniqueness, understood strictly, is a form of closure that tries to contain or cordon off the Holocaust. Here too the issue of generational transmission of holocaust trauma can be raised. See, e.g., the issue of *Psyche* (49 [January 1995]) devoted to this matter.

36. In the case of Celan, this hidden and congealed element may include the seductive sublimity of Rilke's *Sonnets to Orpheus* or the *Duino Elegies*; in the case of Derrida, the *Chimères* of Nerval.

37. See Blanchot on the act of reading and communicating, in *L'espace littéraire* (Paris: Gallimard, 1955), 201 ff. Derrida, it seems to me, by what Blanchot would have called the "errance" of his style—his refusal to sacralize the word "holocaust," for example, or a punning that moves between the demotic and the charged meaning of a word, or marked and unmarked semes ("revenant," "revient")—comes close to "le risque de se livrer à l'inessentiel [qui] est lui-même essentiel" (the risk of abandoning oneself to the inessential, which is itself an essential act; *L'espace littéraire*, 177).

38. This essay is found in Derrida, *Psyché: Inventions de l'autre* (Paris: Galilée, 1987). It is translated by Ken Frieden as "Denials," in *Languages of the Unsayable: The Play of Negativity in Literature and Literary Theory*, ed. Sanford Budick and Wolfgang Iser (New York: Columbia University Press, 1989).

39. A further, symmetrically placed example occurs when he closes *Schibboleth* with the politeness formula "permettez-moi de laisser tomber ceci" (allow me to pass this by), a rhetorical courtesy expressing his sense of the arbitrary character of closure. But translated as "permit me to let this be entombed," it speaks to his hope that Celan's "unbestattete Worte" have been given a tomb, a *tombeau*.

40. *Feu la cendre* was published in 1982 and 1987. The English version, translated, edited, and with an introduction by Ned Lukacher, ap-

peared in 1991 (Lincoln: Nebraska University Press). *De l'esprit* was also published in 1987.

41. In both Heidegger and Karl Mannheim *"Destruktion"* means a methodical destructuring—laying bare—of the unexamined social, epistemological, and ontological assumptions of Western concepts. Heidegger moreover thinks to create a language that has reformative as well as analytic-destructive vigor.

42. See also my "Evening Star and Evening Land," in *The Fate of Reading* (Chicago: Chicago University Press, 1975).

43. *De l'esprit*, 66; my translation.

44. See *Positions*, trans. and ann. Allan Bass (Chicago: Chicago University Press, 1981), 73. There is some advance in theory, of course, partly influenced by Derrida and centering on the concept of intertextuality. Yet theory, it can be argued, by remaining exterior to inventive writing, perpetuates a dichotomy that Derrida seeks to undermine by his "installation."

45. Cf. Geoffrey Hartman, *Saving the Text: Literature/Derrida/ Philosophy* (Baltimore: Johns Hopkins University Press, 1981), 9 ff., 85–86.

46. For the deconstructive or more experimental type of Holocaust or anti-Nazi monument, see James Young, *The Texture of Memory: Holocaust Memorials and Meaning* (New Haven: Yale University Press, 1993).

47. My translation. Quoted in the "Editorial Epilogue" to Adorno's *Ästhetische Theorie* (Frankfurt-am-Main: Suhrkamp, 1970), 538. On the fragment (also "Bruchstück") and disintegration, see also *Ästhetische Theorie*, 73–74.

48. Jean-François Lyotard, *Heidegger et "les juifs"* (Paris: Galilée, 1988), 76. Cf. the difficult reflections on "the beautiful death," understood as the desire to "die well" through choice or a chosen obligation, in Lyotard's *The Differend: Phrases in Dispute* (Minneapolis: University of Minnesota Press, 1988), sections 156 ff.

49. *Lodz Ghetto: Inside a Community under Siege*, ed. Alan Adelson and Robert Lapides (New York: Viking, 1989), 299.

50. Cf. Lawrence Langer, prefacing his collected volume *Admitting the Holocaust: Collected Essays* (New York: Oxford University Press,

1995): "Readers of the essays in this volume will see at once the vivid and lasting impression the views of this Auschwitz survivor have had on my response to the Holocaust experience. [Améry's] line 'No bridge led from death in Auschwitz to *Death in Venice*' must have been engraved on my memory as nothing less than an epiphany." See also 55–57.

51. *Negative Dialectics*, 360.

52. Chaim A. Kaplan, *The Warsaw Diary of Chaim Kaplan*, trans. Abraham Katsh (New York: Collier, 1983), 107.

53. The burden on theory, that is, increases. Adorno affirms an unresolvable difference between theory and practice: their unanimity or alliance would be as sinister, he observes, as an understanding between the police and the criminal element! Yet he knows that to grant the impotence of theory is no improvement. It would merely provide, as he says, an excuse for submitting to the all-powerful ideal of productivity that dominates the capitalistic world of businessmen and bureaucrats. "Since we have gotten rid of Utopian thought and demanded a unity of theory and practice, we have become all too practical" (*Minima Moralia*, 44; translation modified).

54. *Negative Dialectics*, 359.

55. Adorno coincides, at this point, with Franz Rosenzweig's claim in the opening pages of *The Star of Redemption*, trans. William W. Hallo (Notre Dame, Ind.: University of Notre Dame Press, 1985), that philosophy "travels on over the grave that gapes before our feet at every step. It lets the body fall into the abyss, but the soul floats on high and away" (3). The nothing that philosophy applies as a quality of thought, as negation within a system, is simply, according to Rosenzweig, an evasion of that nothingness.

56. In *Fallen Soldiers: Reshaping the Memory of the World Wars* (New York: Oxford University Press, 1990).

57. It was popularized by Lessing's essay "Wie die Alten den Tod gebildet" (1769): "How the Authors of Classical Antiquity Depicted Death."

58. Theodor W. Adorno, *Negative Dialektik. Jargon der Eigentlichkeit*, in *Gesammelte Schriften* (Frankfurt-am-Main: Suhrkamp, 1973), 6:360. My translation.

59. Adorno extends the meaning of *épater le bourgeois* in his bourgeois bashing. The bourgeois, practically speaking, coincides in his thought with the philistine; Hannah Arendt goes so far as to stereotype this social entity as being without civic virtue. The irony here is that the word points to a self-enriching class that is the mainstay of urban life, so that, once again, even while these thinkers insist on city rather than country, as on the importance of deliberative democracy ("le parlement et la ville," so to say), city life as the ideal milieu for democracy (aspiring to the modern equivalent of a Greek city-state) is put in doubt.

60. *Negative Dialektik*, 6:354–58.

61. For Blake, see "The Voice of the Devil" in *The Marriage of Heaven and Hell* (1790–93).

62. Cf. Lyotard, *Heidegger*, 83.

63. Cf. Hannah Arendt, *On Revolution* (New York: Viking, 1963), 84.

64. The strain on the humanistic concept of culture is also evidenced by the many intellectuals in the modernist movement who displayed a supercilious, alarmed view of mass democracy and saw the possibility of higher culture and great art threatened. John Carey makes this point vividly in *The Intellectuals and the Masses: Pride and Prejudice among the Literary Intelligentsia, 1880–1939* (Boston: Faber and Faber, 1992), when he counters Hugh Trevor-Roper's remark that Hitler's ideas on culture were "trivial, half-baked and disgusting" with "there are marked similarities between the cultural ideals promulgated in the Fuehrer's writings and conversation and those of the intellectuals we have been looking at" (198).

65. This audience exaltation is a highly ambiguous phenomenon, however, and context must always be taken into account. So in Nazi Germany a kind of youth-culture protest took the form of "the swing movement": wild dancing to English and American hits even in wartime. This outraged Himmler and brought in the Gestapo. See Detlev J. K. Peukert, *Inside Nazi Germany: Conformity, Opposition, and Racism in Everyday Life*, trans. Richard Deveson (New Haven: Yale University Press, 1987), 166–69, 200–203.

66. "After Auschwitz," in *Negative Dialectics*, 361–65.

67. In his *Classical and Christian Ideas of World Harmony: Prolego-*

menu to un Interpretation of the Word "Stimmung" (Baltimore. Johns Hopkins University Press, 1963), Leo Spitzer sees "a great caesura in occidental history" when the master metaphor of a *musica mundana* reaches the end of its Christian (postclassical) life and wanes: "At the end of the eighteenth century *Stimmung* was crystallized, that is, it was robbed of its blossoming life" (76). Spitzer, who accepted H. Sperber's "Bedeutungswandel ist Kulturwandel" ("Changes in the meaning of words are due to changes in the culture"), regrets this ominous disintegration of a long-lived semantic "field." He does not fully diagnose the crisis, however, except to say that it has to do with the Enlightenment and the waning of Christianity. The fact is, though, as he himself often remarks in his generous footnotes, that eudaemonic themes survive in both philosophy and ordinary language, and the word "*Stimmung*" in particular remains indebted to "an ancient semantic texture" going back to "the first picture of the world seen in a harmony patterned on music, a world resembling Apollo's lute" (7). But where he seems to criticize Kant for his aversion to the eudaemonic (223), which may have helped to destroy the idea of world harmony, we might well take a more nuanced view, given the cultural development noted in this chapter. Spitzer knows, moreover, that Nietzsche disputed this nonagonistic picture of Greek culture. See also the final page of chapter 6 below.

68. Johann Gottlieb Fichte, *Some Lectures Concerning the Scholar's Vocation* (1794), in *Philosophy of German Idealism*, ed. Ernst Behler (New York: Continuum, 1987).

69. My translation. On the "veneration of culture and personality . . . one of the principal pieties of nineteenth-century Germany," in relation to both politics and religion, see Fritz Stern, *The Failure of Illiberalism: Essays on the Political Culture of Modern Germany* (Chicago: Chicago University Press, 1955), 14–15. His chapter "The Political Consequences of the Unpolitical German" is particularly relevant. See also "German Idealism in the Light of Social History," in *Germany and Europe: Historical Essays by Hajo Holborn* (Garden City, N.J.: Doubleday, 1970), 1–32.

70. My translation. The original reads, "Ewig nur an ein einzelnes kleines Bruchstück des Ganzen gefesselt, bildet sich der Mensch selbst

nur als Bruchstück aus; ewig nur das eintönige Geräusch des Rades, das er umtreibt, im Ohr, entwickelt er nie die Harmonie seines Wesens, und anstatt die Menschheit in seiner Natur auszuprägen, wird er bloß zu einem Ausdruck seines Geschäfts, seiner Wissenschaft." See *On the Aesthetic Education of Man*, bilingual edition, trans. and ed. Elizabeth Willoughby and L. A. Willoughby (New York: Oxford University Press, 1967), 34.

71. There was no German nation-state in Fichte and Schiller's time, so that, as already in Herder, speculation on culture, or the cultural nation, had a special poetic and utopian pathos, one that allowed Germans "to overcome the fragmentariness of existence both metaphysically and nationally and to feel a sense of oneness and belonging." See Gregory Jusdanis, "Beyond National Culture?" *boundary* 2, no. 22 (1995): 23–60, esp. 38–39.

72. Friedrich Meinecke, *Cosmopolitanism and the National State*, trans. Robert B. Kimber (Princeton: Princeton University Press, 1970), 12–14.

73. *Minor Prophecies: The Literary Essay in the Culture Wars* (Cambridge: Harvard University Press, 1991), 131.

74. Jacques Lacan's animosity to American ego psychology is a deliberately harsh response to a model of psychic development still dependent on this harmony of integration. Similarly, the schizoanalysis promulgated by Deleuze and Guattari proposes an iconoclastic model of psychic functioning radically suspicious of classicist integration. The Holocaust does not figure explicitly in the thinking of Deleuze and Guattari, who interpret fascism along Marxist lines as a pathological consequence of capitalism, yet they have written, according to Foucault, an "Introduction to the Nonfascist Life." The psyche is reconceived in order to reconceive politics. Another example is Levinas, who launches a radical revision of ethics based on the charge that Greek ontology turned the other (whose recognition is basic to ethics) into the same. A parallel development is found in Paul de Man's critique of "aesthetic ideology," which is correctly linked by Martin Jay to Central European notions of *Bildung* and *Wissenschaft* (see especially his essay on the subject in *Force Fields: Between Intellectual History and Cultural Critique* [New York: Rout-

ledge, 1993]). Jean-François Lyotard's description of modern equivalents of Enlightenment "grand narratives," imprinted not only with
ideas of progress and emancipation but with a—however finely conceived—coercive hope in consensus is also relevant here. The suspicion of system generally, especially when blindly (though in the
name of science) applied to politics and the domain of spirit, pro-
voked what Georges Bataille named "heterology" in the 1930s. Denis
Hollier defines it as "the science of what science does not want to
know, the science of what exceeds knowledge. The science of epistemological residues." Bataille sometimes connects the psychology of
fascism with an attempt to purge everything heterogeneous. See Hollier, *Les dépossédés (Bataille, Caillois, Leiris, Malraux, Sartre)* (Paris:
Minuit, 1993), 127.

75. Introduction to Ellen Fine, *Legacy of Night: The Literary Universe of Elie Wiesel* (Albany: State University of New York Press,
1982), xi.

76. In a brilliant critique of Raymond Williams, David Lloyd and
Paul Thomas point out his overidentification with this particular discourse on culture, which in stressing the whole man idea, or the harmonizing and compensatory function of culture, forgets that, as they
put it, the political "stands for a division of the human into partialities."
One result is that Williams underestimates what E. P. Thompson recovered: the importance of the Chartist movement in the nineteenth century and, more generally, an emerging working-class power of thought.
Another result is that he did not see clearly enough how this Greek or
pseudo-Greek vision of culture as restorative and unifying paralleled—
and so could merge with—a view in which the state (not civil society)
provided that remedy. Their article calls itself, therefore, "Culture and
Society or 'Culture and the State'?" See *Cultural Materialism: On
Raymond Williams*, ed. Christopher Prendergast (Minneapolis: University of Minnesota Press, 1995), 268–304.

77. Letter by a police officer from the East, quoted in Léon Poliakov, *Harvest of Hate: The Nazi Program for the Destruction of the Jews
of Europe*, rev. ed. (New York: Holocaust Library, 1979), 128. See also
Léon Poliakov and Joseph Wulf, *Das Dritte Reich und die Juden:
Dokumente und Berichte* (1955; reprint, Wiesbaden: Fourier, 1989).

78. For the impact of *völkisch* notions on National Socialism, see George Mosse, *The Crisis of German Ideology: Intellectual Origins of the Third Reich* (New York: Grosset and Dunlap, 1964).

79. See Debórah Dwork and Jan van Pelt, *Auschwitz, 1270 to the Present* (New York: Norton, 1996).

80. Wordsworth, 1850 *Prelude* 5.93–98.

chapter five

The Sympathy Paradox:
Poetry, Feeling, and Modern
Cultural Morality

hearing oftentimes
The still, sad music of humanity
　　　　　—WORDSWORTH, *Lyrical Ballads*

Damn humanity, let us have a bit of inhuman, or unhuman truth, that
our fuzzy human emotions can't alter.
　　　　　—D. H. LAWRENCE[1]

Modern cultural morality is well summed
up by Wordsworth when he defines genius as "widening the sphere
of human sensibility for the delight, honor and benefit of human nature."[2] This doctrine, linking genius to the sympathetic imagination,
sees the progress of humanity in terms of an ability to feel for others,
a progress facilitated by a faculty that can acknowledge—represent
from the inside—situations different from one's own. Allowing into
serious public representation an eighteenth-century "underclass"—
a mad mother, an infanticide, an idiot boy, a homeless woman, a
destitute shepherd, an old and disabled servant—constitutes an
advance in realism based on that widening of sensibility.

Little is gained, in Wordsworth's case, by reducing the doctrine
to ideas of *Humanität* in continental historicism or eighteenth-century British sources that deal with moral and sentimental matters.
But there is a complex, unexplained, humanitarian shift in sensibility between the sixteenth and the late eighteenth centuries that
affects the relationship of man to the natural world but shows itself

in England more as a growing "love of nature" than as "love of man." The shift is complex because of the many social and economic factors that seem to have participated in it and unexplained because it is so overdetermined that only the intervention of Wordsworth (but also his reception, which returns the matter to the social sphere) made this longitudinal alteration decisive.[3]

Wordsworth's way, moreover, of bypassing technical philosophy has its own "English" specificity. He avoids hardcore philosophic diction as he does poetic diction. After Coleridge turns away from German philosophical method in chapter 13 of his *Biographia Literaria* (1816), literary theory lapses back into pragmatic and essayistic reflection. There is no systematic engagement in England or America between poet and philosopher, though there is (as in Kenneth Burke, for example) a lot of wonderful, productive bricolage. Indeed, the very distinction between philosopher and poet can be challenged, at least in America, by pointing to Thoreau, Emerson, and William James. If painting is silent poetry, then poetry is silent philosophy. This "tacit dimension" is related to Wordsworth's radical consolidation of a view that valued rural nature's range of quiet and quieting influences.

Wordsworth's own portrait of a philosopher, in an early poem that becomes *The Excursion*, is an itinerant peddler who embodies the northern English countryside and the wisdom of oral tradition. *Lyrical Ballads* already claims to draw a truer language for poetry— a language that widens rather than impedes sensibility—from the way men and woman speak in natural, that is, rural, surroundings. (It is a truer language of poetry but also a truer language of thought, as I will show later. In that sense Wordsworth *is* a philosophic poet.) One might have expected this claim to produce a sense of joy or liberation, because of the new freedom to feel and observe. The very theme of Wordsworth's autobiography, *The Prelude*, is inner growth, liberty, power. Yet most of his ballads about the poor also portray his burdened state of mind.

Blake's poems and pronouncements seem far more liberated in their laughing speech, even when the laughter is bitter. "Damn braces: Bless relaxes" or "Exuberance is Beauty" are among Blake's confident "Proverbs of Hell." "Pity would be no more, / If we did not make somebody Poor" is the opening of "The Human Abstract." Blake uses his imaginative powers less for empathy than for communicating the possibility of an emancipation, or awakening the revolutionary and visionary energies that remain in us, often despite ourselves. For Blake, we stand in our own way, fearing the liberating potential in imagination. For Wordsworth, the simple or suffering people to whom his spirit clings have something permanent and even dignified about them; they are a part of the Nature in which they live, and it is the poet, with his strange fits of feeling, who is perplexed.

Two centuries later Wordsworth's subdued vision seems more realistic—if it is realism one is after. And Blake, in his Prophetic Books or "Bible of Hell," is forced to adopt what Derrida will call a paleonymic style, the basis also of deconstructive practice. Blake installs himself parasitically in traditional visionary concepts so as to destroy them, though with the aim of saving an original vision, of purging it of oppressive politico-theological distortions and so returning imaginative power to its source in the "Poetic Genius . . . the true Man."[4]

The question, though, raised by the history of sensibility, and one that has become unavoidable with the romantic emphasis on the sympathetic imagination, is whether we can deal with suffering that is not only local but general. Wordsworth's *misérables* are mainly of his own neighborhood, yet a shift since his time in the means of representation, an extension of consciousness made possible by photography and telecommunications, uncovers "a wretchedness of global extent." "A radical change occurs in the way the world is known. Epic fantasy gives way to stark realism. And now politics is everywhere and hopeless."[5]

In fact, we have become involuntary witnesses to every sorrow and evil the cameras catch. The transition between local and global is crucial here: it brings a new despair, a hopelessness challenging the possibility of religious consolation or political remedy. And so we are left too often with "the dismay of images"[6] and an unappeasable conscience. Photographs of the dying, the mutilated, the mute, the devastated are harder to modify than verbally mediated pictures. Utopian visions dim. Snapshots of ordinary or happy life are increasingly like promotional inserts, ads that persuade us to buy life, to go on living. The reign of images, its stark realism, imposes a responsibility that cannot be met, feelings that cannot be acted on, and a resentment that may actually shut those "doors of perception" that the romantic revolution in sensibility wished to open wide, on all creation, all creatures, in an infinite, nonenvious expansion of the humanitarian covenant. How infinite or flexible are the humanitarian feelings that art seeks to develop and that Matthew Arnold saw culture as disseminating and perfecting?

The paradox of the sympathetic imagination is that the more successful an expanding sensibility becomes, the more evidence we find of actual insensibility. Must we, then, consider human beings callous by nature? What we do know suggests rather the economy of moral sentiments: emotional defenses and self-protective doctrines come into play to limit an intolerable burden on feeling. (Psychoanalysis might talk here of countertransference, or the negative aspect of empathy.) Even when there is bliss or happiness, the contrast between present and past, or the vacillation of moods itself, may prove too painful and lead to a desensitization.

The consciousness of a link between sensitivity and desensitization has always been there *in art*. The art of art allows strong feelings to emerge, even toward what is strange or estranged, for "things silently gone out of mind" or "things violently destroyed." The binding together of differences into a harmonious "empire" is never given up.[7] In art this is accomplished by an economy of form or by limits of representation that keep the spectator of the suffering (oneself or others) from being overwhelmed.[8] The rules of poetics, unless reduced to dry prescriptions, have always implied a "science" of the feelings, what was later generalized as aesthetics; a "grand elementary principle of pleasure," according to Wordsworth, makes distress (and, at times, ecstasy) more bearable. Aristotle's *Poetics* is basically a descriptive set of rules derived from a mimesis that gives pleasure even when, as in tragedy, it deals with intense and painful events.

Human development does not start with a sensibility open to every impulse or sentiment. To a great extent feelings are taught, being the result of nurture as well as nature. They are guided by collective morality, restrained or encouraged by it. Art participates in that educative process. John Stuart Mill praised Wordsworth's poetry as a "culture of the feelings." (Even indifference, as Fichte once said, is not the absence of passion but rather a kind of passion itself.) From the very beginning of life feelings are worked on, and passions shaped, by a symbolic order. Love too must be reinvented, as Rimbaud declared.

Consider Coleridge's haunting poem "The Rime of the Ancient Mariner" in the light of the need for sentimental education. A wedding guest is stopped at the door of the festivities by a hypnotic storyteller. His marvelous tale, basically of a fall into and recovery from insensitiveness, implies that, of the two kinds of love, *agape* is of greater importance than *eros*. "Man and bird and beast" should be the true community; compared to it, the communion of man and woman in the sacrament of marriage is too exclusive and not sufficient to overcome radical human solitude:

> O Wedding Guest! this soul has been
> Alone on a wide, wide sea:
> So lonely 'twas, that God himself
> Scarce seemed there to be.

The Mariner's tale acts like an inverse banns, cautioning against marriage and sending the Wedding Guest away a "sadder and a wiser man." Yet sentimental education, mediating between solitude and society, covers much more in life than the courtship and marriage relation.

Here Wordsworth's importance returns. His autobiographical poem *The Prelude* is our first comprehensive (if still highly selective) consideration of how we develop into social beings. Examining the birth, growth, and binding of the affections in a rural setting, the poet shows that the imagination's quest for autonomy—for other worlds or a world of its own—could end in solipsism. The most remarkable of his early experiences, those for which *The Pre-*

lude is famous, are suffused by terror or ghostly feelings. How then does imagination become a socializing faculty? How do we achieve what the eighteenth century called philanthropy, that is, a communitarian "love of mankind"?[9]

Wordsworth holds that love of nature, though alloyed by fear and inspired by early life in rural surroundings, leads to love of humankind in a way that expands rather than narrows sensibility. The relevance of that claim is twofold. An early, intense and unconscious, intercourse with the sights and sounds of nature is essential to personal development. The imagination is saved for this world by being substantively imprinted by rural nature. The poet's argument, part original myth, part empirical observation, is that by age seventeen the link between nature and his inner life had become so strong that he "coerced" all things into "sympathy." As late as his college years he experiences "consciousnesses not to be subdued," so that to "even the loose stones that cover the highway, / I gave a moral life." Nature in its phenomenality has captured the imagination, or the imagination has adapted itself to the world and given up some of its self-involvement. This "mutual domination" of external and internal worlds results in what Keats will call "soul making."[10]

It is, then, in the heroic age of childhood and adolescence that nature bonds with imagination and becomes the basis of memory. However, the strength of those early, unmediated, and sometimes ecstatic encounters also works against memory. The spin Wordsworth puts on this impasse between memory and ecstasy is that a sublime sense of what happened remains, even if the details, the exact contents of the original experience, are effaced. He often tries to interpret positively such traumatic effacement.

It is important to understand that Wordsworth's anxiety about the past goes beyond the absence of specific images (for some continue to be present) to the absence of the affect that once accompanied them. The grown man suffers from an empty if still motivating sense of sublimity.[11] What we grieve for is often the capacity for feeling itself. The images before our eyes, the scenes that seemed to greet us then, are now viewed apathetically, though with a clear consciousness of loss: the gleam, the "splendor in the grass," has faded. Only here and there a sudden, as if irrational, access of emotion returns to startle and waylay. "That glimpse of glory, why renewed?"[12] Such moments recall the preternatural strength with which imagination once "wedded" nature and may, so goes the hopeful argument, wed it again.

In terms of societal progress, moreover, if most of the world is still undergoing a change from rural to industrial urban, Wordsworth's understanding of nature as a prior and indispensable reality connection supports the hope that this transition, even in modern, speeded-up conditions, can be made less traumatizing.

I am not positing the existence of a peasant sensibility as something uniform or immutable or suggesting that the world was better off in the agrarian age. Nor that there is curative virtue in a *déjeuner sur l'herbe* or that one's daughter should live, in Yeats's wonderful phrase, "like some green laurel / Rooted in one dear perpetual place" ("A Prayer for My Daughter"). But what historians call modernization often involves a catastrophic transition: displacement into cities, coerced collectivization, large-scale rather than local war, the rupture of traditional rhythms and habits. Writing at the end of the eighteenth century and toward the beginning of brutal changes, Wordsworth acted as a seismic indicator and registered all the nuances of a severe alteration that should have produced a transformation, not just a retrospective glow, but has continued as a series of disasters.[13]

To illustrate how Wordsworth deals with these matters, and how deeply his thought engages with the paradox of the sympathetic imagination, let me bring an early poem to your attention:

Old Man Travelling
Animal Tranquillity and Decay
A Sketch

The little hedge-row birds,
That peck along the road, regard him not.
He travels on, and in his face, his step,

His gait, is one expression; every limb,
His look and bending figure, all bespeak
A man who does not move with pain, but moves
With thought.—He is insensibly subdued
To settled quiet: he is one by whom
All effort seems forgotten, one to whom
Long patience has such mild composure given,
That patience now doth seem a thing, of which
He hath no need. He is by nature led
To peace so perfect, that the young behold
With envy, what the old man hardly feels.
—I asked him whither he was bound, and what
The object of his journey; he replied
"Sir! I am going many miles to take
"A last leave of my son, a mariner,
"Who from a sea-fight has been brought to Falmouth,
And there is dying in an hospital."

A genre picture from daily life, the "sketch" does not try to arouse pity. Paradoxically, it is more concerned with envy of a state of insensibility or with a natural stoicism. It intuits feelings that were, yet are no more. We see a man "insensibly subdued / To settled quiet," whose years have moved him closer to "animal tranquillity" as well as decay. (The placement of "insensibly" suggests a nontraumatic passage from sensitivity to its absence, as if the inner perception of a feeling's loss could itself be injurious.) The bending figure of the old man curves back to nature, to the ground that seems to be his destination. The very sensibility that made a sketch like this possible produces in the poet a consciousness of unselfconsciousness[14] and suggests how attractive such "quiet," "patience," and "peace" can be. Should we retitle the poem "Still Life with Birds"?

Let us not accuse Wordsworth too quickly, however, of projecting or giving in to an illusion. Had the poem stopped at line 14 and become a blank verse sonnet concentrating on a wishful idea of composure or impassibility,[15] it would still have evoked a mode of existence *between* animate and inanimate. The poet's depiction of this border state diminishes anthropomorphism and arouses what he called a "sentiment of Being": the sense that there is no "line where being ends." Structures of meaning, or habits that compartmentalize Being into such categorizing dichotomies as nature and man, mute and speaking, inanimate and animate, local and universal, can limit rather than liberate perception.

The "life" of this man who moves along almost unperceived, almost at one with the natural scenery ("The little hedge-row birds . . . regard him not"), remains unknown, as does, by inference, nature's own life. Yet the absence of a self-regarding consciousness does not mean there is no life. Wordsworth conveys this animistic vision without rhetorical emphasis (except for an increase in negative locutions), but he does let us know that our knowledge is incomplete by way of a surprise: the final verses. There the nearly inanimate speaks, and the pity that was not aroused, or had no place, in the first part comes back as a specific kind of pathos and opens on a tragic perspective.[16] For the stately speech of the old man reveals that his destination was not a return to nature: he is traveling to a specific place in time, a hospital at Falmouth during England's war with France. Instead of a young person journeying to an old man's deathbed, it is, unnaturally, an old man who makes his way to his mortally wounded son.

Freud's "the aim of all life is death" holds, ironically, for the second part of the poem as well, but the contrast of the two parts causes a startling shift in perspective, as the image of a human life cut short follows abruptly on the impression of natural and peaceful decay. The element of drama in this reversal also occurs on the level of diction. The poet's complex, intuitive description of a nontraumatized mode of being in lines 1 through 14 is displaced, though not invalidated, by the simple, forthright wording that expresses the old man's resolve.

Wordsworth's contemporaries often failed to see the point of writing about such ordinary encounters. But Wordsworth draws from them a subtle, nontransfigurative mode of description, though it may come close to suggesting an omen. A being near death's door turns before our eyes into a wayside monument and speaks.[17]

A voice from nature, from a source apparently mute and insensate, is always there as the eerie ground of Wordsworth's poetry. His sensibility opens to the metasound of mute speech or nonevent: he records, by his exquisite attention to nature's life, the slightest change in a remembered landscape or "one soft impulse saved from vacancy."[18] It is generally the still small voice and not the cataclysmic fiery apparition that counts: Wordsworth would have turned from Sinai's thunder as a "gross and violent stimulant"! There is a great deal we have not fathomed in his peculiar sensitivity to the minimal, to that which, precisely, is *not* eventful, not part of a *histoire événementielle*. Daily, common life is his domain.

"I begin," he writes in a poem of 1800, celebrating his settling at Grasmere in the Lake District,

> Already to inscribe upon my heart
> A liking for the small grey Horse that bears
> The paralytic Man; I know the ass
> On which the Cripple in the Quarry maimed
> Rides to and fro[19]

Wordsworth's representation of landscape and his feelings toward it establish, for the first time in English poetry, a relationship that is strongly personal yet not exploitative. Instead of assuming a fixed position, the poet is both creator and receiver, involved in a complex exchange tested by each poem. It is partly his own act, his "creative agency," that must establish a "brotherhood" between himself and the Vale.[20] The newcomer "inscribes" things on his heart, discovers or recovers their link to the affections. As a Wanderer who may never be satisfied with locality, he makes, as well as finds, a home at Grasmere.

Yet a displacement in the above passage from human to animal accentuates the *bearing* element: that which is quietly supportive in Nature. Vulnerabilities are not passed over. Wounds (the crippling, the paralysis) are shown as a physical thing, and often an accidental meeting or a chance return of memory suggests another kind of vulnerability: that of the psyche, which is not, despite the poet's hopes, "from all internal injury exempt."[21] Moreover, in quasi-apocalyptic moments, Nature takes on a severe or fearful aspect. Ominous episodes give warning of the mutability and even mortality of the natural world and react on a mind that needs to think of that world as permanent and basically unchangeable.

The poet feels himself called on to save nature for imagination by a nonviolent kind of representation, learnt, as it were, from rural nature itself in its ordinary, unthreatening aspect. He apposes nuances, *Abschattungen*, "all shades" in nature or consciousness, to admonitions "from another world."[22] This representational nonviolence, affecting both stimulus (nature) and response (poetry as "authentic comment"), pervades even a scene of election in which Wordsworth is *called*, like a prophet of old:

> I made no vows, but vows
> Were then made for me; bond unknown to me
> Was given, that I should be, else sinning greatly,
> A dedicated Spirit.[23]

How different this defining moment is from the summoning voice of God that sets the tongue and hair of Jeremiah or Ezekiel on edge. Wordsworth hints at a "timely utterance" ("vows"), but he does not record it as a specific and startling episode. He seems to have experienced it unconsciously. No voice comes from nature to declare, "Thou art my son, my chosen poet." Yet a quiet myth like that informs, without transforming, his self-awareness. This art of semidisclosure is typically Wordsworthian. An omen is acknowledged, but the supernatural intimation comes from a "common dawn," however magnificent. It is as if Nature still gave him a choice: "Stop here, or gently pass." However violent or disruptive imagination might be, however foreboding of its separateness or transcendental impulses, Wordsworth, as nature poet, will connect nature once more to our minding of it.

Wordsworth's subduing of supernaturalism is, to sum up, only as important as his refusal to modify perception by loud and conventional techniques, such as a voice (of the genius loci or other personified entity) rising up to admonish the passerby. (In some poems he does succumb to the old rhetoric and its inflation.) Poetry modifies sensibility, or conventional and synthesizing categories by which we limit "the line where being ends," through the "natural" means of daily language. In this sense we can say that Wordsworth's poetry is philosophical: it cleans the plaque from the arteries of thought, speech, and perception; it dissolves dichotomies and fixations produced—ironically in the same cause—by the "unnatural" diction of both philosophy and traditional religious vision.

Though Wordsworth is exemplary, Keats, Shelley, and Coleridge also give voice to the power of sympathy while disclosing its limits. But they are less wary of traditional poetic diction, which often substitutes an artificial language of ecstasy for a truer "language of the sense." The first stanza of Keats's "Ode to a Nightingale," for example, beginning "My heart aches, and a drowsy numbness pains / My sense," is melodically richer than almost anything in Wordsworth and more direct about the paradox involved. It evokes an involuntary self-emptying that suggests how fatally close empathy and ecstasy can be. Not only is the human capacity for in-feeling limited in a quantitative sense but when, as here, empathetic identification is especially strong it becomes a danger to the poet's "identity," a word used by Keats in the modern sense. "When I am in a room with People . . . then not myself goes home to myself: but the identity of everyone in the room begins to press upon me that, I am in a very little time an[ni]hilated."[24]

Coleridge, Wordsworth's closest friend, also registers loss of joy and spontaneous emotion: his eye is "blank" as he looks, emulating Wordsworth, at the sunset sky, "with its peculiar tint of yellow green." He sees, but cannot feel, its beauty. He converts what Keats once called "the feel of not to feel it" into his special fate. Accepting the role of *poète maudit* (the curse, in his case, is loss of nature-motivated inspiration) he contrasts himself with Wordsworth. "My genial spirits fail," he laments in *Dejection: An Ode*. "I may not hope from outward forms to win / The passion and the life, whose fountains are within."

One way to follow the sympathy paradox is by tracing the rise of Gothic from the later eighteenth century to the present. The mode has maintained itself: think of the continuing popularity of horror movies, of science fiction with aliens, and other assorted assaults on the maiden consciousness. The Gothic is, no doubt, an overdetermined development in the history of fictional representation. But formally and chronologically it is closely related to the dream of reason—which breeds monsters. In an Age of Reason the censored thing rebels and the mad side of sympathy relegitimates itself. At the same time, art mobilizes a modern *apatheia*, freezing the blood through fiction: the very means that should have stimulated rather than blocked the sympathetic feelings.

Yet the challenge to sympathy comes less from an extreme rationalism than from the imagination itself. As the demand to cultivate and expand our understanding of otherness dilates toward infinity, we realize how woefully inadequate our capacity for sympathy is. In Mary Shelley's *Frankenstein* the key episode is the scientist-creator's failure to acknowledge his offspring, to look on it, like the God of Genesis, and bless what he has made. Frankenstein is repelled by his creation; a redeeming sympathy falters. Gothic fiction, which testifies to our repressed feelings, is at the same time a chilling confession of their limits, of a guilty emotional coldness and the fear of being vamped.[25]

Gothic remains, however, a playful and self-inflicted mode. Its sinister sublime is not meant to overwhelm but rather to institute a special relation between text and reader. The original template of gothic is a pseudonarrative full of strange incidents that challenge reason or keep it in suspense, though a naturalistic explanation is eventually offered.[26] This literary structure, the *surnaturel expliqué*, displaces attention from ambiguously realistic—borderline surrealistic—plot events to an introspective and burdened imagination. We frighten ourselves playfully with ghosts or monsters that vacuum our feelings and even identity. "Gothic" as a new literary form prevents realism from (1) overloading the feelings and (2) totally disenchanting the real. It keeps romance going in an age of realism. The complexity of the Gothic as the kernel of modern ghostliness includes the surprise of art as something astonishing to ourselves.

In short, as the "pain of sympathy" (Bentham) increases, the burden to encourage a widening sphere of sensibility that defines genius falls on imaginative literature. From Wordsworth to Jane Austen, Shelley, Keats, Tennyson, Browning, and George Eliot (to enumerate only English authors), the imagination is formally recruited for the task of empathetic insight. Yet the specter of a failure—of lack of response or inspiration—accompanies this effort: *The Prelude*, after opening with a promissory flood of verses addressed to Liberty, immediately records such a failure, despite "aeolian visitations."

There are many issues I do not have time to raise. They are crystallized by T. S. Eliot's concept of the "objective correlative" and his negative reception of most romantic poetry. Sentimentalism, the pathetic fallacy, misdirected emotion, or even the marketing, through fiction, of sensations as a commodity are among these issues. But I certainly do not see in the romantics that "dissociation" of sensibility from thought diagnosed by Eliot as a modern discontent emerging first in the seventeenth century.[27] I observe instead the deepening awareness of a principle of *association* that continues to operate in poetic, quixotic, and often unconscious fashion. Eliot himself described the poet's mind with the analogy of a complex chemical medium, "a receptacle for seizing and storing up numberless feelings, phrases, images, which remain there until all the particles which can unite to form a new compound are present together."[28] The *cognitive* advance in literary studies comes from an acknowledgment of this associative flow and a charting of its structures. John Livingston Lowes's *The Road to Xanadu* (1927), an analysis of the disorder of images and allusions that resolved itself into Coleridge's "Kubla Khan" and "The Ancient Mariner," is contemporaneous with Eliot, as is I. A. Richards's neurological paradigm of mental connectivity in *Principles of Literary Criticism* (1924). These developments are relatively independent of Freud, though *The Interpretation of Dreams* (1900) gave a more scientific basis to eighteenth-century associationism and what Coleridge had called the mind's "streaminess."

Today the debate continues as to how poetry retains its contact with unconscious and neural process. But the issue has broadened to include cultures, or structures of collective identity. The dominant metaphor now is that of symbolic and narrative construction, and the problem is described as one of a superfluity of myths or stories, of how to overcome their chaos, their potential anarchy, as they at once underwrite and undermine claims of identity.[29]

Yet Eliot had spotted the sympathy paradox. In his view a coarsened sensibility accompanies, in the modern era, a separated and increasingly self-conscious intellect. Impressed by the English church's *via media* efforts to maintain a unified Christian society, and impose a symbolizing and imaginative discipline toward that end, he never really valued the freer, mythmaking romantics but championed an affinity between the school of Donne and modernist verse. He saw a certain toughness in both, a wry, paradoxical, and elegiac sense of the lost unity. His poetics of culture were entirely nostalgic, despite the more radical direction of his verse.[30] He tried to hold the line by a restricted economy of feeling and neoclassical ideals such as impersonality and the objective correlative. Eliot's influence lasted into the 1950s; it was well after the Second World War that the study of romanticism began to recover from charges of subjectivism, irrationalism, spilt religion, adolescent *Schwärmerei*, unstructured emotion, unbridled nationalistic fervor, and other schismatic sins. The situation Eliot diagnosed, and for which he offered an anti-self-consciousness therapy, moved steadily toward deeper forms of crisis. European civilization would not be able to fall back on such a therapy after a second world war, the Holocaust, and disintegrating colonial regimes.

Today the limits of human sensibility have become clear. They oblige us to review cultural morality rather than to clutch a conservative and retrospective ideal of unity or to solace our conscience with clichés about progress and humanitarianism. The liberal ideal of culture, whose latest form is multiculturalism, has not questioned forcefully enough its residual religious pathos or dogmatic politics of sympathy.[31] Even when promulgated without condescension, it demands a *disponibilité* of the heart that used to belong to Mary as the Mother of Christ. There was, however, no greater collective failure of sympathy in a mainly Christian Europe than what happened in the Holocaust.

The status of being human was denied the Jews; all pity, all feeling was withdrawn from them, even within their native German land. War dehumanizes the enemy—that is bad enough—but these were noncombatants. If Nazism had triumphed, slavery would once again have become an institution and extermination accepted state policy. It is a hard truth to acknowledge that neither Christian universalism nor liberal culture actively prevented the genocide, any more than it halted slavery or, after its abolition, slavelike conditions. In the case of the Jews, moreover, many blamed the victims, alleging their failure to assimilate entirely into a Christian or national community. In Nazi Germany two further beliefs contributed to the abrogation of a cultural morality based on compassion and the sympathetic imagination. The first was a hierarchic, Manichean, and totally exclusive doctrine of racial purity. It declared assimilation impossible and promoted an idea of culture from which every alien element—often defined arbitrarily— was purged. Culture meant total integration into the national community as defined by the party leadership and the *Führer-prinzip*. The second belief was the pseudo-Darwinian teaching of "life unworthy of life" (*unwertes Leben*), which was used to justify the killing of the mentally ill or handicapped, homosexuals, and so-called social misfits.

The crucial question is now as always: how does one maintain compassion; what familial or formal pedagogy can achieve a widening of sensibility when that widening soon exhausts itself?[32] The pro-life debate in America as well as the animal rights movement are symptoms of a deep unease: they exhibit an imagination drawn to whatever is mute or helpless and they view that extension of feeling as the test of our humanity. But feelings are finite and so, as the sympathy paradox teaches, become overinvested, dogmatic, and even schizoid. As one segment of a forgotten or neglected reality is recovered, another fails, is not responded to, or is construed as unredeemably alien. This self protective indifference, however, does not always anesthesize conscience: often what is rejected hurts like a phantom limb. The perceived absence of compassion can then turn into a deliberate and dangerous coldness and seek to justify itself ideologically.

An awareness of these failures has influenced the *academic* idea of culture. I use "academic" descriptively, and not at all to mock the debate on culture in the universities. The attempt to achieve an ethos of inclusion, to enjoy the "rainbow" of ethnic difference, to prevent the withdrawal of sympathy from stigmatized groups, and to recognize fully the difficulties encountered as we pursue such ideals: these have deeply formed our discourse and established an as yet informal discipline, that of xenology.[33]

It would take a Shakespeare and his comedic revels, however, to cool our inflamed contemporary sense of identity, to bring it back once more from tragic fixation to an enjoyment of its humorous variety. What we see mainly around us is pathology: a stressed sympathetic imagination and doctrines or defenses resulting from that. This pathology emerges most blatantly when cultures or nations different from us are demonized or one's own country is viewed not as a beloved community, an extension of family and a way of accommodating the finiteness of our energies and feelings, but as a sacrificial abstraction.

It is true that a large gap remains between discussion in the academy and the actual politics of culture waged in the less protected world outside the university. Ideals are flammable and convictions seem to demand blood, like the shades of the dead in Homer's underworld. I have no answer for the question of why ideals turn bloody. Karl Mannheim says matter-of-factly: "Political discussion possesses a character fundamentally different from academic discussion. It seeks not only to be in the right but also to demolish the basis of its opponent's social and intellectual existence." He adds that this "will to psychic annihilation" is perhaps harder to bear than physical repression, but we have learnt that, in the world of politics, it does not stop with psychic annihilation.[34]

I offer one guiding precept in this tract for the times: do not give up the concept of aesthetic education.[35] Art is not a luxury, a snobbish indulgence, but basic to a measure of freedom from inner and outer compulsions. The aesthetic sense is essential for this growing freedom and establishes links even with physics, that is, with a world not of our making, which is attractively sensuous yet open to intellectual scrutiny. My own focus has been on aesthetics as a science of the feelings and on limits of representation that art both acknowledges and expands. They reflect the strength, but also potential anarchy, of compassion as a passion.

I have also implied that we are too defensive about the contemplative life. Its *otium* is not otiose. We should recognize more firmly its achievements and its relation to a certain spaciousness, especially that of a shrinking rural world. Not to heed Wordsworth's understanding of the ecology of mind jeopardizes the bond between nature and mind. The spacious ambience of nature, when treated with respect, allows physical and emotional freedom; it is an outdoor room essential to thought and untraumatic (that is, relatively unforced) development. To curtail it adds to the damage done to the culture of civil society by the totalizing and controlling demands of political religions.

Media pressures too can create a modern form of claustrophobia, through imposing a *souffrance à distance*, a vampiristic demand for universal empathy. The result is, as we already see, an antipastoral world, where no one is allowed to be at rest and the idea of home (or of a homeland) is exploited by reactive political nostalgias impossible to satisfy. To call oneself a citizen of the world is as unthinkable today as it was courageous in the eighteenth century. It is unthinkable because the social and political suffering of the world bears down on us so strongly that, like Keats in company, we are in a very little time "annihilated." Some idealize diaspora rather than native country or local attachment, but homelessness is always a curse, not an ideal. The consequence of this turmoil is too often a severance of delight from knowledge, a turning away from both the theoretical sciences and the pleasures of meditation, as if they were escapist.

I have told a story of Sense and Insensibility. The fateful question raised by Freud on the last page of *Civilization and Its Discon-*

tents whether love can prevail as compassion and loving-kindness in the face of forces that side with aggression and aim for a state of nonfeeling, a perverse kind of invulnerability—this question remains in the balance. On the side of hope I have enlisted the convergence rather than divergence of romantic and Enlightenment endeavors. The slogan of the Enlightenment, which Kant affirmed in his pamphlet on the subject, was "dare to know." The romantic poets added "afford sympathy": dare to feel. Wordsworth stated his hope that mature knowledge would not have to be "purchased" by the loss of power, where by "power" he meant the "infant sensibility / Great birthright of our Being" and its evolution into "A virtue which irradiates and exalts / Objects through widest intercourse of sense."[36] To extend his proposition: power too, power in the worldly sense as a capacity for social action, should not be purchased by loss of knowledge, by forgetting or slandering a more contemplative existence. "The growing good of the world," George Eliot declares at the end of *Middlemarch*, "is partly dependent on unhistoric acts."

NOTES

1. From a letter of 11 December 1916 to Cynthia Asquith

2. Preface (1800) to *Lyrical Ballads*. By "sensibility" Wordsworth means a sensitivity that has taken hold, become organized or even a second nature.

3. See especially Keith Thomas, *Man and the Natural World: Changing Attitudes in England, 1500–1800* (New York: Oxford University Press, 1983). Thomas admirably seeks "to reunite the studies of history and literature" (16), but by this he means bringing to bear (as in the New Historicism) a wonderful array of neglected sources in a growing discourse on "Meat or Mercy" (as he wittily summarizes it), which reflects an increasingly humanitarian attitude in England toward other species and the conquest of nature generally.

4. *All Religions Are One* (circa 1788).

5. Terrence Des Pres, *Praises and Dispraises: Poetry and Politics, The Twentieth Century* (New York: Viking, 1988), xvi. The first extension of serious, rather than comic, realism came through the great realistic novel, which reached its apogee in the period between Jane Austen

and Thomas Mann. For modern realism as an achievement, see especially Erich Auerbach, *Mimesis: Dargestellte Wirklichkeit in der Abendländischen Literatur* (Bern: Francke, 1946).

6. Arthur Kleinman and Joan Kleinman, "The Appeal of Experience, The Dismay of Images: Cultural Appropriation of Suffering in Our Times," *Daedalus* 126 (1996): 1–25.

7. See the second epigraph to this book, taken from the 1802 preface to *Lyrical Ballads*.

8. Cf. Adam Smith, *Theory of Moral Sentiments* (1759). Smith posits an impartial spectator and a sufferer who wishes to reach him or to arouse a sympathy that is not taken for granted and not to be mistaken for empathy. Both, therefore, have to form an image of the other's state of mind. John Wilson, a close reader of Smith, himself later to become professor of moral philosophy at Edinburgh, writing when only seventeen years old an appreciative letter about *Lyrical Ballads* to Wordsworth, complains that, in the case of Betty Foy, the Idiot Boy's mother, "we are unable to enter into her feelings, we cannot conceive ourselves actuated by the same feelings, and consequently take little or no interest in her situation." He declares, alluding to Smith's theory of moral sentiments, that this "inability to receive pleasure from descriptions such as *The Idiot Boy*" is "founded upon established feelings of human nature." See appendix C in *Lyrical Ballads: Wordsworth and Coleridge*, ed. R. L. Brett and A. R. Jones (London: Methuen, 1963), 329. The issue of what role imagination can play in bridging the distance between observer and sufferer is explored not only by Smith but in much of eighteenth-century ethical philosophy from Shaftesbury on. See, on this matter, especially Luc Boltanski, who brings the problematic into the present in *La souffrance à distance: Morale humanitaire, médias et politique* (Paris: Métailié, 1993), and Esther Schor, *Bearing the Dead: The British Culture of Mourning from the Enlightenment to Victoria* (Princeton: Princeton University Press, 1994). Schor sees a shift, already in Hume, from a "spectator" theory to a "conversation" theory and relates it to a more rhetorically and aesthetically conscious "politics of sympathy."

9. The term became politically freighted, however, with the French Revolution. See especially Kenneth R. Johnston, "Philanthropy or Trea-

son? Wordsworth as 'Active Partisan,' " *Studies in Romanticism* 25 (1986): 371–409.

10. My summary is based on 1805 *Prelude* 2.405 ff., 3.121 ff; and 1850 *Prelude* 14.81.

11. Cf. Wordsworth's "Ode. Intimations of Immortality from Recollections of Early Childhood."

12. From "Composed upon an Evening of Extraordinary Splendour and Beauty" (1820).

13. The term "urban landscape," on the one hand, suggests deceptively an unrealized *rus in urbe*, while we know, on the other hand, that peasant life, before as after industrialization, was often immensely cruel and brutal.

14. To say that the old man "does not move with pain / but moves with thought" may imply that thought usually pains but does so no longer.

15. Indeed, with the second edition (1800) of *Lyrical Ballads* and subsequent printings, Wordsworth ends the poem at that line.

16. David Simpson suggests that Wordsworth is recording and then reversing his misunderstanding: he "thinks the man serene who is in fact absorbed in grief" (*The Academic Postmodern and the Rule of Literature: A Report on Half-Knowledge* [Chicago: University of Chicago Press, 1995], 177). Simpson's *Wordsworth's Historical Imagination: The Poetry of Displacement* (New York: Methuen, 1987) has important pages on what he calls the "Politics of Sympathy." See chapter 6, 160–84.

17. We cannot even claim that a *figure* of speech is involved, a "prosopopeia" that animates what is mute or inanimate, for the figure is literally that of the old man who evokes (like many of these peculiar ballads) an archaic, anti-Enlightenment sense of something ghostly; this seems to be the only polemical design.

18. See "LINES Left upon a Seat in a YEW-TREE . . ." and "The Brothers," both in *Lyrical Ballads*.

19. I quote from MS B, ll. 721–727, of a poem unpublished in Wordsworth's time. See *Home at Grasmere: Part First, Book First of The Recluse*, ed. Beth Darlington (Ithaca: Cornell University Press, 1977), 82.

20. See especially the passage in 1850 *Prelude* 2.396–411, which is his transposition of Hartley's "associationism." Like Coleridge, probably

his informant, Wordsworth wishes to overcome the taint of passivity, of simple determinism, in that principle.

21. 1850 *Prelude* 5.67.

22. Ibid. 7.635–49.

23. 1805 *Prelude* 4.341–44.

24. Letter to Richard Woodhouse, 27 October 1818. For Keats the great exemplar of the sympathetic imagination in literature is Shakespeare; Wordsworth is acknowledged but thought to be limited by what Keats names the "egotistical sublime."

25. Moreover, reason itself becomes a passion, though it always thinks it is in control. While Wordsworth pays tribute to the dawn of the revolutionary period in Europe, when Reason became a "prime Enchantress," this romance of Reason soon degenerated, according to him, into a self-deceiving intellectual turmoil:

This was the time when, all things tending fast
To depravation, speculative schemes
That promised to abstract the hopes of Man
Out of his feelings, to be fixed thenceforth
For ever in a purer element,
Found ready welcome. Tempting region *that*
For Zeal to enter and refresh herself,
Where passions had the privilege to work,
And never hear the sound of their own names
(1850 *Prelude* 11.223–231)

26. For a fine structural analysis, see Tzvetan Todorov, *The Fantastic: A Structural Approach to a Literary Genre* (Ithaca: Cornell University Press, 1975).

27. See "The Metaphysical Poets," in *Selected Essays* (London: Faber and Faber, 1932), 288.

28. "Tradition and the Individual Talent" (1919), in *Selected Essays* (London: Faber and Faber, 1951), 19.

29. For this problem of *surnomie*, a term I prefer in this crowded context to Durkheim's *anomie*, see Geoffrey Hartman, *The Fate of Reading*, 101–13.

30. Here is how Peter Ackroyd, a sympathetic biographer, describes

Eliot and other disaffected Americans: "They grew up in a time of great ethical and social confusion—the intercontinental railways were changing the shape of the country, just as the vast tide of immigrants from southern and eastern Europe was radically reforming the idea of what an 'American' was. This was a society which offered no living or coherent tradition, a society being created by industrialists and bankers, and by the politics and the religion which ministered to them" (*T. S. Eliot: A Life* [New York: Simon and Schuster, 1984], 24).

31. For a somewhat more sustained critique, see my "Art and Consensus in the Era of Progressive Politics," *Yale Review* 80 (1992): 50–70. Cf. also the skeptical reflections on an exclusively rights-based morality in Richard Rorty's writings.

32. I must signal here the interesting distinction made by Hannah Arendt in her attempt to give politics a principled basis in conceptual argument. "Terminologically speaking, solidarity is a principle that can inspire and guide [political] action, compassion is one of the passions, and pity is a sentiment. . . . Pity, taken as the spring of virtue, has proved to possess a greater capacity for cruelty than cruelty itself" (*On Revolution* [New York: Viking, 1963], 84–85). She also says, like Blake ("Pity would be no more / If we did not make somebody poor"), "by virtue of being a sentiment, pity can be enjoyed for its own sake, and this will almost automatically lead to a glorification of its cause, which is the suffering of others" (84). I would reply that poetry (*Dichtung*, fiction), which she appreciates, having based the above reasoning on Dostoyevsky ("The Grand Inquisitor") and Melville (*Billy Budd*), has a power of argument of its own that mediates—however sensitively, precariously—between the muteness of compassion and the sentimental eloquence of pity. It is a part, not always recognized, of worldly space or what she defines as the political realm.

33. Cf. the discussion of "xenology" in Aleida Assmann and Jan Assmann, "Kultur und Konflikt: Aspekte einer Theorie des unkommunikativen Handelns," in *Kultur und Konflikt*, ed. Jan Assmann and Dietrich Harth (Frankfurt-am-Main: Suhrkamp, 1990).

34. *Ideology and Utopia: An Introduction to the Sociology of Knowledge*, trans. Louis Wirth and Edward Shils (New York: Harcourt, Brace, 1936), 34–35.

35. As a concept, it was launched in the 1790s by Schiller's famous *Letters on Aesthetic Education* (1795) and a group around Hegel, which may have included Schelling and Hölderlin, inspired by both Schiller and Fichte. We know this through a manifesto surviving in fragmentary form and published by Franz Rosenzweig as "The Oldest Systematic Program of German Idealism." See Franz Rosenzweig, "Das älteste Systemsprogram des deutschen Idealismus," in *Zweistromland: Kleinere Schriften zur Religion und Philosophie* (Berlin: Philo, 1926). A translation can be found in *Philosophy of German Idealism*, ed. Ernst Behler, The German Library, vol. 23 (New York: Continuum, 1987), 161–63.

36. 1805 *Prelude* 2.285 ff. and 5.449.

chapter six

A Culture of Inclusion

All human forms identified . . .

—WILLIAM BLAKE

In the spring of 1995, with Jacques Chirac succeeding François Mitterand as head of state, a new ministry bearing the wordy title "De l'intégration et de la lutte contre l'exclusion" (For integration and the battle against exclusion) was announced. The issues recognized by the new French ministry preoccupy this book, but they are not analyzed in the context of immigration, daily politics, the French republican model, or political science.[1] My context is an idea of culture that has overtaken us and the hopes and dangers that it presents. This idea—better, ideal—seeks a politics of inclusion whose boundaries are difficult to draw.

Without being explicitly Christian, indeed, without having any formal relation to established religion, the ideal as a political program often uses an evangelical rhetoric; in the United States the "New Deal" is thus replaced by the "New Covenant." If faith is involved it is vested in technology, in our ability to remedy the ills of society by administrative and technological competence. This faith, at the same time, has been weakened (in academic rather than government circles) by Adorno and Horkheimer's critique—and its offspring over the last fifty years—of the "pact" between Enlightenment and domination, a pact made irreversible by technology, administrative reason, the media, and other embedded institutions that represent themselves as progressive and productive.[2]

The idea of culture, therefore, is by now deeply divided against itself. It supports the progress made possible by what has been

called technopoly[3] yet remembers forms of life much less dependent on it, and it seeks not only to preserve but to organize these
into a viable alternative. This alternative cannot do without *including* nature, or ecology—a nature more ravaged than repaired by
technology and increasingly scarred by global wars and the demo-
graphic time bomb. Both sides of this conflicted idea of culture,
then, focus on issues of integration and inclusion, which remain
essential topics of sociopolitical discourse on the modern nation as
a fully participatory community of citizens or residents,[4] though a
parallel discourse on the habitat of all living beings and our responsibility toward them, while not absent and remaining the subject of
poetry, has been inadequate.[5]

I wish to turn specifically to the relation between culture, politics,
and the university. My topic so far has been culture rather than politics, but it is hard to separate the two. There are reasons for this,
and they are not all good. It is usually politics that impels the "invention of tradition" by which nationalism fosters, however anach-
ronistically, its claim for the existence of an early, even primordial,
ethnic consciousness.[6] That claim comes with little evidence except
from the realm of imaginative writing, such as epic fragments
whose historical context must be reconstructed. As Carlyle wrote:
"Any historical light emitted by these old Fictions is little better
than darkness visible."[7] Poetical relics are impressed to invent a history and a tradition; this evidence is always edited and sometimes
forged or of composite inspiration. William Blake spoke more literally than he knew when he asserted that all "religions" (he meant
national ideologies or established religions) were a "derivation from
the Poetic Genius."[8]

   Those who aspire to make history in modern times do not give
up a tradition-inventing memory that is often deliberately mobi-
lized against the accelerating pace of contemporary life. In fact, as
the memory link between generations weakens because of mobility and displacement, our attention is directed to an older, "collective" form of memory, more legendary and oral, akin to storytelling.
Pierre Nora describes it as an "integrated, dictatorial memory—

unself conscious. . . . A memory without a past that ceaselessly rein vents tradition, linking the history of its ancestors to the undifferentiated time of heroes, origins and myth."[9]

This earlier form of memory, strengthening today, evokes literature's proximity to myth and inspiration. There is a craving for "imagined communities" (Benedict Anderson) and a sense that art has lost its public function and become solipsistic. There is also an explosion of monuments and memorials, each the subject of dispute, at least in the democratic part of the world. Still, whether commissioned by kings, popes, or patrons in the Renaissance, or by Kennedy-inspired American administrations in the 1960s, or by the extension of "Camelot" into France under André Malraux as minister for cultural affairs, the public context that surrounds these modern works with programmatic and propagandistic statements enlivens the hope that art can help to renew a sense of community.[10] Moreover, artists and scholars will often attribute works whose historical context has been lost to a "popular" memory such as the one Nora describes. It is supposedly preserved in songs about "far-off things, / And battles long ago." A genealogical fiction supports a *present* culture war by adducing the idea of an indigenous *ancient* culture.

The fabulous content and speculative character of such folk or popular memory would seem to protect it from politics or the presumption of literal truth. However, the nation-state (as it comes into existence) appropriates this memory lest it turn into a subversive countermemory. Both academic and nonacademic manifestations of culture are easily politicized. Such cultural steering (*dirigisme, Kulturlenkung*) is not a new phenomenon: in the seventeenth century, for example, Richelieu's patronage was decisive for the evolution of both French culture and national feeling. The British empire too and then the American were not slow in retailing myths of justification, which made their way into high as well as popular culture.[11] But today literature and literacy also play a more hidden or "Foucauldian" role in fortifying social cohesion and the national consciousness. Educational institutions, in particular, come under close scrutiny as agencies of the state. Given the fact that parliamentary democracy seems always closer to disorder than order—like the plurality of interpretations in literary studies—and that the contemporary nation is more than ever a mixture of immigrants, there are civic as well as national motives for what the 1938 Modern Language Association called "the cultural needs of a civilized democracy."[12]

Cultural politics, pervasive and inevitable, are now in bad repute. This is due to a fundamental disappointment. Our wish persists that the means-end relationship in this matter prove to be on the side of culture: politics should be the means to an end, namely, a richer quality of life. In historical fact this desired means-end relationship is reversed, so that culture is instrumentalized to serve a political end. This can happen in covert ways or as coercive public policy. We have recently experienced the terrible human damage inflicted by regimes that engineered a culture politics to legitimate their militant aims. The idea of empire, directed previously to territories outside the central nation, turns against "foreign" elements within the nation.

A "sinister unification of voices," as Kenneth Burke called it in the 1930s,[13] led to massacre and genocide as well as to suppression of dissent. Neither the most lofty claims for unity and collective action on the totalitarian side nor an enlightened emphasis on rationality and universality on the democratic side prevented what Adorno and Horkheimer denounced as the moral bankruptcy of culture (their own metaphor is culture's *Ausverkauf*, literally "sell-out" or "going-out-of-business sale"). The culture of the *Kulturvolk* failed utterly in the face of the determined political onslaught of Nazism. At the same time, Stalinism enjoyed a similar triumph over the intellectual "guides" of the masses. No wonder a new wariness has emerged about culturalist claims or prophecies. All such claims are being nervously inspected not only by historians but also by social and literary theorists.

This is clearest in the emphasis on social construction, a theory that acknowledges the imaginative and artificial elements in all human arrangements. The theory has noble antecedents. Indeed, the modern humanities found their grounding as early as the first half of the eighteenth century in the work of Giambattista Vico. He based humanistic study, distinct from theology as a science of the divine, on the axiom that we can know only what we have made. Thus, while human beings cannot know God or His designs other than through revelation, they can know history, which is made by themselves. (Increasingly, of course, even God's domain of nature was opening to the eyes of science, despite its nonhuman genesis and uncertain teleology.) Structuralism, a major form of cultural analysis in the aftermath of the Second World War, extends systematically the *homo faber* concept (which includes Huizinga's *homo ludens*) into the area of everyday life and civic institutions. What seemed natural, or was accepted as such, is now viewed as a social, hence modifiable, construct: modifiable in terms of meaning, symbolic content, value. Culture is redefined as a "continuous and unending structuring activity" that "constitutes the core of human praxis, the human mode of being-in-the-world" carried out through tools and language, the principal means of manual and mental labor.[14]

The special contribution of literary studies enters when cultural texts, ancient or modern, are shown to contain a diversity of voices. The literary-critical methodology developed since the 1930s, as well as a hermeneutic anthropology influenced by it, questions the unity of received national myth or master narrative and discloses instead an intricate tension, a web or montage that includes contrary and ambivalent positions. We have even begun to define the literary itself in terms of such a dialogic or polyphonic structure.[15] The purposiveness of art is revealed: like nature itself, it seems to combat "sinister unification."

Yet as the vision of inclusion expands, strengthened by an appreciation of art's many voices (including an internal "heteroglossia"), we are confronted by limiting phenomena. The most obvious of these is related to a question that won't go away: is not identity, personal or collective, always partially based on exclusion, on physical, mental, or doctrinal characteristics that indicate a distinctive difference? The enemy-brother syndrome morever seems to show that sameness too is intolerable, so that we often create distinctions and attempt to make them meaningful. Even when a democratic frame of mind establishes itself and the equality of individuals becomes an important human and legal principle, how can we *not* exclude what is oppositional? Or is co-optation a genuine form of inclusion? What ideal of synthesis or unifying dialectic does art, in particular, foster? As literary language becomes more aware of its multivocal or equivocal character, the distance between literature and actual politics increases.[16]

The "order-in-variety" paradigm, for example, favored by many eighteenth-century artists, seems undynamic and unprogressive, modeled as it is on the English garden as a little wilderness. And though we admire Blake's proverb that "Opposition is true Friendship" (which was formulated in part against the English garden ideal of order-in-variety), can it lead to any settled form of statecraft? Even should culture genuinely accommodate rather than co-opt opposition, can what is productive in *culture* give a law to *politics*?

What we do know is that art, as a stratified rather than monolithic structure, and historiography, which tends towards a convulsive revisionism, bring what is suppressed to light. (What we kill in the present we revive in the past.) Sometimes, in fact, the victims— those left behind by "progress"—partially conquer the victors: the latter are assimilated into a preexistent and resilient culture. ("Cultures rarely die," Philip Rieff says, "they merely marry.")[17] The classic instance of this pattern is found in Virgil's *Aeneid*. The older culture of Latium, supported by Juno, must fall to the Trojan conquerors, supported by Jupiter. Yet Juno exacts a compromise from Jupiter which turns defeat into a kind of victory. This is her petition to him:

> Never command the land's own Latin folk
> To change their old name, to become new Trojans,
> Known as Teucrians; never make them alter
> Dialect or dress. Let Latium be.

And Jupiter aquiesces:

> Ausonian folk will keep

Their fathers' language and their way of life
. . . .
. . . The Teucrians
Will mingle and be submerged, incorporated.
Rituals and observances of theirs
I'll add, but make them Latin, one in speech.[18]

Yet the recovery of territory by the defeated forces does not always work in favor of Juno's compromise of a more inclusive politics made in heaven. It may foster instead dogmatic adhesion to an imagined *arche*, to a foundational and fundamentalist myth of strength through purity. In the case of minority cultures, a doctrinal consolidation often takes place, while new majority cultures may mount a defense against modernity or dissent, as if these were counterrevolutionary. Inclusion meets fierce resistance in the form of identity politics, and precisely from those previously excluded.[19]

There is also a second limit, related this time not to the vicissitudes of war and politics but to the utopian character of inclusion. For even progressivist spirits who believe that an open society can be achieved, not just in one country but globally, realize by now that heroic measures are needed for this. These measures, however, undertaken in the name of national or global unification or in the name of scientific progress, tend to be repressive. For technology—a Promethean gift—is so far our only means to pursue a struggle with nature that has always defined the presence of mankind on earth. That struggle, a competition to acquire or expand limited resources, links culture with agriculture, science, the economy, and ultimately with planned social structures. Thus it becomes at the same time a struggle to reform humanity itself. It is tragic, then, that the sciences are increasingly used for destructive purposes and develop ever more deadly technologies.[20] If Nature is "red in tooth and claw" and exerts an indifferent triage, if Society defines itself and fends off fears of disintegration by exerting this triage more deliberately, Science, which harnesses the laws of physics and turns them against Nature, is potentially the most destructive agency of all.

The idea of an "organic" development arises in this context. It serves to counter domination over nature or nation. In urging *local* attachments, the organic idea responds to a fear of losing a "natural" connection with traditional forms of life. By its rhetoric of roots it opposes westernization or globalization, indeed any large-scale attempt to impose a rationalized economy, especially in rural areas.

Yet when the organic idea is co-opted, which happens easily enough, it becomes, as in Nazi Germany, aggressively segregationist and imperialist rather than protective of local cultures. It too begins to speak in the name of science as well as nature (think of *Rassenwissenschaft*, the pseudoscience of race) and uses their combined authority to impose a triumphal and murderous vision of ethnic evolution. A myth arises that even though nature—or nature in cooperation with providence—created a particular national culture, only a heroic war can maintain it against the existence of enemy forces seeking to conquer the culture or contaminate it from within by racial admixture.

What is true in the mixture of half-truths that accompany the organic idea is also, ironically, what discredits it: an irreducible, permanent tension between nature and culture. From the beginning of recorded time culture has been an extraordinary achievement, a heroic imposition on nature or natural tendency. Culture takes on nature, as a cultivator does the soil, which is itself the protoepic subject of Virgil's *Georgics*. There is also, we might say, a human soil to be made fertile. But this transition from *humus* to *homo* includes a testing, by the gods or man himself, of human nature, which may encourage its autonomy *or* forge a link between culture and domination similar to that between the *Georgics* and the *Aeneid*.

In recent ethical discussion we discern therefore a caution about heroic philosophies of action. Heroes have a way of oppressing as much as liberating mankind. Yet what is difficult to describe without martial or agonistic metaphors is *mental labor*: the activity that creates, maintains, and transplants cultural achievement. Even though geography matters, and one climate may be more benign than another, and being born in a certain region or coming from a certain stock may also be an advantage, culture is not a permanent endowment transmitted primarily through the good earth or by descent. It is not nature but a second, "man-made" nature.[21]

The relation between culture and this secondariness—between culture and *poesis*—is reinforced by contemporary literary criticism, its understanding of the density of texts. Texts are complex mediations, not charters, and stand in the way of revelation as well as reveal. The sense that we are increasingly at a distance from events, even though the media give off the illusion that they bring us nearer, rouses a "modern" impatience. How do we get back to nature, or to human essentials, and avoid the clutter of historical consciousness and civilized existence? As the dream of an unmediated vision recedes, as an emphasis on agency or the means of disclosure displaces transparency of truth, our *creative* nihilism becomes more explicit. The human imagination, in Coleridge's famous definition, "dissolves, diffuses, dissipates, in order to re-create"; the energy of genius, in Emerson, is not on the side of stability but of transition and revolutionary intellectual classification; in Goethe's *Faust*, the lure of the eudaemonic ideal is contested even as it grows stronger. In continental Europe, where there are, as Arnold already noted, Academies, or cultural institutions closer to the central authority of the state, thinkers often see themselves as archeologists who must deconstruct the site of writing in order to emerge into their own discourse.

Unless we argue, then, that there is a culture of nature, that our minds must bend back to it and find institutions that have grown, like certain trees, "too slowly ever to decay," cultural achievement is bound to be at once pervasive and precarious.[22] It must be renewed from within each generation rather than passively inherited. There is no spontaneous, plantlike rejuvenation, despite the comforting German expression of *Nachwuchs* (intellectual growth and dissemination occurring in the environment of a great scholar) or other organicist and biological metaphors. To pass achievement on, to keep it from mutability or entropy—including the depression that comes from an embarrassment of cultural riches[23]—is a near-heroic task. We may not like what Coleridge named a clerisy, a disciplined and articulate elite comparable to Plato's guardians, yet some culture bearers are necessary, though they need not be en-robed and designated as such.

Since a culture that seeks to be independent of the state is often checked by specific historical conditions or denatured by politics, it is remarkable that groups do maintain their cultural capital over time and define themselves, at least in part, by that accomplish-ment. Wariness about culture politics need not turn into a self-defeating pessimism. Every individual who comes in contact with a canon, with works that stand in a mutual and mutually renovative relation, understands what culture means as a collective endow-ment. The canon, in short, is more of an immune system than a vulnerable reflection of national ideology. It can provide too much security, of course—Ortega already warned against "cultura-seguri-dad"—and in reaction a revolutionary type of decolonization seeks to eliminate all cultural activity that distracts from the overthrow of the colonizer.[24] But in all other respects recent calls to go "beyond culture" make no sense at all, however elitist, or bourgeois-con-formist, the concept of culture may seem to have become.[25] Juno's compromise remains the best we can hope for.

Yet, as I have intimated, even in the context of relative peace we confront the fragility and pitfalls of the endeavor to improve and dis-seminate the quality of public life. Mindful of this, some cultural historians have questioned the disinterestedness of intellectuals who cooperate with the modern nation-state's centralizing authority. Culture, they argue, which always constructs and modifies symbols, should be a revealing, not just an ordering; and as such it is closer to art.[26] Yet cognitive perspectives grow to be so strong after the Enlightenment, and the corrective (legislative) impulses so tempt-ing, that "culture" becomes the ideology of the intellectuals. "The intellectual ideology," Bauman writes, "was launched as a militant, uncompromising and self-confident manifesto of universally bind-ing principles of social organization and individual conduct." This harms a culture of inclusion. For diversity of life, accordingly, is esteemed to be "a temporary phenomenon, a transient phase to be left behind in the effort aimed toward a universal humanity." As an ideal, the so-called republic of letters sought to bring about "the

constitution of knowledge as power; the establishment of a privileged, foolproof access to right knowledge as the legitimation of the
right to tell the others, deprived of such access, what to do, how to
behave, what ends to pursue and by what means."[27]

Such a critique (only partially correct, I think) reveals an unexpected continuity between Enlightenment and the premodern age
of absolutism. It also changes our view of romanticism's relation to
the Enlightenment. Romanticism is a vortex, a time when rationalism and rationalization are challenged and nationality (or a schematic and unifying national pedagogy) is asked to respect local
forms of life and the *pouvoirs intermédiaires*. What does not change
is a fundamental issue: How can local traditions be passed on, or
integrated into a national or imperial culture that sees only their
"morbid resilience"? Can inclusion prevail?

The consciousness that reading brings is necessarily a historical one, communicating freely with historical tradition. It has a certain justification,
therefore, if we identify, like Hegel, the beginning of history with the emergence of a will to transmit, to memorialize permanently.

—HANS-GEORG GADAMER[28]

When a major political transition or *passation* takes place—as
when the French or the American presidency changes with ceremony and pomp—there is a feeling of relief that "power" has been
transmitted without a crisis. A fear that it will jump the tracks, burst
out of bounds, heightens the emphasis placed on ceremony. The
transmission of culture may not seem as hazardous a process as
political change, yet a recognition that cultural continuity is at risk
is quite old. For the West it was already expressed by the formula of
a "transfer of empire and learning" (*translatio imperii et studii*),
which also signaled the passing of cultural hegemony from East to
West. Starting with the Holy Roman Empire, the concept provided an apology for imperialism by envisaging the joint advance of
political power and culture.[79]

Yet the *translatio* concept was more than a conquering ideology.
It accepted learning and protected it, and though the arts under its

sway were neither liberated nor (in the modern sense of the word) liberal, they were guaranteed some maintenance and did not lose their status. Moreover, despite great tensions between pagan classicism and Christianity, another formula, that of *Santa Maria sopra Minerva* (the New Church built upon the Old), came down on the side of cultural appropriation rather than excision and guaranteed the residual survival of an older learning and even—as the Renaissance progressed—an older culture.

Today we are at a dangerous juncture, at a passage moment, because the will to transmit a body of learning (*translatio studii*) has weakened. This has occurred despite the university system and related institutions of civil society. We have become uncertain about the disinterestedness of knowledge, a knowledge suspected of contributing to power politics and involving the university as an "apparatus" to institutionalize and disseminate it. Since Nietzsche, Foucault, Althusser, and Bourdieu, we obsessively examine the genealogy of received or acquired ideas, seeking not only clarity but purity. Instrumental reason likewise is discredited, all the more so after imperial adventures, two world wars, and the Holocaust. We apply a "hermeneutics of suspicion" to everything, and our awareness of former complicities often promotes a new, sometimes arrogant puritanism. At the same time, a challenging question is evaded: is it possible to divorce knowledge from power; can we see knowledge once more as disinterested, without an instrumental linkage to a power that supposedly is good?[30]

The problematic of exerting power—especially state power—in order to achieve a "good" cultural result became clear long ago. It certainly became clear by the time of the first modern and democratic form of despotism. The effort of the Jacobins to centralize France, which was followed by the administrative policy of the Napoleonic empire, created a unified state at the expense of provincial cultures or emerging nationalities. The ensuing state tyranny, however enlightened, led to a convergence of opinion between Edmund Burke and Benjamin Constant, political thinkers whose judgment about the liberating potential of the French Revolution was otherwise totally at odds. "I will insist, to the great scandal of modern reformers," Constant declared, "that if I knew a people to whom one would have offered the most perfect institutions (metaphysically speaking), and who refused them in order to remain faithful to those of their ancestors, I would esteem that people and think it more happy, because of its moral and spiritual bearing, even under its defective institutions, than it could have been with all the proposed improvements."[31]

Since we cannot, today, join transmission of culture to transmission of empire—we have entered a postcolonial era and have realized the danger of a state-regulated or preplanned culture—is any redemptive politics, inclusive and global, any politics with that form of universality, still possible? Or, rejecting the possibility, are we fated to reprovincialize ourselves and to engage in endless culture wars?[32]

There are those who say that the French Revolution was never completed. Its doctrine of human rights (to which a right to be different has recently been added) and the utopian solicitation, especially in the United States, of participatory or populist democracy (with Walt Whitman as its bard), continue to have immense appeal. They foster a concept of heroism that envisions not so much a struggle against nature as a struggle against governmental or other established and oppressive forces. In line with this point of view, cultural discontinuity is blamed on centralization and *force majeure*. In modern localism, every culture emerging from the smithy of the racial or ethnic soul is viewed as a rightful natural growth, part of a God-given diversity—or else as an embattled Antigone. If the attainment of culture (really *cultures*) requires effort and struggle—and the "smithy" image evokes that effort and struggle—it is less to transmit a mixed and multilayered heritage than to achieve recognition for something that always already exists, though repressed, persecuted, or slighted as provincial.

I am suggesting that political idealism—what is left of it—has taken refuge in a *representation* of culture: culture as a collective and destined form of identity. Unfortunately, this development not only sins against the inner dynamics of culture, its creative and unpredictable potential, but allows cultural issues to become a political pawn in the ethnic wars besetting nation-states. For, while the dirty or cynical part of this war is assigned to politics ("politics as usual"), the transcendent and inspired part is linked to culture. Culture motivates political action *even as it consecrates the split between them*, between a self-interested, instrumental politics and a culture at once immanent and transcendently defining.

It is here that critique can begin, for now the concept of "society," not only of "nature," pulls away from that of "culture," especially in the context of democracy. The more a particular culture is viewed as a collective form of destiny, with immanent features that amount to an essentialized difference, the more alien it seems to the dynamic mixture of interests and classes, to the mobility of roles fostered by a democratic system. We see that the ineffability previously attributed to what is individual (*individuum est ineffabile*) has been taken from the person and transferred to a collective (this or that culture) that asserts its difference, often in a spectacular way. "A diminished will to power," Jean Baudrillard has written, "and a problematized will to knowledge, today bequeath us everywhere the will for spectacle." War is the expression of such a will, one that cannot be satisfied without a spectacular event, a provocative difference.[33]

There is an obvious paradox related to this exaltation of difference. Total integration into the group, with near-mystical overtones (a doctrine that, adapting the French word, one could call "integrism"), promises an altruistic loss of self at the level of the individual. This self-loss, however, is then compensated at the level of the group: the corporate (incorporated) individual continues to seek distinctiveness as well as national or ethnic symbols to reinforce his claim. Moreover, in order to affirm nation or ethne as a collective individual, history is reduced to a limited set of memories that entail the deliberate neglect or amnesia of many others. The political collective suffers, like Freud's hysterical individual, from "reminiscences," from anachronistic events implanted by memory envy.[34] The modern nation, and perhaps the modern sensibility in general, cannot exist, it seems, without inventing and extroverting a collective unconscious of archaic origin. A competition between nationalitics imposcs defining memorics that flag each culture's iden tity in a spectacular manner.

If the integrist rather than integrationist view of culture seems counterproductive to thinkers concerned with strengthening social democracy, it also runs into difficulties with those who do not want to overlook the challenge of culture to society. Here indeed opposition is friendship, for norms are not identical to standards of excellence. Adorno is suspicious of culture critics insofar as their oppositional pronouncements assume their personal distinction (*Vornehmheit*) or imply that, as a class, intellectuals have transcended the contested norms. He holds that every surplus of consciousness must become self-critical. This does not alter the fact that culture remains "high culture."[35] Accordingly, culture provides, as in the Arnoldian tradition, an undogmatic yet uncompromising standard of excellence or, in Adorno and Co., an unrelaxing consciousness of self and society, by no means a refusal of vision but a meticulous critique about how it can go bad and become totalitarian.[36] Every least sign of "bad totality" is recorded. The idea of culture yields a criticism of life for person and nation alike.

The inclusivist concept of culture, then, as it seeks to complete the French Revolution without becoming despotic—without extending, that is, mastery over nature to the world of nations—is still as invasive as an older and more heroic ideal, and perhaps as wishful and unrealistic. A counterrevolutionary tradition, coming in the wake of the French Revolution, already attacked what it called the abstract or metaphysical nature of the doctrine of human rights. So Joseph de Maistre declared in his *Reflections on France* (1797) that he had learnt, thanks to Montesquieu, that Persians existed but that he had never encountered the Abstract Man (*l'homme "en soi"*) posited by French revolutionary doctrine. Benjamin Constant, similarly, denounced inspirational slogans like "the great empire" and "the entire nation" as fostering dangerously vague notions. "They serve to immolate real beings to abstract beings."[37]

Yet the aim of both contemporary and older appeals to "culture" is not that of turning everything into an item of knowledge that can be manipulated in order to bring about domination, whether by a benevolent or a malevolent order. It is *to redeem imagination from abstraction*, to achieve, with or without the state, a more embodied and less alienated way of life. The earliest societies we know of seem to have been religious for that reason. They may have suffered from the same feeling of ghostliness moderns suffer from, which I described in my first chapter. That there is another life within or beyond our life and from which we have become separated—that "the true life is absent" (Levinas)—motivates collective fantasies of reembodiment. Blake thought that the poet Cowper went mad "as a refuge from unbelief," and Robert Musil saw nationalism as "only a special case of forced yearning for belief."[38] The aspiration to totality on the part of both religious and postreligious cultures is, I speculate, a reaction to an intolerable sense of decadence, or ghostliness, or alienation from the sources of life.

No wonder the newer concept of culture also breeds doctrine and a degree of fanaticism. It can foster a political, not only a civil, religion.[39] Yet as long as it discourages groupthink or the tyrannical enforcing of a particular embodiment, that is, as long as it does not create self-segregating, ethnic, or lifestyle sects, it opens toward a plenitude of social forms and the possibility of their coexistence.[40] Cultural differences should be the subject of comedy, not of tragedy: ethnic humor, swiftly disappearing in a politically correct society, was always based on such (often interchangeable) characteristics.

In brief, *the function of individual cultures remains the same throughout history: to convert longing into belonging.* Culture is always site specific in that respect. (The site includes language in its density.) If Schiller and Herder can be said to typify culture thinking at the threshold of modernity, then their quite different conceptions spring from the same source. Herder, the father of multiculturalism, does not see an inevitable conflict between the totality that marks each nonclassical culture and the internal harmony attributed by Schiller to classical antiquity, especially to an exemplary Greece. From a European perspective, nevertheless, the cultural pluralism arising in the period we call romantic poses a challenge: given that it continues to take local attachment seriously, how can a citizen participate fully in several cultures? Is not that as improbable as the older ideal of becoming a citizen of the world? Multiculturalism remains undertheorized and seems as unrealistic or abstract as the cosmopolitanism it intends to replace.

The question also arises—and with an edge to it—of what purpose is served by knowing about other cultures. The obvious answer is that such knowledge increases tolerance. Yet the chances are that this knowledge will either undermine patriotism or foster chauvinism. It may even intensify longing rather than belonging, as well as the guilt that comes from being unable to prefer the rightness of one's own existence. It is here that we glimpse the importance of an institutional space, the university, that leaves us free to examine this new and expanded consciousness, this cultural pluralism, and mediates between it and exigencies of allegiance in the political and practical world. I would also put it this way: learning about other cultures is part of our culture rather than of our politics. Yet the road to politics must go through that detour.

What we get to know, as students and scholars, is the past, though not a uniform or single past. Rather, as light yields a colored spectrum, so the past, through the skilled social, political, and literary historian, reveals something dynamic and multicolored, where many possibilities, many alternate forms of historical life jostle. Most of these forms, aborted or defeated, continue to lead an underground existence because of their "weak messianic power" (Walter Benjamin). What survives is, moreover, tinged with the sadness of what might have been. Learning, in short, though it may reinforce and justify what is, though it may legitimate a certain line of thinking or conduct, can also retrieve lines of evolution that were cut off and recover history as a more complete kind of memory. To turn learning into culture (no mean task) is to *live* with the fullness of that kind of memory; only when that phase has been honored can there be a moral culture politics, one in which we chose our relation to the past and a retrieved, particular history becomes a motive for action.

The university plays an essential role in the cultural space I have evoked. It is concerned with learning, not with the support of specific cultures; at the same time, by encouraging learning, it surrounds every subject of study with the critical and imaginative fullness mentioned above. There is a culture of criticism that should precede, in the university, all affirmation. The arts too play a special role in this, for they are a nursery of forms as well as a powerful and complex means of appealing to memory. Their mode of presentation can breach the walls of the academy and reach a broad public. They make memories, personal or historical, more actual; memories that are not always furnished by academic learning, though they often are. The sadness of having a past—not a historical past alone but also an intimate past, fugitive moments of ecstasy or identity— *that* sadness does not derive from the sense of personal mortality alone but also from achieving whatever is achieved through the sacrifice of other possibilities.

I have tried to clarify the link between a culture of inclusion and a certain idea of freedom: specifically, freedom to learn, to imagine, to speak one's mind in public. This link prevails despite the fact that culture, from early on, is related to more heroic ideas of labor, dominion, nation building, empire.[41] Today we continue to put "development" on the side of inclusion, even though the word is often mocked by groups educating local populations in the third world about global pressures that lead to a new, postcolonial type of economic exploitation.

For a time, modern imperialism, especially a British and nationalist version of historical progress, actually appropriated the paradigm of *translatio imperii et studii*. It argued that the Spirit of Liberty that had founded Greek culture moved from East to West to settle in the "Western Isle," whose empire would disseminate that freedom in politics and the arts alike. The Big Bird theory, as it might be called, represented the Angel (Eagle) of liberty deserting decadent regions in the Middle East—and then the Continent— for England, its new and destined clime. Liberty and empire were incongruously joined.[42] The myth of the frontier, which spurred American imperialism, is of related inspiration.

The shadow side of such stately progress, however, in British or other imperialisms, is the cost involved in passing from one era or civilization to another, because earlier ones are generally imagined as having been closer to nature. This cost was already expressed by Virgil, both in his creation of a new literary mode, the pastoral, and in the final books of the *Aeneid*, where the killing of Sylvia's stag is the first event of an action in which Turnus and his native country (with close ties to Faunus's woodland domain) are defeated by the Trojan invader. Those imperfect transitions from nature to civilization contribute to the birth of an acute historical consciousness and then to the movement called historicism. What I have named Juno's compromise establishes the rights of local or minority cultures or allows their mingling with the victorious civilization, but this never quite erases nostalgia for a more primal, powerful, natural realm. The triumphalism characterizing the progressive concept of culture is, in any case, often accompanied by a distinct note of pathos for this realm, portrayed as having had an integrity of its own. Indeed, the myth of the noble savage has persisted so long in Western history that it has attained a kind of universality.

Europe in the throes of industrialization and modernization adds the sentimental myth of the noble peasant. In "The Question of Our Speech," I pointed to an ominous development, a new convergence of culture and politics centered on the myth of rural virtue. That this virtue is ideal rather than real only deepens regret. Half-received and half-created, it entices us with the wonderfulness of *Waldeinsamkeit*, with a retreat into inwardness or subjectivity for which music is the high expression, with the phantom idea of an "organic community" and local attachment (*Heimat*),[43] with a wholeness prior to modern specialization and the corrosiveness of capitalism, and with a "natural," tacit or taciturn, speech that expresses an integrity of character deeper than what is possible for the mobile, hurried, overstimulated citizen of the modern age. These qualities are also among the topics of romanticism, where, however, they are treated with ambivalence, irony, or consciously visionary devices.

Indeed, the shrinking of a rural culture marks an epoch in the history of memory. We become aware of a memory haunted by ruins and cemeteries, by deserted or inorganic sites (topoi, loci, *lieux de mémoire*), once its relation to a living or unself-conscious milieu weakens.[44] A new alliance between poetry and memory begins to operate in the shadow of a lost rural domain: the mind tries to find again what it fears has vanished, by meditating on traces of the past in a landscape that may itself soon turn into such a trace.

Wordsworth's "Tintern Abbey" is paradigmatic for this attempt to stabilize time through memory, to arrest its flow for reasons beyond love of the moment (also beyond the moment of love that motivates Lamartine's "Le lac"). Conscious of the acceleration of history, Wordsworth saves what Georges Poulet will call "human time," as Thoreau does later, in New England. Kant asks us to "dare to know" in order to achieve a worthwhile future; Wordsworth "dares to hope," though changed, "that in this moment there is life and food / For future years."

In the political sphere, unfortunately, simplification and demagogic exploitation make the appeal to the (lost) land and landed virtues, to native soil, *pays, patrie, Heimat, Heimatland*, a dangerous weapon of the revolutionary (i.e., counterrevolutionary) Right. The land and the dead buried in it combine to create a powerful topos of demagogic lamentation. Spirit of place (the genius loci) becomes not only a nostalgic subject of study but also a source for retroactive nationalistic or identitarian claims. The Left, too, even when "green" rather than "red" in outlook, does not manage to articulate a philosophy of culture that escapes sentimentality or the suspicion that it is merely incubating another fanaticism or impractical political religion.

To continue to maintain, as has been maintained for centuries, that peasant experience is marginal to civilization, is to deny the value of too much history and too many lives. No line of exclusion can be drawn across his-

tory in that manner, as if it were a line across a closed account.
—JOHN BERGER, *Pig Earth*[45]

I have suggested that the newer idea of culture, which includes multiculturalism, has all the strength and weakness of utopian vision. Its main weakness is that it forgets where its strength comes from: that it was created in the *wake* of an older idea of culture, by the latter's heroic, historical struggles for land or against the land. Without those struggles, which are deeply secular even if involved in ideas of transcendence and religion, there would not be a plurality of cultural "species."

Only Thoreau, perhaps, in his understanding of natural economy, which excludes exploitation of the land by capitalistic farming or industrial development, had the imaginative force to depict an alternative culture. But Thoreau's vision is not without a self-contradictory tension: the sparse life in natural surroundings that he provisionally lives at Walden is conveyed by a literary exuberance that escapes his ascetic bonfire. Literary devices compensate for, even while they subvert, his message. Thoreauvian hyperboles delight yet also recall the extraordinary rather than ordinary life. The beauty of his flowers of speech is not that of flowers of the field that neither toil nor spin. We appreciate, for its political lesson, the ornery turn in "Many are concerned about the monuments of the West and the East, —to know who built them. For my part, I should like to know who in those days did not build them,—who were above such trifling" (*Walden*). What are we to make, however, of his description of *nature*'s bonfire, a Bataille-like image of reckless expenditure and consumption, introduced by the kind of expression more suited to the bourgeois tourist? "I love to see [!] that Nature is so rife with life that myriads can be afforded to be sacrificed and suffered to prey on one another; that tender organizations can be so serenely squashed out of existence like pulp,—tadpoles which herons gobble up, and tortoises and toads run over in the road; and that sometimes it has rained flesh and blood!"[46]

Perhaps this is satire, or self-satire: inner counterpoint to his scrupulous account keeping in the face of something so much larg-

er, which his "experiment in living" seeks to confront without defenses. He does foresee the possibility of "*human* culture," of cultivating the mind so that it too can dwell in nature, nourished by it.
But this is clearly not what is usually called art or civilization, and
he emphasizes that even religion has simply fostered an exploitative and alienating economy. "We now no longer camp as for a
night, but have settled down on earth and forgotten heaven. We
have adopted Christianity merely as an improved method of *agriculture*" (*Walden*). True culture—for Thoreau, human culture—
has not advanced to the point where it can be transferred from the
independent individual to organized society. The distance between
nature's news and what mechanized or institutionalized ears perceive is just too great for anything but a humorous transfiguration:

> When I reached the railroad in Plaistow, I heard at some dis-
> tance a faint music in the air like an Aeolian harp, which I
> immediately suspected to proceed from the cord of the tele-
> graph vibrating in the just awakened morning wind, and ap-
> plying my ear to one of the posts I was convinced that it was
> so. It was the telegraph harp singing its message through the
> country, its message sent not by men but by gods. Perchance,
> like the statue of Memnon, it resounds only in the morning
> when the first rays of the sun fall on it. . . . I heard a fairer
> news than the journals ever print.[47]

Returning to the contemporary world, irrevocably organized
and industrialized, I want to illustrate what is at stake in sustaining
any culture, any humane economy, under the continuing pressure
of moving from country to city. To show how widespread the awareness of the problem is I go to films rather than classic works of art.

If I omit in what follows any comment on the visuality of the
movie medium, it is for fear of being lured into a long excursus on
the role the ordinary world of sensory perception (sometimes so
ordinary as to be insensible) plays in and against this effort to give
culture durable and objective status. Film, in particular, consumes
as well as innovates images: it cannot be reduced to a signifying
momentum in which everything adds up. It purloins but also ques-

tions the stabilizing force in perception, particularly the relative muteness and thingness of objects in the rural world. It creates a consuming visuality of its own, from which the senses emerge shaken yet renewed or simply happy to return to normalcy. Yet since film has entered and partially transformed the visual field of theater and spectatorship, the optics it proposes must imply (either generally or at the level of the individual picture) an aesthetic politics rather than an aestheticization of politics.

The first of the two films to be considered is a grade B French movie whose main distinction lies in the acting of Simone Signoret. In *Les granges brulées* (The burnt barns), she plays a woman of integrity in a distinctive setting. She lives on a large farm, which she owns only in part, that is worked by her husband and two grown (and very handsome) sons, one of whom has married a girl who wants to escape the peasant life. A murder that occurs near the isolated farm intrudes "city" suspicions into the country and brings a young investigating judge (*juge d'instruction*) into contact with Signoret. The frame of the detective story proves to be, as often in fictions of this kind, a device to illuminate the opacity of a certain kind of life. What is discovered by the judge is trivial: the (city-oriented) wife of one brother is unfaithful to him with the other brother, and the murder was a gratuitous act by totally unrelated drifters. The real mystery turns out to be Signoret's character, associated here with life in the country; in a sense it is no mystery at all but an unexplained, attractive mode of integrity.

The identification of country life with strength of character is naive, yet not entirely so, for the film also exploits the tension between younger and older generations: Signoret is trying to hold on to not only a patrimony but a way of life, to what we would now call a *culture*. That the tension expresses itself principally as one between city and country is not irrelevant, no more than it is in Wordsworth's very great poem "Michael." But the interesting and disconcerting thing is the convergence of culture (understood as a traditional way of life) and of character or *ethos*.

The word *ethos*, as I use it here, points not only to character disclosed by habits and choices but, as already in Aristotle, to a quality that need not reveal itself in *dianoia*: the reasoned utterances of people. Signoret is presented as a modern woman; at least there is no sign of her deep dissent from that kind of life or any extreme attachment to the farm. Yet it seems as if the film, in order to evoke an image of integrity, had to fall into a stereotype that draws its force from the double mystery of Signoret herself, the mature woman acting the part of the mature woman (a return, within theater, from theater to nature) and the peasant motivated by something *dianoia* cannot reach.

The word "culture" points always, in its new and proliferating as well as in its more traditional sense, to that kind of (lost) integrity. How dangerously nostalgic this "pastoral" desire for an original integrity can be is shown by Michael Ignatieff in his aptly titled book on today's ethnic and civic nationalisms, *Blood and Belonging*.[48] This political and pernicious form of pastoralism was equally there in fascism and has dominated the cultural and political landscape since the later nineteenth century.

I turn now to a second film, distinguished again by a star characterization. *Nell* is an American version of the French "wild child" theme.[49] Jodie Foster plays a girl of about fifteen who appears like a foundling in the modern world. She has the shyness and obsessive habits of a stray animal and speaks an unintelligible language. The doctor who finds her and the psychologist whose aid he seeks soon face a dilemma beyond the scientific task of seeking to decode Nell and the humane task of drawing her into some kind of relationship to society.

The question of how to understand this creature—strange and other enough to suggest that here is not a sick, aberrant human being but one with her own integrity—is immediately complicated by the intrusiveness of those who study her. This intrusiveness characterizes both science and modern life. It raises the existential issue of whether this strange, vulnerable being can be civilized, whether the wildness of the young woman (who strikes the modern sensibility as having been arrested or fixated at a primitive stage of development) is a deeply archaic good that cannot pass into our kind of life, our kind of culture. The film confronts this issue, though it then chooses a happy ending. The two doctors who study Nell spy on her with tape recorder and video camera, a spying pushed beyond bearable limits by the public media when they learn of the wild girl: in a terrifying scene, a helicopter is used to survey and pursue her. Must she end in a hospital, because it is the only place that can look after her safely, that can protect her enough to allow her to evolve and eventually to rejoin "civilization"? Somehow, after being retraumatized by her contact with the modern world, Nell recovers, and in its final scene the film stages a psychoanalytic fiction: her original trauma, relived in a benign context, dissolves, and she is promised full entry into the human family.

Nell is abused not by evil persons but by an impasse in cultural development itself. The film attributes her backwardness, or woodland nature, to a superstitiously religious upbringing that isolated her totally from the evil of the world. The loss, moreover, of her only childhood companion, a twin sister, induces in her an enigmatic ballet of memorial gestures and sounds. In order to develop, Nell must leave her world behind. An insistence coming from modern times, as from developmental psychology generally, that reality must be faced whatever the consequences and that modernity is an inevitable part of this reality gives the story of the wild child a happy ending and fashions a nostalgic rather than tragic film. We are allowed to enjoy—quite shamelessly—twilight glimpses of a mysterious and expressive mode of being with its own language and body. Nell's poetry is in her pathos, her doomed integrity (even if it is an integrity based on a mistaken principle of nurture), and this pathos is close—too close for comfort—to the vulnerability of all poetry within a civilization that should, yet cannot, keep it a vital principle.

As a realistic myth, Nell recalls not only Wordsworth's Boy of Winander but also his Lucy, who dies into nature before reaching maturity, whose violetlike privacy is not to be violated. This sensitivity to a privacy jeopardized by the conditions of modern life (industrialization, urbanization, and the rise of intrusive media, all of which are explicitly questioned by Wordsworth in his preface to *Lyrical Ballads*) yields one reason why in the course of intellectual history since the end of the eighteenth century the word "culture" begins to stand in contrast to its synonym "civilization."[50] Personal loss associates itself with a larger loss, exacted by an increasingly technocratic society.

However, even as poetry becomes the guardian of a private realm, of a shy vitality (culminating in Emily Dickinson, the ultimate Nell), interpretation emerges as the guardian of poetry. It finds a way of keeping an "archaic" endowment alive by inventing a new kind of dialogue with it. The "itsy-bitsy spider" rhyme, which calms another girl, an autistic patient shown toward the beginning of the film, anticipates the self-hypnotizing but unintelligible rhymes that send Nell into a trance. The desire to draw her back into ordinary, communicative language is what motivates the doctor. Several episodes in the film turn on his near-magical attempt to break through Nell's terror and solipsism, to establish contact with her by accepting her "idioglossia." So he affectionately repeats her own speech, her nonsense syllables; he talks to her in her own way. Through this fact—that here the interpretive act does not impose a different way of speaking, a scientific metalanguage, but respects the other's idiom while extending it tenderly—human solitude is comforted rather than profaned. It is not precipitated into deeper trauma. Interpretation becomes dialogic, participatory, able to honor an older speech (in this case, distorted biblical phrases), however superstitious and even harmful that speech might have been.

Yet culture, in modernity, although protective of a disappearing mode of life, also identifies with "civilization" or civil society and seeks to influence the public realm. The forms of art, beginning with romanticism, reflect a deepening tension between something elegiac—their sense of a mode of being that is lost, or deeply privatized, and to be recovered only by a retrospective as well as introspective method—and culture as a creative and contestatory force, helping to cancel old and form new institutions and even the "personality" of nations.

The "fateful question" Freud poses at the end of *Civilization and Its Discontents* concerns humanity's survival in the face of a discordant and perhaps permanently antithetical force. Culture,[51] he concludes, must control the vital yet aggressive energies that build it up, energies that tend to defeat themselves because they react explosively to frustrations imposed by the very advance of culture. Indeed, since Freud's analysis of 1930, "culture" has itself become a fighting word. One might have hoped that the erotic libido ("Eros, builder of cities") would help to counteract or even tame aggression. According to Freud, however, eros conspires with death in seeking a return of the organism to a more inert, less burdened state, even one that is quasi-inanimate, so that, to adapt a famous saying, we call peace what is really desolation.

The note of tragedy and even impasse introduced by Freud goes back to Rousseau's indictment of culture, of the arts and sciences insofar as they rouse human desires rather than assuaging them. "All the values of culture and civilization are phantoms, which we must renounce if we are not to be forever led astray, forever drinking from the cask of futility."[52] But Freud, of course, does not posit an original or pure state of nature, not even as a benign and hopeful fiction. He stands closer to Kant's renunciation of such eudaemonic ideals, which both inspire and frustrate progressive concepts in history, ethics, and culture. Freud's vision of death-in-life, even of death-in-love, is closely connected to evidences of mourning, from ancestor worship to monumental ceremonies, and generally to symbol systems that temper the loneliness and ghostliness of individuated being. I would include among these evidences nationalism's cult of the dead and other dangerously nostalgic aspects of modern politics that play on the fear of national decadence by invoking heroic ideals.[53]

From the more private history of sensibility too we learn that loss is difficult to overcome, that the death of someone we have been close to takes away a part of us as surely as if it were a limb. We also then mourn for ourselves, either for the recognition that we too are not immortal or for our inability to feel grief longer and more intensely. We wish to encrypt the lost person or ideal into our continuing life or to separate absolutely (from it, from us) the taint of death. Through this courageously perverse effort to sustain the lost object by means of imagination we come often to understand our own finitude.

Freud's analysis, though deeply pessimistic, leaves open the possibility that love might still detach from self-destructive impulse and preserve what it has helped to build. He knows that regression moves *away from* the inanimate, not only *toward* it. The overhead of living in civilized society, the anxiety of demand it generates and that involves feelings as well as mind, leads to a search for reanimation not all that dissimilar from what poetic myths suggest when they evoke a sympathetic cosmos, or a partnership between all creatures, human, animal, and floral. Yeats's "News for the Delphic Oracle" ends with "Nymphs and Satyrs / Copulate in the foam," but this erotic "Know thyself" is not the whole story.

From childhood to maturity we continue to be fascinated by legends about an original unity, often imaged as a symbiosis of nature and humankind. We reenvision Blake's "Animal Forms of Wisdom" and tame them into transitional objects that, as we grow up, comfort moments of loss and separation. But if maturity is a specifically human form of survival, do we not also seek biological wisdom of a more radical kind, one that "looks through death," as Wordsworth said, or faces "death without mediation," in Terrence Des Pres's words, and "embrace[s] life without reserve"?[54]

Julien Benda foresaw, writing between the wars and in the era of Freud, that the political feelings would form "une masse passionelle compacte" and swallow all other passions, attaining a universal presence not previously known. Politics condenses, according to him, into a small number of simple hatreds attached to the deepest roots of the human heart.[55] The fateful question, restated in this light, is whether an idea of culture can be formulated that remains generous, that is not the pawn of politics and does not rationalize suicidal acts of collective self-differentiation.

It is ironic that "tribalism," as the movement toward secession and segregation is sometimes called, has failed to make us rethink nature as the destined habitat of other species, as a principled ecol-

ugy in which nonhuman beings too live and differentiate them
selves. Given present misery, bloodshed, and waste of life, it is quite
a task to maintain Kant's thesis that the final aim of "nature, the
great artist" is to develop all human capacities in order to produce
"a harmony amongst men against their will and indeed through
their discord."[56] My favorite poet wrote the following lines near the
beginning of an epic-sized poem, the first ever devoted to the
growth of the mind and the development of the individual. The
honest yet heightened language of these lines makes you aware of
how precariously the eudaemonic ideal is maintained:

> Dust as we are, the immortal spirit grows
> Like harmony in music, there is a dark
> Inscrutable workmanship that reconciles
> Discordant elements, makes them cling together
> In one society.[57]

NOTES

1. The creation of this ministry responded to (1) pressure to restrict
the *jus soli* that grants automatic citizenship to those born on French
soil, even when their parents are noncitizens, and (2) the perception
that there were too many *"exclus,"* either through poverty or because
they were not following the assimilationist pattern of previous immi-
grations but showing *intégriste* tendencies.

2. *Dialektik der Aufklärung.* Originally published as *Philosophische
Fragmente* (New York: Institute of Social Research, 1944; reprint, Amsterdam: Querido, 1947).

3. Neil Postman, *Technopoly: The Surrender of Culture to Technology* (New York: Vintage, 1993). An important counterstatement to
"postmodern" suspicions of technological science is found in Yaron
Ezrahi, *The Descent of Icarus: Science and the Transformation of Contemporary Society* (Cambridge: Harvard University Press, 1990). Ezrahi
examines fully the relation of liberal democracy to the rise of the "attes-
tive" (rather than "celebratory") gaze enabled by modern science, its
creation of a new visual culture and instrumental exposure of the
politician. Ezrahi is wary of the "delegitimation of grand social and

political engineering and the decline of instrumental rationality in the context of public affairs," fearing a return to kitsch and pleasing illusions, to that aestheticization of politics Benjamin had already discerned in fascism.

4. On the two main patterns of dealing legally with integration, those of the French *jus soli* and the German *jus sanguinis*, see the informative book by Rogers Brubaker, *Citizenship and Nationhood in France and Germany* (Cambridge: Harvard University Press, 1992).

5. The idea of a vast community of creatures (humans and nonhumans) remains relegated to religion or to visionary eccentrics like Christopher Smart in *Jubilate Agno*. It does not seem reconciliable with the idea of nation. There is, of course, a growing literature discussing "biota" and "biodiversity." But the combination of science, sociology, and politics required for an effective discourse in this area seems far away.

6. Eric Hobsbawm and Terence Ranger, eds., *The Invention of Tradition* (Cambridge: Cambridge University Press, 1983). See Benedict Anderson, *Imagined Communities: Reflections on the Origin and Spread of Nationalism* (London: Verso, 1983). See also Gregory Jusdanis, "Beyond National Culture?" *boundary 2* 22 (1995): 24–60, for an account of how the idea of national culture anticipated and promoted the absent nation-state. It is important to mention here that my comments target simplified ethnocultural claims that stretch into a mythic past and use that as a basis of exclusionary politics. It does not target what Brubaker has called "an enduring consonance between a legal formula" (*jus soli* or *jus sanguinis*) "and a political-cultural self-understanding," since the "nation-state is not only, or primarily, an ethnodemographic phenomenon, or a set of institutional arrangements" but also a crucial way "of thinking about and appraising political and social membership" (Brubaker, conclusion to *Citizenship and Nationhood*, 186, 188).

7. "The Nibelungen Lied" (1831), in *Carlyle's Unfinished History of German Literature*, ed. Hill Shine (Lexington: University of Kentucky Press, 1951), 50.

8. *All Religions are One* (1788), in *The Complete Poetry and Prose of William Blake*, ed. David V. Erdman (New York: Doubleday, 1988), 8.

9. "Between Memory and History: *Les Lieux de Mémoire*," *Representations* 26 (1989): 8.

10. See, for example, two case studies of recent public art: Casey Nelson Blake, "Between Civics and Politics: The Modernist Moment in American Public Art" (unpublished); and James Young, *The Texture of Memory: Holocaust Memorials and Meaning in Europe, Israel and America* (New Haven: Yale University Press, 1993).

11. The most ambitious and interesting recent book on that subject is Edward W. Said, *Culture and Imperialism* (New York: Knopf, 1993).

12. "The Aims of Literary Study," *PMLA* 53 (1938): 1367–71. For the larger picture, see Gregory Jusdanis, *Belated Modernity and Aesthetic Culture: Inventing National Literature* (Minneapolis: University of Minnesota Press, 1991). Bill Readings, influenced by Jean-François Lyotard, claims that there is a "breakdown of the metanarrative that centers the university around the production of the national subject" and that "the strong idea of 'culture' arises with the nation-state, and we now face its disappearance as the locus of social meaning" ("University Without Culture?" *New Literary History* 26 [1995]: 465–93). Marc Fumaroli goes so far as to assert in *L'état culturel: Essai sur une religion moderne* (Paris: Fallois, 1991) that after Malraux's ministry the French "mission civilisatrice" turned from the lost colonies to target the "indigènes" of the homeland. See also John Guillory, *Cultural Capital: The Problem of Literary Canon Formation* (Chicago: Chicago University Press, 1993).

13. See "The Rhetoric of Hitler's 'Battle,' " written shortly after the Munich conference and collected in *The Philosophy of Literary Form: Studies in Symbolic Action*, 3d ed. (Berkeley: University of California Press, 1973), 191–221. This "sinister unifying" is also defined as "curative unification by a fictitious devil-function [i.e., anti-Semitism]" (218).

14. Zygmunt Bauman, *Culture as Praxis* (London: Routledge and Keegan Paul, 1973), 55–57. A parallel development is the fact that, in postmodern North America, many can chose "when and how to play ethnic roles" (Herbert J. Gans on "Symbolic Ethnicity," quoted in Jusdanis, "Beyond National Culture," 52 ff). Whether poststructuralism is a significant critique of structuralism rather than a widening of it remains unclear to me. Heidegger's difficult reflections on technology, however, which reintroduce the concealed presence (to be revealed by

art rather than technology) of a nonanthropomorphic nature, run counter to, in particular, the Marxist understanding of construction.

15. This does not mean, as is sometimes charged, that contemporary criticism "privatizes" literature or that it prefers the personal to the communal. Although Bakhtin, as the major source of this critical method, analyzed the novel, the newly fashioned critical instruments are used just as effectively on the lyric, despite its idiosyncratic and (often) enigmatic language. The lyric, in fact, precisely because it is both formal and personal, becomes the preferred object of theoretical desire, a desire to show how art remains connected, though not necessarily subordinated, to the sociolect as well as specific historical conditions.

16. Two essays in Denis Hollier's *Les dépossédés (Bataille, Caillois, Leiris, Malraux, Sartre)* (Paris: Minuit, 1993) center on this: "De l'équivoque entre littérature et politique" and "L'adieu aux plumes." See also Jean Starobinski's account of the Jaspers-Lukács debate at a Geneva conference on "the European spirit" immediately after World War II. Lukács was unable to speak candidly, given the absence of free debate in the Soviet sphere of influence. "He had to *translate* into another language his idea of an alliance between the democratic nations" (Starobinski, *Table d'orientation: L'auteur et son autorité* [Lausanne: L'Age d'homme, 1989], 205–6).

17. "Toward a Theory of Culture: With Special Reference to the Psychoanalytic Case," in *The Feeling Intellect: Selected Writings*, ed. Jonathan B. Imber (Chicago: Chicago University Press, 1990), 325.

18. Book 12, in Robert Fitzgerald, trans., *The Aeneid. Virgil* (New York: Random House, 1983), 398.

19. On the dynamics of identity politics, especially in the university, see Todd Gitlin, *The Twilight of Common Dreams: Why America is Wracked by Culture Wars* (New York: Holt, 1995). He describes the dynamics succinctly as "the recognition of a collective hurt, followed by the mistaking of a group position for a 'culture,' followed by the mistaking of a 'culture' for a politics" (147–48).

20. In their *Dialektik der Aufklärung (Dialectic of Enlightenment)*, Horkheimer and Adorno found the contradictions in the concept of rational and scientific progress even in Homer's *Odyssey*.

21. By adding "man made" to "second nature" the shadow arises again of an administered or reified social reality whose sinister end result can be state-sponsored genocide. Culture can veer toward domination once more. Here the necessity of an ethics based on the sympathetic imagination shows itself more clearly than ever.

22. Wordsworth, " Yew Trees" (1803). Our famous and augmenting powers of mechanical reproduction do not alter this precariousness: things easily preserved are also easily forgotten or weary themselves out of the memory by the excess of multiplicity.

23. "The advance of culture continually presents man with new gifts; but the individual sees himself more and more cut off from the enjoyment of them. And what is the good of all this wealth which no single self can ever transmute into its own living possession?" (Ernst Cassirer, *The Logic of the Humanities [Kulturwissenschaften]*, trans. C. S. Howe [New Haven: Yale University Press, 1961], 185). Cassirer, after Georg Simmel, identifies this fact with civilized man's tragic "discontent" "from which no intellectual development can free us, for the defect is inherent to the very nature of intellectual development" (185, 216). Yet Cassirer shifts, at the end, to a vision of collective *Bildung* (as in Herder's vision of *Humanität*) that pretends to override the individual consciousness, the pathos he has just described: "It is of decisive significance that in his speech, his art, and all the rest of his forms of culture, man has created, so to speak, a new body which all men share in common. . . . that part of himself which he puts into his work . . . is *embodied* in language and art and endures henceforth through it. It is this process which distinguishes the mere *transformation* [*Umbildung*] taking place in the sphere or organic emergence from the *formation* [*Bildung*] of humanity"(216). Despite my respect for Cassirer, I think this is a purely verbal solution, one which returns us to the desire for embodiment that I analyze in chapter 2, "Culture and the Abstract Life."

24. Ortega y Gasset, *Meditaciones del Quijote* (1914). On colonization, see Frantz Fanon, *Les damnés de la terre* (Paris: François Maspero, 1961). In an essay of 1932 Ortega also presciently posed the question: "Can we live on our classics today? Is not Europe suffering from a strange proletarization?" He reminds us that a "patrician" was a Ro-

man who could make a will and leave an inheritance, whereas "prole-tarians" were descendants but not heirs ("In Search of Goethe from Within," in *The Dehumanization of Art and Other Writings on Art and Culture* [Garden City, N.Y.: Doubleday, n.d.], 125).

25. See Lionel Trilling's analysis of the attempt to escape bourgeois norms in *Beyond Culture: Essays on Literature and Learning* (New York: Viking, 1965) and, more recently, Bill Readings, "The University Without Culture?" Critical Theory, the movement led by Adorno and Horkheimer and so named because it explores the possibility of cri-tique in modernity, contributes most to our heightened consciousness of the culture problematic in the West.

26. See Heidegger, *The Question Concerning Technology and Other Essays*, trans. William Lovitt (New York: Harper and Row, 1977), esp. 26 ff.

27. Zygmunt Bauman, *Intimations of Postmodernity* (New York: Routledge, 1992), 9. Bauman extends the critique of Adorno, Hork-heimer, Gramsci, and Foucault. I present the more idealized view of the "republic of letters" in chapter 2 above. Ezrahi too, in *The Descent of Icarus*, presents a more careful picture, showing how modern sci-ence is one of the cultural foundations of liberal-democratic politics. Bauman, it seems to me, generalizes implicitly from the special case of Communist intellectuals, considered as "intellectual workers" in the service of party or state, whose function it was to indoctrinate the recal-citrant masses. But the function of culture, at least since the Enlightenment, has always been determined by two factors, not a sin-gle one: public opinion about national character or destiny, and the importance to personal development or civil society of free (leisure) time, often associated with ancient debates about *otium* as well as a newer concept of "humanity."

28. "Lesendes Bewußtsein ist notwendig geschichtliches und mit der geschichtlichen Überlieferung in Freiheit kommunizierendes Bewusstsein. Es hat daher seine Berechtigung, wenn man wie Hegel den Anfang der Geschichte mit der Entstehung eines Willens zur Überlieferung, zur 'Dauer des Andenkens,' gleichsetzt" (*Wahrheit und Methode: Grundzüge einer philologischen Hermeneutik* [Tübin-gen: Mohr, 1960], 369).

29. There is a vast literature on the *translatio* concept. For an incisive treatment of its relevance to modern literature, see Frank Kermode, *The Classic: Literary Images of Permanence and Change* (New York: Viking, 1975). That modernity might have legitimated itself illegitimately—by a failed *translatio* and progress called "secularization," which in fact reduced and repressed premodern religion rather than absorbing it—is argued in Hans Blumenberg's *Legitimacy of the Modern Age*, trans. Robert M. Wallace (Cambridge, Mass.: MIT Press, 1983), originally published in German in 1966.

30. Said acknowledges this "demystification of all cultural constructs" by what he calls "consequential metropolitan theorists" but brings evidence, at the same time, of how vast the breach still is between them and the "contribution of empire to the arts of observation, description, disciplinary formation and theoretical discourse" (*Culture and Imperialism*, chapter 4). I would add that, because modern art is less under the sway of learning, we might be able to distinguish formal knowledge from the arts and ascribe to the latter a more instinctive and autonomous domain, which can succumb to indoctrination but may also have this inbuilt resistance. Shakespeare is modern in this sense, for his learning, though considerable, and his interests, though deeply involved in the question of succession and the maintenance of empire, cannot be subdued to a particular fidelity. Modern science, however, often tries to bypass instrumentalism as a moral issue by understanding knowledge as competence.

31. See Constant's chapter "On Uniformity" in his *Spirit of Conquest and Usurpation in Its Relation to European Civilization* (1814) in *Political Writings*, trans. and ed. Biancamaria Fontana (Cambridge: Cambridge University Press, 1988), 73–79.

32. On the complex relation between imperialism and the provincial and how it helped to determine literary value, see Kermode, *The Classic*, especially chapter 1.

33. I interpret in my own way Jean Baudrillard, *La Guerre du Golfe n'a pas eu lieu* (Paris: Galilée, 1991), 24: "La pulsion spectaculaire de la guerre reste entière. A défaut de la volonté de la puissance, bien diminuée, et de la volonté du savoir, problématique, il reste partout aujourd'hui la volonté de spectacle, et, avec elle, le désir obstiné d'en sauver le spectre ou la fiction."

34. See also my remarks in "Public Memory and Its Discontents," in *The Longest Shadow: In the Aftermath of the Holocaust* (Bloomington: Indiana University Press, 1996).

35. With Pierre Bourdieu, of course, and with roots in Rousseau, there is an attack on the category of "distinction" as a historically developed and often classist category that appropriates and aestheticizes culture.

36. For the problematic of gaining a vision of the whole, see appendix 2, "On Methodology."

37. "On Uniformity," 73–79. Cf. Coleridge's scathing remarks on political economists: "They worship a kind of non-entity under the different words, the State, the Whole, the Society, &c. and to this idol they make bloodier sacrifices than ever the Mexicans did to Tescalipoca" (*The Collected Works of Samuel Taylor Coleridge*, vol. 4, *The Friend*, ed. Barbara E. Rooke, Bollingen ed. [Princeton: Princeton University Press, 1969], 1:299).

38. See Emmanuel Levinas, *Totality and Infinity: An Essay on Exteriority*, trans. Alphonso Lingis (Pittsburgh: Dusquesne University Press, 1969), 33 ff. Levinas establishes, from within metaphysics, a critique of totality. The remark about Cowper is found in Blake's annotations to Spurzheim's "Observations on Insanity," in *The Poetry and Prose of William Blake*, ed. David V. Erdman (New York: Doubleday, 1965), 652. Blake suggests (through Cowper) that he too is mad for that reason. Musil makes his comment in unpublished drafts of 1923 collected by Burton Pike and David S. Luft under the title "The German as Symptom" in Robert Musil, *Precision and Soul: Essays and Addresses* (Chicago: University of Chicago Press, 1990), 161.

39. The names associated with these concepts are Eric Voegelin (political religion) and Robert Bellah (civil religion). Marc Fumaroli (n. 12, above) calls the "culture state" a "modern religion."

40. The problem on the level of practical politics is obvious, and a ministry "against exclusion" within a particular nation does not settle the issue of the exclusion of those outside the nation, the strangers at the gates. In its visionary aspect, the generation and toleration of all kinds of social groups is another development within the Great Chain of Being, a concept Arthur Lovejoy traced in his book of that title.

European romanticism inaugurated the idea of a "symphony" of distinctive nations or cultures, although multiculturalism *within* the nation state had to await the present era.

41. But culture is never fully conciliable with either state or church, religion or politics. I will not distinguish at this point between religion and culture, except to say that, as a historical fact, freedom of imagination and intellect, of learning and the arts, associates itself, in the modern period, primarily with culture and the European idea of a republic of letters.

42. See, e.g., Bishop Berkeley's "Verses on the Prospect of Planting Arts and Learning in America," in *Works*, vol. 7, ed. A. A. Luce and T. E. Jessop (London: Nelson, 1948–57), 367–71, for one version of this westering with strong providential overtones. Berkeley's five-act drama of history conflates imperial and millennial themes, the *translatio*, and the five ages or kingdoms Jerome had deduced from the Book of Daniel. Cotton Mather's *Magnalia*, interpreting pious Aeneas's emigration as a *translatio*, foresees America as a new and sacred foundation. The concept of a *translatio* had also served to glorify Elizabethan politics and culture. On the Continent, we find parallel theories supporting the ideas of a Northern (as well as Western) *translatio* in Hölderlin's poetry, for example.

43. An important account of the appeal and post-Nazi survival of the notion of *Heimat* is found in Celia Appelgate, *A Nation of Provincials: The German Idea of Heimat* (Berkeley: University of California Press, 1990). She remarks on the fact that the prevailing primary meaning is that of local culture, close to regionalism (her "provincialism") but also associated, especially after the Nazi destruction, with a fertile and pastoral countryside. See her fascinating portrait on pages 206–7 and 236 of Kurt Kölsch, the Nazi *Gaukulturwart* who after the war becomes a poet of the Pfalz ("Hier ist der Acker und hier ist die heilende Erde," etc.). For an acccount of the destructiveness of the notion, see Henryk M. Broder, *"Heimat? No, Thanks,"* in *Jewish Voices, German Words: Growing Up Jewish in Postwar Germany and Austria*, ed. Elena Lappin (North Haven, Conn.: Catbird, 1994).

44. See Pierre Nora's theoretical introduction to his collective work *Les lieux de mémoire* (Paris: Gallimard, 1984–92): "Consider, for exam-

ple, the irrevocable break marked by the disappearance of peasant culture, that quintessential repository of collective memory whose recent vogue as an object of historical study coincided with the apogee of industrial growth" ("Between Memory and History: *Les Lieux de Mémoire*," *Representations* 26 [1989]: 7). But that "for example" is surely disingenuous. It is the single most important instance of the modern "acceleration of history." See also Eugen Weber, *Peasants into Frenchmen: The Modernization of Rural France, 1870–1914* (Stanford: Stanford University Press, 1976), part 3.

45. Berger's trilogy (I quote from the introduction to the first volume of *Into Their Labours*) describes peasant life in France, not England. Almost two centuries after Wordsworth, he tries, seemingly closer than Wordsworth to the laborers and in a "spirit of solidarity with the so-called 'backward,' " to recall their "experience of survival." Brutal as their life is, he suggests it is less brutal than what is brought about by "corporate capitalism in all its brutalism." It is their survival skill, even as they disappear (the trilogy is his *Tristes tropiques*), from which he claims we must learn if we are to survive.

46. *Walden*, chapter 17, " Spring."

47. *A Week on the Concord and Merrimack Rivers.* I owe a debt to Stanley Cavell, especially to his *Senses of Walden* (New York: Viking, 1972), even when I differ from him in my view of Thoreau.

48. *Blood and Belonging: Journeys into the New Nationalism* (New York: Farrar, Straus, and Giroux, 1994).

49. "The Wild Boy of Aveyron" appeared in 1800 (a Wordsworthian year!). The story of the attempt to educate and bring him back to civilized life is told best by Roger Shattuck in *The Forbidden Experiment: The Story of the Wild Boy of Aveyron* (New York: Farrar, Straus, and Giroux, 1980), which is alluded to in *Nell*. Shattuck was partly inspired by Truffaut's version in *L'enfant sauvage* (1970). Kaspar Hauser, another wild boy, surfaces in Germany in 1828; killed by an unknown person, he became the focus of a play by Peter Handke, a film by Werner Herzog, and a poem by Georg Trakl.

50. See appendix 1, "On 'Culture' and 'Civilization.' " Brook Thomas has drawn my attention to a significant essay entitled "The Right to Privacy," by Louis Brandeis and Samuel Warren, in *Harvard Law Review*

4 (1890). 193–220. After lamenting the "intrusion upon the domestic circle" of the daily papers, the authors make the following remark: "The intensity and complexity of life, attendant upon advancing civilization, has rendered necessary some retreat from the world, and man, under the refining influence of culture, has become more sensitive to publicity, so that solitude and privacy have become more essential to the individual." See Thomas, "The Construction of Privacy In and Around *The Bostonians*," *American Literature* 64 (1992): 719–47. See also Stacey Margolis, "The Public Life: The Discourse of Privacy in the Age of Celebrity," *Arizona Quarterly* 51 (1995): 81–103. Increased networks of communication, a factor in the rise of nation-states, according to Karl Deutsch, problematize the boundary between private and public.

51. Freud uses *"Kultur"* but tells us he does not make a distinction between it and *"Zivilisation."*

52. Cassirer, "The 'Tragedy of Culture' " in *The Logic of the Humanities*, 183.

53. Cf. Terrence Des Pres, *The Survivor: The Anatomy of Life in the Death Camps* (New York: Oxford University Press, 1976), 5: "One of the functions of culture is to provide symbolic systems which displace awareness of what is terrible. . . . Through death the hero takes upon himself the condition of victimhood and thereby grants the rest of us an illusion of grace."

54. Wordsworth, "Ode: Intimations of Immortality"; Des Pres, *The Survivor*, 207.

55. *La trahison des clercs* (Paris: Grasset, 1927), chapter 1.

56. See "Of the Guarantee for Perpetual Peace" in his treatise "On Perpetual Peace" and the fourth thesis of his "Idea for a Universal History from a Cosmopolitan Point of View." I have used L. W. Beck's translation in *Kant: On History* (New York: Bobbs-Merrill, 1963).

57. Wordsworth, 1850 *Prelude*, 1.341–44.

appendix 1
"Culture" and "Civilization"

The reader might find it useful to have an overview (but one that does not aim at comprehensiveness) of the important history of the words "culture" and "civilization" from the later eighteenth century to the Second World War. They designate highly charged concepts, often defined in opposition to each other. A magisterial treatment of their contrast is found in Norbert Elias's work on the civilizing process.[1] But Elias basically deals with the sociogenesis of the German concept of "Kultur" and its difference from French "civilisation." I can add little to his sociological analysis summed up in the following paragraph: "The French concept of civilisation reflects the specific social fortunes of the French bourgeoisie to exactly the same degree that the concept of Kultur reflects the German. The concept of civilisation is first, like Kultur, an instrument of middle-class circles—above all the middle-class intelligentsia—in the internal social conflict. With the rise of the bourgeoisie, it comes to epitomize the nation, to express the national self-image."[2] Without denying the importance of this kind of analysis, I focus my study on certain semantic developments within these concepts and add the English idea of "culture," which is neglected by Elias but has its own development and cannot be merged with either "Kultur" or "civilisation."[3]

"Culture" is a crucial word in Fichte and Schiller. They change it from denoting something antithetical to nature—or its radical improvement—to what could restore us to nature, after our basic connection with it has been endangered by . . . well, culture, understood broadly as human inventiveness in art, craft, technology. The paradox is clearly stated by Schiller in the sixth letter of his *Aesthetic Education* (1795), a remarkable summary of what inspired classical humanism in Germany. The nostalgia for a presumed Greek balance and wholeness is, as later in Hegel, unashamedly expressed, though its loss, like another fortunate fall, might be transcended by mankind on its way to personal and political maturity.

Schiller describes modern fragmentation with zest and elegance. "Forever chained to a single and tiny fragment of the whole, individual man can only fashion himself as a fragment; hearing forever only the monotonous sound of the wheel that he is turning, he can never develop the harmony of his being, and instead of expressing more fully humanity in its very nature, he becomes a mere imprint of his occupation, of his specialized knowledge."[4] What wholeness remains in the form of the state, together with the very sense of life in all its richness, becomes—and it is a word that we often meet—"abstract." Citizens, estranged from their government, receive its laws with indifference (*Kaltsinn*). The all-unifying nature (*alles vereinende Natur*) that supplied forms of life to the Greeks is contrasted with the all-dissecting reasoning (*der alles trennende Verstand*) of Schiller's age.

This distrust of reason as the "false secondary power that multiplies distinctions" is familiar to readers of English literature from Wordsworth's *Prelude* and Coleridge's fanciful discrimination between fancy and imagination. But in England it is not set off historically, or not so intensely, by the fiction of Greek wholeness. And while English as well as continental romanticism is the source of restorative antiselfconsciousness theories, rarely are the motifs so clearly elaborated as in Schiller. "Culture itself," he writes in the sixth letter, "inflicted this [totality-destroying] wound on modern humanity."[5] In a classic move on a remarkable chessboard of arguments, a move we also find in Rousseau and Hegel, *what inflicts the wound must also be its remedy*. This homeopathic "remède dans le mal," as Starobinski calls it, citing a lost Greek tragedy in which the hero Telephus can only be cured by the rust of Achilles' spear, which caused his wound, allows for progress, but of a precarious, dialectical kind.[6] In order to achieve a degree of development even higher than that of the Greeks, humanity has to pursue a new totality despite and through such fated fragmentation. "This antagonism of forces," Schiller writes, perhaps borrowing a dialectical principle from Kant, "is the great instrument of culture, but only its instrument"; it is a means and never its end. The totality, he concludes, "which artifice [die Kunst] has destroyed, must be recovered again through a higher art."[7]

As the term "higher art" implies, the culture that restores wholeness and quality of life is associated with what we would now call "high culture," a product of classical humanism in Germany, of its combination of Aufklärung and Humanität. It displaces French refinement. The fall into division (including division of labor and the class structure) provokes a compensatory principle of unity that counterbalances accelerating pressures of modernization. These pressures are also noted by Wordsworth in the 1800 preface to Lyrical Ballads. He suggests that his unconventional and minimalist ballads will cultivate a sensibility endangered by his era's increasing search for violent stimulants, by a sensationalism ascribed to the combined forces of industrialization, urbanization, the press, and cheap fiction. Poetry reinforces nature to prevent what will soon be called "overcivilization," understood both as an excessive, unbalancing emphasis on practical, philistine, acquisitive, and materialist as against contemplative factors and as an excessive, unbalancing emphasis on cerebral and skeptical analysis: "We murder to dissect" (Wordsworth). By the time of Mill, Arnold, and Ruskin this anxiety about the superficial and unnatural effects of civilization begins to valorize the word "culture."[8]

It was probably Coleridge's On the Constitution of Church and State (1830), rather than a foreign source, that was most influential in England. In chapter 5 of his treatise, Coleridge twice indicates that civilization is "a mixed good," even a corrupting influence, which creates "a varnished [rather] than a polished people; where this civilization is not grounded in cultivation, in the harmonious development of qualities and faculties that characterize our humanity." A nation, he concludes, "can never be a too cultivated, but may easily become an over-civilized race."[9]

With this distinction, moreover, Coleridge also introduces the idea of a national "clerisy" as an *enclesia*, that is, an estate or class composed of "the learned of all denominations," analogous in its function to a national (i.e., established) church, and creating a coalition of "clerks," of bookmen and churchmen. A religion of culture is envisaged, though still within the aegis of the church. It is a canny English adaptation of Fichte, who was the first to define the destiny or vocation of such a learned class in his *Die Bestimmung des Gelehrten* (The destiny of the scholar) of 1794.

But the decisive intervention in England was Arnold's *Culture and Anarchy* (1869). It not only subsumes all the strands of the debate, but, by staying away from theory or system, by being so cannily both a political pamphlet engaged with the speeches and newspapers of its time and a comprehensive, nonparochial vision of what Arnold calls "*humanized* knowledge," it exemplifies the genre of cultural critique. Arnold must first save the word "culture" itself from political and utilitarian despisers who mock it for being the cant of the day, a high-sounding word that refers to nothing more than a smattering of Greek and Latin. At the same time, without setting the word systematically against "civilization," Arnold must persuade his readers that culture, in England, has "a weighty task to perform, because here that mechanical character, which civilisation tends to take everywhere, is shown in the most eminent degree." He takes for granted that, since we esteem it so much, we know what "mechanical and material civilisation" is, and he concentrates instead on defining what culture is: an indispensable aid in the pursuit of perfection, not "a having and a resting, but a growing and a becoming." Culture, he reiterates, "is a harmonious expression of *all* the powers, which make the beauty and worth of human nature, and is not consistent with the over-development of any one power at the expense of the rest." Even religion, then, is only a way station: we are to be nourished, and not bound, by "the best that has been thought and known in the world current everywhere." Where religion was, culture will be, and its diffusion, carried from one end of society to the other, will go beyond "the clique of the cultivated and learned" and "do away with classes."[10]

Arnold's gospel of perfection (a word that, in his usage, has connotations of moral inner striving as well as external, social progress) breaks with the idea of civilization or culture as something already achieved; moreover, that which has been achieved must be diffused and pervade all strata of society.[11] The Marxist concept of society, as Raymond Williams saw, is at once similar and very different.

Like Arnold, Williams wants to save "culture" from its despisers or those who wish to reduce it to a superstructural mystification. The question is whether "culture," as it breaks with "civilization" and comes to be at once "a noun of 'inner' process, specialized to its presumed agencies in 'intellectual life' and 'the arts' " and "a noun of general process, specialized to its presumed configurations in 'whole ways of life' " could be valued by the prevalent Marxist concept of society.[12] This question is more than theoretical. It involves an understanding of a complex historical development and Marxism's willingness to evolve: can it face "not concepts but problems, not analytic problems either but historical movements that are still unresolved."?[13]

Marx was Arnold's contemporary, and Williams singles out as a decisive element Marx's understanding of civil society and as an unresolved element his concept of culture. European civilization, according to Marx, is a specific historical rather than permanent form: a "bourgeois society created by the capitalist mode of production." But while "society" and "economy" now become, through Marxism, basic analytic concepts, cultural history tends to be viewed as a pawn of idealist historiography. Marx's view of economic and social production, at the same time, when combined with Vico's axiom that man makes his own history, leads, according to Williams, to a new understanding of human creativity and "the most important intellectual advance in all modern social thought": the "emphasis on 'man making himself' through producing his own means of life." He produces himself or his culture, as well as consumable objects.[14] Roland Barthes and Clifford Geertz develop a later but parallel concept of culture, based on Weberian sociology and semiotics and more intent on continuing to change the world through understanding. "Believing," writes Geertz, "that man is an animal suspended in webs of significance he himself has made, I take culture to be those webs, and the analysis of it to be therefore not an experimental science in search of law but an interpretive one in search of meaning."[15]

Marx, while reintroducing the concept of culture as an essential ingredient in human self-fashioning, did not resolve the antinomy between culture as a social or collective process and culture as the province of individual and often rebellious creation.[16] What is stressed in Marxism is cultural history as a material process that effects "a recovery of the wholeness of history." This "wholeness," however, remains a vague ideal. Williams acknowledges that deficiency: to sideline culture as a mystification of material processes is not only reductive of culture but subversive of Marxism. It is a mistake, in fact: "the reproduction, in altered form, of the separation of 'culture' from material social life, which had been the dominant tendency in idealist cultural thought." What Williams calls "the full possibilities of the concept of culture as a constitutive social process" has not been achieved, though *Marxism and Literature* shows what progress has been made, as well as delineating the scope of the problem.

The striving to imagine and reconstruct a lost wholeness was given a postfictional pathos by Hegel: an elaborate historicizing narrative that established and dominated cultural history at least to Lukács's *Theory of the Novel* (1915). Lukács argues that the novel as a paradigm for modern art is marked by Western culture's "transcendental homelessness," by the loss of a Greek "totality" he himself will not give up even in his later, Marxist phase. (It turns up in Marxism as a cultural memory with revolutionary, because utopian rather than ironic, potential.) The idea that art and, beyond it, an artful political structure might reintegrate the fragmented individual moved the idea of culture into a *critical* position vis-à-vis both "civilization" (marked by overrefinement rather than robustness) and "anarchy."

That "culture" will cure "civilization" is an idea that culminates in Spengler, but it also appears in the form of a politicized antithesis that contrasts German *Kultur* with French *civilisation*. ("It is clear," Elias writes, "that the function of the German concept of *Kultur* took on new life in the year 1919, and in the preceding years, partly because a war was waged against Germany in the name of 'civilization' and because the self-image of the Germans had to define itself anew in the situation created by the peace treaty.")[17] In Jacques Rivière's *L'Allemand* (1918), the reflections of a prisoner of war who had returned from Germany, that antithesis is poignantly examined, mainly by way of a polemic between the future editor of the *Nouvelle Révue Française* and the neo Kantian philosopher Paul Natorp. Both sides agree, despite their different valuation of the fact, that *"civilisation"* is the "culture" of France. But when that culture becomes no more than a national characteristic, despite universalist claims so memorably stated by Rivarol—who acknowledges national differences and the wars arising from them[18]—a relativizing shift takes place.

The notion of culture as national or regional, as an organic emanation of spirit-of-place, not only brings into play its root meaning (culture of the soil) but gains strength in reaction to the advances of (1) technology and (2) relativism. "We must recognize that civilization is nothing but the aggregate of the techniques, of the means with which we dominate this brave and ingenious animal, nature" is Ortega y Gasset's opinion in "Sobra los estudios clássicos" (1907). As to cultural relativism (or pluralism), it at first benefits from the alliance of humanistic and Enlightenment ideas, especially their counsel of toleration.

Herder's philosophy of history and a historicism nourished increasingly on Vico as well are remarkable products of that alliance. Herder was the first, in fact, to use "culture" in the modern sense of an *identity culture*: a sociable, populist, and traditionary way of life, characterized by a quality that pervades everything and makes a person feel rooted or at home. In its liberal version, the idea that each nation has its own culture, contributes to respect of local traditions, increases what A. O. Lovejoy calls the "plenitude" of the

Great Chain of Being,[19] and, while recognizing each culture as an organic or distinctive growth, seeks to understand it through imaginative empathy [*Einfühlung*].[20]

Herder in his famous anthology *Stimmen der Völker in Liedern* (Voices of the nations in song) harmonizes national differences by his literal metaphor, and even in the fully developed era of European nationalism Martin Buber still adheres to this liberal version. In their striving for culture, he claims, nations are motivated not by expansionism or a territorial imperative but by their realization of

> individual nuance. What happens is that folk-souls become self-reflective [*Selbstbesinnung der Völkerseelen*]. The unconscious development of the national psyche is being made conscious; the specific qualities of blood and tribe [*eines Blutstammes*] are being turned into poetry and creatively deployed; the instincts of the collectivity are rendered more productive by proclaiming each type [*Art*]. Goethe's dream of a World Literature assumes new forms: only when each *Volk* speaks out of its essential being [*Wesen*] does it augment the shared treasure.[21]

But historicist thinking of this idealizing kind—fueled by French humanitarian epics of the nineteenth century, from Ballanche and Quinet to Victor Hugo and Leconte de Lisle, as well as by Dilthey's *Lebensphilosophie*[22]—also led to Spengler's morphological and hyperbolic schematism, in which "cultures" are irreducibly distinct while undergoing an identical evolution from barbaric robustness to a decadent phase labeled "civilization" and then back by way of their rebarbarization to a renewed cycle of life. Robert Musil, who dismissed the attempt to distinguish between culture and civilization as "an old and really fruitless quarrel," nevertheless saw it as a symptom of modernity's growing complexity, of the burden of technological advances and knowledge diffusion that characterizes "civilization" as against "culture" where a single ideology reigns. "Intellectual organization," as he calls it, cannot keep up with either population growth or knowledge growth. "What characterizes and defines our intellectual situation is precisely the wealth of contents that can no longer be mastered, the swollen facticity of knowledge (including moral facts), the spilling out of experiences over the surfaces of nature, the impossibility of achieving an overview, the chaos of things that cannot be denied."[23] F. R. Leavis's pamphlet of 1930, "Mass Civilization and Minority Culture," expressed a similar diagnosis and sought a qualitative solution by way of a university program of English studies.

"A phrase charged with sacred pathos demonizes its antonym."[24] That is the effect of *Kultur* and *civilisation* on each other. *Civilisation* too, as Starobinski points out, is sacralized after the French Revolution in the writings of Condorcet, Michelet, Victor Hugo, and others. Yet it designated from the outset not only an achieved state but as a long-term and progressive action subject to constant revaluation.[25] Baudelaire, enemy of all easy philosophies of progress, declared that civilization was simply a "grande barbarie éclairé au gaz."[26] When "culture," then, is opposed to "civilization" as an incontestable value, a retotalized totality that cannot be judged except from within, on its own terms, a tension disappears that had marked the concept of "civilization" and made it critical of itself as well as self-satisfied toward others.[27]

Indeed, "culture" grows to be a sacred term in the German domain and denotes an ideal consonance of person and nation, or even a *Bestimmung*, a destined harmony of the self, of the state, of self and state. Fichte's identity philosophy claims that the highest drive in mankind is for identity, for a being-in-tune with oneself ("vollkommene Übereinstimmung mit sich selbst") that leads to perfect accord also beyond oneself. Culture, in turn, is defined as "the last and highest means to that end."[28]

It is revealing, given this imperious emphasis on harmony over any kind of difference or tension, to compare Wordsworth's struggle to render, in the emerging *Prelude* (his autobiographical poem, written between 1798 and 1806), a more complex music of identity. The growth of the individual mind is represented there as a precarious harmonizing of discordant elements, as a unity-of-being achieved by nature's "dark, inscrutable workmanship." Arnold too is wary of coercive teleologies, of culture as an explicit system of ethical or national ideals. But in Fichte, or the German tradition of identity philosophy, the concepts of personality and nation-state are aligned. Scholars, intellectuals, and even artists—basically Coleridge's "clerisy" or *enclesia*—are considered as functionaries, prophets in the service of the state, and not as "intellectuals" in the modern, contestatory sense of the word. When Spengler's quasi-biological idea of health and decay, joined to a strict determinism, challenges that other "scientific" determinism, namely Marxist sociology, this trend is reinforced, and many intellectuals become history's ambulance chasers.[29]

After the First World War and Spengler's *Decline of the West*, every writer on culture starts taking the pulse of his nation and vacillates between manic optimism and doomsday bodings. There is a often a *Kulturpessimismus* or "generalized despair about Western civilization" (Stephen Spender). An intensified era of grand cultural narratives begins.

A difference emerges, however, between the Old and the New World, specifically between the United States, on the one hand, and Europe and England, on the other. In the United States "culture" had to overcome two liabilities: its connotation of (English) gentility and a conviction that America could not have a high culture but only a vulgar, material, and crankish one. Francis Hackett caricatures an upper-class woman, a Brahmin who "wrings her fair hands" over "the materialism of all classes," "the influx of a racially and socially inferior population," and "the idolatry of science" and, worst of all, is unable to envisage her ideal's "supersession by another culture to which orthodox culture has no clue."[30] Van Wyck Brooks, lamenting "the absence both of an intellectual tradition and a sympathetic soil" that might "develop the latent greatness we possess," sees America shamed, in European eyes, by typifying "the universally externalizing influences of modern industrialism." It is unable to condense the "religious energy of the race," which has become "ego-centric and socially centrifugal."[31] Randolph Bourne, a sharper mind, calls this attitude of cultural humility humiliating. He differentiates the older American critic from the new. though both are hospitable to the fact that culture is international, only the younger critic dares to be nonconformist, takes what suits his "community of sentiment," and views culture as "a living effort" opposed to all affectation of the mind. "He began to see in the new class-consciousness of poets the ending of that old division which 'culture' made between the chosen people and the gentiles."[32] In this loaded scriptural allusion there is considerable ambivalence (is it the people who have true culture and the gentiles who are over- or falsely civilized?). But the poets are seen as a class, as a separate yet potentially unifying force, and the need felt by Bourne and his contemporaries for intellectual or cultured community recalls Goethe's sense of the isolation of Weimar in a German society that was fragmented and had no city like Paris "where the outstanding minds of the whole realm are gathered in a single place."[33]

In continental Europe, of course, the other side of this centrality—the centralized state, its propagandistic power and educational dirigisme—proved to be the problem. A belatedly unified Germany now joins the game. The state seems to play an ever-larger role in determining what culture, or its official image, will be. Journalists emerge as an opinion-forming class, and scholars too construct or reconstruct cultural history, often framing a defense of the West and attacking symptoms of decadence. As nationalism grows, culture politics becomes noisy, a press-and-propaganda spectacle. Julien Benda writes in his famous tract of 1927, The Treason of the Intellectuals: "With a self-consciousness never before attested (strongly stirred up by men of letters) each people now focuses on itself and squares off against the others in its language, its art, its literature, its philosophy, its civilization, its 'culture.' "[34]

That Benda puts culture in quotation marks indicates the rise of the word in its nationalist connotation. He also quotes Treitschke, the German historian, to the effect that "this consciousness of themselves assumed by the nation-states, and which culture cannot but fortify, this self-consciousness will have as a consequence that war can never disappear from the earth, despite the closer linkage of those nations' interests, despite the convergence of manners and external forms of life."[35] Not without irony Benda calls the fact that political war now implies culture war "an invention of our era which assures it a signal place in the moral history of humanity."

The most tragic turn of events in this "moral" history takes place in Germany, where *Kultur* had become a philosophy of life. More even than in Victorian England, a bourgeois ideology of continuing education (of *Bildung*, or self-culture) took hold and fostered a cosmopolitan appreciation of learning and art wherever they were found. This needs no elaboration here: it has been assiduously documented and studied. German Jews were in the vanguard of this development. By 1914 *they* had become the *Kulturvolk*. Statistics show their disproportionate registration in the universities, their massive role in theater and the press, their dissemination of Lessing, Goethe, Kant, and the concept of *Bildung* itself—all of which the Nazis turned against them.[36]

I restrict myself to noting the complete reversal effected by Nazi ideology basing itself on *"völkisch"* (nationalistic-populist) currents.[37] Already the First World War was often represented in Germany as a decisive battle between German "culture" and Western "civilization."[38] *Kultur*, imbued with a devotional and almost messianic fervor, *Kultur* as a lifelong task, permeating like religion all aspects of personal and social being, undergoes a coup d'état and is deployed by the Nazi regime not only against French *civilisation* but against all so-called non-Aryans in Europe. Particularly against the Jews. A tomb in the Weissensee cemetery, the main Jewish graveyard of Berlin, identifies the person buried there as a "Jünger der Menschheit": a disciple of humanity. This cosmopolitan perspective was denounced as an internationalist conspiracy against German blood and *Volk*.

It is interesting that the culture/civilization distinction has not disappeared even today. After German reunification in 1989, the playwright Heiner Müller argued in the following terms that socialism was reformable but that the West was "colonizing" East Germany: "The former Federal Republic—a civilization economically overdeveloped and culturally underdeveloped—attempts to eradicate, by means of contempt and bureaucracy, the culture that once flourished in the former East Germany in opposition to Stalinist colonization."[39]

NOTES

1. *The Civilizing Process*, trans. Edmund Jephcott (Cambridge: Blackwell, 1994). This combines *The History of Manners* and *State Formation and Civilization* in a one-volume edition. The core of Elias's book goes back to an enlarged *Habilitationsschrift* finished in 1936. It is impossible not to notice his dedication, which indicates that Elias's mother died in Auschwitz in 1941, two years after the Basel edition of his work in 1939.

2. Ibid., 40–41.

3. See also Jeorg Fisch's compendious article "Zivilisation, Kultur," in *Geschichtliche Grundbegriffe: Historisches Lexikon zur politisch-sozialen Sprache in Deutschland*, ed. Otto Brunner, Werner Conze, and Reinhart Kosselek (Stuttgart: Klett-Cotta, 1992), 7:679–774. This overview is rich in quotation and has important analytic insights; it is again, however, strongest in the German and French language domains and weak when it comes to English developments.

4. *On the Aesthetic Education of Man*, bilingual edition, trans. and ed. Elizabeth Willoughby and L. A. Willoughby (New York: Oxford University Press, 1967), 34. My translation. Cf. chapter 4 above, 123.

5. *On the Aesthetic Education of Man in a Series of Letters*, trans. Reginald Snell (New York: Ungar, 1965), 39.

6. Jean Starobinski, *Le remède dans le mal: Critique et légitimation de l'artifice à l'âge des lumières* (Paris: Gallimard, 1989), chapter 5. The Parceval legend also transmits the image of this remedial wounding.

7. *Aesthetic Education* (1965), 45. Kant's "Fourth Thesis" in his "Idea for a Universal History from a Cosmopolitan Point of View" (1784) introduced the notion of such an "antagonism," or an "unsocial sociability," necessary "to bring about the development of all the capacities of men" and leading to "a universal civic society." Cf. *The Difference Between Fichte's and Schelling's System of Philosophy*, trans. H. S. Harris and Walter Cerf (Albany: SUNY Press, 1977). On contradiction, see also Martin Jay, *Force Fields: Between Intellectual History and Cultural Critique* (New York: Routledge, 1993).

8. The source of this idea of overcivilization was, of course, Rousseau, though it is already found in the elder Mirabeau, who coined the word *civilisation* from the verb *civiliser* and talked of a "false civilization" (Elias, *The Civilizing Process*, 31–33). Hence the distinction between "culture" and "civilization" found already in Kant's "Universal History": "To a high degree we are, through art and science, *cultured*. We are *civilized*—perhaps too much for our own good—in all sorts of social grace and decorum. . . . The ideal of morality belongs to culture; its use for some simulacrum of morality in the love of honor and outward decorum constitutes mere civilization" (*Kant: On History*, trans. L. W. Beck [New York: Bobbs-Merrill, 1963], 21). It is interesting that in his remarkable essay "On the Teaching of Modern Literature," collected in a book entitled *Beyond Culture* (New York: Viking, 1965), Trilling does not use the word "culture" to indicate what is challenged by modern literature but rather "civilization:"

> Arnold's historic sense presented to his mind the long, bitter, bloody past of Europe, and he seized passionately upon the hope of true civilization at last achieved. But the historic sense of our literature has in mind a long excess of civilization to which may be ascribed the bitterness and bloodiness both of the past and of the present and of which the peaceful aspects are to be thought of as mainly contemptible—its order achieved at the cost of extravagant personal repression, either that of coercion or that of acquiescence; its repose otiose," etc.   (16–17)

9. Bollingen edition of *The Collected Works of S. T. Coleridge*, vol. 10, *On the Constitution of Church and State*, ed. John Colmer (Princeton: Princeton University Press, 1976), 42–43, 49. See also *The Friend* (1818), Essay IX, with an allusion to France: "Never can society comprehend fully, and in its whole practical extent, the permanent distinction, and the occasional contrast, between cultivation and civilization; never can it attain to a due insight into the momentous fact, fearfully as it has been, and even now is exemplified in a neighbour country, that a nation can never be a too cultivated but may easily become an overcivilized, race" (3:494). Cf. Raymond Williams, *Keywords: A*

Vocabulary of Culture and Society (New York: Oxford University Press, 1976), s.v. "Culture."

10. Cf. the tenor of Emerson's "Culture." Emerson makes no significant distinction between culture and civilization, but neither this nor his essay "Civilization" are particularly inspired. Culture for him is primarily personal culture, and his conception of that owes something to the French ideal of the unostentatious, conversational *"honnête homme."* One of his few pithy sayings is that "culture corrects the theory of success."

11. While I agree with Richard Poirier's understanding of how the idea of "genius" works in Emerson to unsettle and even unravel its original performances and how this volatility might explain why Arnold rather than Emerson became the dominant literary-cultural figure in American criticism, I think he somewhat underestimates the subversive quality in Arnold's ideas of perfection and diffusion. They too suggest, together with Arnold's fluid style, a receding horizon or transcendental perspective that puts into question any dogmatic fixation of the imaginative energy displayed in particular works. It is true, however, that Arnold's perfection is progressive and recoils from the "anarchy" that might result if "genius" undermines its own effects as too mechanical and therefore also its potential contribution to cultural reform. See Poirier, *The Renewal of Literature* (New York: Random House, 1987), 85.

12. Raymond Williams, *Marxism and Literature* (New York: Oxford University Press, 1977), 17.

13. The discussion that follows is based on Williams's first chapter, "Culture," in *Marxism and Literature.*

14. Cf. "Si l'homme est ce qu'il fait, alors nous dirons que la chose la plus urgente aujourd'hui pour l'intellectuel africain est la construction de sa nation" (Frantz Fanon, *Les damnés de la terre* [Paris: François Maspero, 1961], 185).

15. *The Interpretation of Cultures* (London: Hutchinson, 1975), 5.

16. For a move in that direction, see Herbert Marcuse, "Die Permanenz der Kunst. Wider eine bestimmte marxistische Ästhetik" (1977), in *Schriften* (Frankfurt-am-Main: Suhrkamp, 1987), 9:196–239. The question of the subject, as it is often called, or who it is that can think con-

cretely, at once from within specific historical conditions yet, at the same time, freely and critically, is posed by many neo-Marxist thinkers who do not identify that subject exclusively with the proletariat. An echo of that kind of thinking is found in the Williams of *Marxism and Literature*, when he begins the chapter entitled "Culture" by defending a "hesitation" before "the richness of developed theory and the fullness of achieved practice" that has the "awkwardness, even the gaucherie, of any radical doubt." There are, in brief, "historical movements that are still unresolved" (11). Williams acknowledges the influence of Lukács but also of Goldmann. Goldmann saw an analogy between basic concepts of Lukács and Heidegger, centering on the fact that "l'homme n'est pas *en face* du monde qu'il essaie de comprendre et sur lequel il agit, mais *à l'intérieur* de ce monde." (posthumous fragments edited by Youssef Ishagpour, *Lukácz et Heidegger: Pour une nouvelle philosophie* [Paris: Denoël/Gonthier, 1973], 65).

17. *The Civilizing Process*, 7. Elias, who sees the *Kultur/civilisation* contrast emerging from the class struggle, also shows that these concepts seek to express a larger, more unified consciousness: that of the West as a whole or of particular nations. The concepts, then, eventually transcend their sociogenesis or evolve into ideas that seem to surpass a class-based motivation (Elias characterizes this development as a recession of the social and advance of the national element). "Civilization" becomes, for example, an evangelical slogan in Napoleon's imperial war. "Soldiers," Napoleon harangues his troops as he sets off for Egypt in 1798, "you are undertaking a conquest with incalculable consequences for civilization" (quoted in Elias, *The Civilizing Process*, 41). The concept's transcendence of class or estate in this context is suspicious and suggests "false consciousness," but again and again critique does not avail in the face of the desire for a unity that would overcome division.

18. See the opening of *L'universalité de la langue française* (1783).

19. A. O. Lovejoy, *The Great Chain of Being* (Baltimore: Johns Hopkins, 1933).

20. The most subtle account of Herder's originality remains that of Isaiah Berlin in *Vico and Herder: Two Studies in the History of Ideas* (New York: Viking, 1976).

21. Martin Buber, "*Jüdische Renaissance*" (1900), in *Die Jüdische*

Bewegung: Gesammelte Aufsätze und Ansprachen, 1900–1915 (Berlin: Jüdischer Verlag, 1916); my translation.

22. See the wonderfully informative and neglected book of Herbert J. Hunt, *The Epic in Nineteenth-Century France: A Study in Heroic and Humanitarian Poetry from Les Martyrs to Les Siècles Morts* (Oxford: Basil Blackwell, 1941). Wilhelm Dilthey's Hegelian linkages produce a prose version of these *Kultursysteme*, all independent yet connected, a fascinating if endless schematism that seeks to secure the distinctiveness of the *Geistes-* or *Kulturwissenschaften*. Though *Kultur* does not become a battle cry for him, Dilthey sees Germany ("Dies Land der Mitte, der inneren Kultur") as the place of their second flourishing in the nineteenth century (the first was the Reformation), and he inserts the speculation that this second renaissance motivated his country's intuitive historical scholarship. "Such epochs of a blooming spiritual life elicit in historical thinkers a greater strength and variousness of lived experience [*Erlebens*], a heightened power to understand and reconstruct [*nachzuverstehen*] the most diverse forms of being" ("Der Aufbau der geschichtlichen Welt in den Geisteswissenschaften," in *Die Philosophie des Lebens: Eine Auswahl aus seinen Schriften*, ed. Herman Nohl [Stuttgart: Teubner, 1961], 230 ff). My translation.

23. In unpublished notes of 1921 on Spengler. See Robert Musil, "On Culture and Theory," in *Precision and Soul: Essays and Addresses*, ed. and trans. Burton Pike and David S. Luft (Chicago: University of Chicago Press, 1990), 134–49.

24. Starobinski, *Le remède dans le mal*, 33.

25. See, e.g., M. Guizot, *Histoire de la civilisation en Europe depuis la chute de l'empire romain*, a course of lectures delivered between 1828 and 1830 and first published in 1840. Guizot's first chapter defines civilization as perfectible, both in the social and personal domain, and distinguishes between ancient and modern types of civilization by ascribing to the latter a politically beneficial diversity.

26. This plays on the earlier contrast of "civilized" and "barbarian." Ortega's view of "civilization" is also, basically, that of a materialistic progress that leads to the stupidity of overspecialization. See his *The Revolt of the Masses* of 1930, trans. Anthony Kerrigan (Notre Dame, Ind.: University of Notre Dame Press, 1985).

27. I should emphasize, though, that "culture" in the France of the 1930s rarely took on the German meaning. The word developed as an exact though nuanced synonym of "civilization." It evoked, like the latter, a heritage formed over a considerable length of time, one that included organized knowledge and social institutions as well as the arts. But the word often introduced a personal factor, which emphasized the creative role of the individual and countered the idea of a collectivist or racial imprint. The clearest ideological manifestation of that tendency is found in Emmanuel Mounier, whose "personalism" encouraged a national and communitarian renaissance to rival and resist the totalitarian temptation. See his *Manifeste au service du personnalisme* (Paris: Aubier, 1936), esp. the chapter "La culture de la personne."

28. Johann Gottlieb Fichte, *Über die Bestimmung des Menschen* (1784). Martin Jay defines the ideal of *Bildung* as featuring, in addition to cosmopolitanism, "a fervent faith in the values of a harmonized personal culture, aesthetic self-fashioning, and the realization of innate capacities of individual growth" ("Response to George Mosse and David Myers," *Judaism*, no. 178 [1996]: 160).

29. Yeats's *A Vision* (1925) is symptomatic as a post-Spenglerian exercise yet also exceptional because of its ironic and self-complicating structure. It is a sort of master mobile, at once abstract and constructivist, providing a new machinery for poetry rather than a history.

30. See *A Modern Book of Criticism*, ed. Ludwig Lewisohn (New York: Boni and Liveright, 1919), 190–93. I use this anthology because it reflects the American situation shortly after the First World War, as the immigrant generations were (like Lewisohn himself) attempting to enter the universities and the field of arts and letters. Hackett's ideal of culture is aggressively democratic and (without knowing the term) multicultural. He mocks the Brahmin lady as follows. "There is only one culture, our own. Perhaps in steerage you can evoke noises from a Lithuanian that sound like human speech. Yes, but soon that Lithuanian will have the 'locutions of the slum.' Beware of Lithuania. Do not pat the strange dog. He might bite a piece out of your culture. What if the young Jewess on the immigrant ship glows with assent when, without Russian or Yiddish or German, you query: Dostoevsky? Gogol? Tchekov? Lermontov? Tolstoy? Schnitzler? Suderman? Artzi-

bashef? Ibsen? Strindberg? . . . The suppresion of such names is the first great necessity of a pinhead conception of culture."

31. Ibid., 194–98. The extract is entitled "An External Civilization."

32. See "Our Cultural Humility," in *History of a Literary Radical and Other Essays* (New York: B. W. Huebsch, 1920), and *A Modern Book of Criticism*, 206–10.

33. Elias, *The Civilizing Process*, 23–24.

34. "Avec une conscience qu'on n'avait jamais vue (qu'attisent fortement les gens de lettres) chaque peuple maintenant s'étreint lui-même et se pose contre les autres dans sa langue, dans son art, dans sa littérature, dans sa philosophie, dans sa civilisation, dans sa 'culture' " (*La Trahison des clercs* [Paris: Grasset, 1927], 29; my translation).

35. Ibid., 30 n. 1.

36. See George L. Mosse, *German Jews Beyond Judaism* (Bloomington: Indiana University Press, 1985), especially chapter 3, "Intellectual Authority and Scholarship." See also Peter Gay, "Encounter with Modernism: German Jews in German Culture, 1888–1914," *Midstream* 21 (February 1975): 23–65, and the work in progress of Paul Mendès-Flohr.

37. For the rise of the idea of a *völkisch* state, see especially George L. Mosse, *The Crisis of German Ideology: Intellectual Origins of the Third Reich* (New York: Schocken, 1981).

38. "Im Kriege hieß es, der Kampf spiele sich ab zwischen deutscher Kultur und westlicher Zivilisation" (Walter Sulzbach, "Die Juden unter den Deutschen," *Der Jude* 3 [1926]). Karl Dietrich Bracher writes in his *German Dictatorship: The Origins, Structure, and Consequences of National Socialism* (New York: Penguin University Books, 1973): "Even in the pre-racist stereotype, the Jew was thought to be incapable of creativity and spirituality. He was the embodiment of everything negative which, under the heading 'civilization', was counterposed to the higher value of true 'culture' " (54). Thomas Mann, in *Reflections of an Unpolitical Person*, composed between 1914 and 1918, while displaying no anti-Semitism, criticizes "civilization" as a term pervaded by a literary mentality derivative of France, and he opposes to it a combination of specifically German qualities, including "*Menschendienst*" ("serviceability," or willing obedience) and musicality. While insisting that his position does not exclude cosmopolitan openness, Mann clear-

ly sees the First World War as a culture war and insists on Germany's special role in Europe, its *Sonderweg*. (See also his reply, in the same book, to Romain Rolland's attack on his defense of *Kultur*.) Equally telling is Friedrich Sieburg's *Gott in Frankreich?* (1929), especially the chapter "Blut und Geist" and others under the heading "Zivilisation." Sieburg represents the Great War as an ideological crusade against everything opposed to the Latin-French idea. France, he asserts, must "sacrifice its concept of civilization, if it wishes to live on [among the nations]." A curiosity is Bernard Grasset's "Lettre sur la France," which accompanied the 1930 edition of Sieburg's book and was reprinted during the Occupation in *Dieu est-il français?* trans. Maurice Betz (Paris: Grasset, 1942), 285–322. "Entre nous," writes Grasset, "tout se joue autour de ce mot 'Kultur.' " He also says (and I translate),

> For someone who is not German, culture means quite simply "what a person retains, after long commerce with spiritual matters," a totally inner kind of wealth that cannot be exchanged for other goods . . . not "the sum of knowledge" but its "quality," quality at one with mind, quality close to what we mean by the word "humanism."—For you, culture is something entirely different: an ensemble of scientific knowledge and means that permit and justify one country's domination of others. Thus your idea of Kultur comprehends both the latest refinements of the telephone or of armaments—which seem to anticipate your triumph—and the immortal works of Goethe, which seem to justify it.

Grasset then cites E. R. Curtius on the German misunderstanding of the French idea of *"civilisation"* as if it referred only to "l'existence matérielle et mécanisée" in opposition to soul, art, and mind.

39. Heiner Müller, "Bautzen oder Babylon," *Sinn und Form* 4 (1991): 664.

appendix 2
On Methodology

The possibility of doing cultural theory, of generalizing about the character and tendency of particular cultures, becomes more problematic in the absence of a religious perspective or its totalizing equivalent. Without a supervisory or adversary vision admonishing a present state of affairs, can we attain to a criticism of life, let alone the life of an entire culture? How can we talk about a culture as a whole if that culture is split or disunified and even takes a certain pride in the fact? And once the zeitgeist gives up its ghost,[1] so that the very idea of a synchronous unity is considered a false construct, ripe only for deconstruction? What can be used as a standard of judgment in comparing one's own culture to that of other societies, when the very concept of a superior culture is constantly being questioned? In a post-Marxist era especially, sociologists or cultural critics must then contend with a frustrating empiricism: close observation, close reading, detailism, and inventory skills kept alive by an unorganized idealistic hope in the mind's organizing powers.[2]

I sense that dilemma in Perry Anderson's influential 1968 essay "Components of the National Culture"[3] and more generally in Marxist critics such as Terry Eagleton. Already in *Exiles and Emigrés*, Eagleton's 1970 book on modern English literature, the question arises of how one can understand events in their totality. Eagleton revises *totalization* to mean "the act of grasping the elements of a culture in their living and changing interrelations," and *transcendence* "not [as] a spiritual movement beyond history and culture, but the historical action of projecting oneself beyond the limits and pressures of a particular settlement into a wider perspective." These qualities, he claims, are lost to British culture. The romantic poet or the great nineteenth-century novelist could still manifest them; according to Eagleton, each displayed "a relationship of intimately detailed intimacy with his society; yet he is also able to grasp that society as a totality, in a way which one might have expected to be genuinely available only to an outsider free of its most immediate pressures. It is integral to the imaginative achievements of Blake, Wordsworth, Dickens and Eliot that they can "totalise" and "transcend" those pressures without damage to the quickness and specificity of their feel for concrete life."[4]

Eagleton, in short, finds an equivalent in this nineteenth-century English *imaginaire* to the idealistic construction Lukács uses in his *Theory of the Novel* (1915), which contrasts the wholeness of epic (a genre that reflects an "integrated" society) with the fallen and fragmentary realities expressed by the novel as a modern epic equivalent in a "problematic" society. Lukács, turning Marxist, questioned that idealistic premise and methodology, but does he overcome it? In many Marxist critics the utopian premise of a classless society or a similar "principle of hope" becomes a golden age replacement.

For Eagleton as for Anderson, empiricism, a strong and intimate aspect of Englishness as a national ideology, limited the possibility of reaching anything like a totalizing vision from within *contemporary* English culture. The achievements that their own time displayed, in the sciences or the arts, were mainly the work of anglophone but non-English exiles and emigrés. "The unchallenged sway of non-English poets and novelists in contemporary English literature," Eagleton concludes, thinking of Conrad, Joyce, Yeats, Eliot, and Lawrence, "points to certain central flaws and impoverishments in conventional English culture itself. That culture was unable, of its own impetus, to produce great literary art: the outstanding art which it achieved has been, on the whole, the product of the exile and the alien."

Taking that thought to its limit, it may turn out that a vision of the whole, one that could challenge a particular society, is bound to be extrinsic to it or utopian. "If . . . a holistic view of society,"

Martin Jay writes in his *Fin-de-Siècle Socialism*, "—indeed any generic view of society—is no longer a valid object of discourse, one major reason for this contention derives from the now widespread hostility to any epistemological vantage point claiming totalistic knowledge." Yet he goes on to quote Laclau and Mouffe on the necessity of constituting a utopian vision radical enough to admonish a particular culture by the quality of its *imaginaire*. "The presence of this imaginary as a set of symbolic meanings which totalize as negativity a certain social order is absolutely essential for the constitution of all left-wing thought."[5]

The methodological issue I raise was also at the core of Adorno's reflections. Martin Jay has analyzed his position: Adorno viewed culture both anthropologically, as a material complex of norms, and from an "elite" point of view that presupposed a transcendent or redemptive position.[6] The critical potential of theory was the important thing, not intellectual mastery as such. The question of how it was possible to criticize culture remained alive in the very act of criticism. Yet what is resolutely unresolved cannot become an ideal: it should not lead to the uncritical acceptance of an incomplete theory. There is no happy conceptual ending to Adorno's conflictual position, as Jay makes quite clear.

I want to supplement and generalize this analysis. For a critical perspective on culture to establish itself creatively—that is, in a way that is involved with art, *even becoming art*—might mean, as in Eagleton's England, an exilic perspective, a language disturbance that goes back to cultural displacement. Aesthetic incompatibility, to use Marcuse's phrase, is connected with the exilic and alien through what is most material in the process of socialization: the acquisition of language-based codes. Adorno's own criticism achieves (and sometimes suffers from) a self-inflicted linguistic disturbance; the symbols of music, their removed referentiality, may have reinforced, like his American experience, a critical distance from the very speech he uses, creating an exquisite and sometimes mandarin discourse.[7]

I also question what seems unquestionable: the very concept of integrity that keeps returning, hydra headed, after "totality" is disavowed. How honest can one announce oneself to be? Adorno's and Horkheimer's proto-Foucauldian insight, "To speak of culture was always contrary to culture" (because it encourages a discourse that "brings culture within the sphere of administration") may protest too much. (It remains valid *for us* because it recalls the endless culturalist noise and claptrap of Nazism and Stalinism.) Jay remarks in conclusion that there were, for Adorno, "no ways to derive undamaged ideas from a damaged life," and he calls this constant theme the "measure of Adorno's remarkable integrity as a thinker."[8] Yet if "integrity" here means only consistency, like that of a juggler who always recovers, this comment is honorific rather than adequate. Integrity as the promise of wholeness, or of a restoration to wholeness, is itself the problem as well as the challenge.

NOTES

1. A Viennese refugee in the United States, Leo Spitzer, the great literary scholar of the Romance languages, tried to save a synthesizing *Geistesgeschichte*, contrasting it with A. O. Lovejoy's "scientific" History of Ideas, which substituted recurring combinations of unit ideas for larger unifying or synthetic structures. The word *Geist* included, for Spitzer, "*all* the creative impulses of the human mind" (*Leo Spitzer: Representative Essays*, ed. Alban K. Forcione, Herbert Lindenberger, and Madeline Sutherland [Stanford: Stanford University Press, 1988]) and, as John Freccero has remarked in a foreword introducing this selection of Spitzer's essays (xi–xx), he tried to fashion a conception of total coherence or ultimate intelligibility that functioned somewhat like the medieval exegete's "*mystificatio*," that is, "the [hidden] principle of intelligibility in terms of which disparate elements might be understood." Spitzer was unsuccessful in conveying to literary studies more than a personal, if strongly admonitory, ideology. But his insistence on the constructive rather than vicious nature of Schleiermacher's hermeneutic circle (the paradox that the whole cannot be understood except through its parts, while the parts cannot be understood except from the standpoint of the whole) and his reliance on what Freccero calls "the widening gyre of context" to resolve obscure or ambiguous phrases did become accepted features of literary studies.

229

2. The contemporary and rather helpless emphasis on "positionality" shows that the desire for vision or the grounds of its possibility stays very much alive. Even if we no longer accept the Marxist identification of the working class as the "subject" of history that has all along, though unacknowledged, created history (and therefore can understand it better than the bourgeoisie), Lukács's description of the "Antinomies of Bourgeois Thought," reaching from the German idealist philosophers to his time, remains fascinating. See *History and Class Consciousness: Studies in Marxist Dialectics*, trans. Rodney Livingstone (Cambridge, Mass.: MIT Press, 1971), 110 ff.

3. *New Left Review*, no. 50 (July–August 1968): 3–58.

4. All my quotations from Eagleton are from the introduction to *Exiles and Emigrés: Studies in Modern Literature* (New York: Schocken, 1970), 10 f. Eagleton himself points to the affinity between his thesis and Anderson's essay. Eagleton's closer affinity, though, is with Raymond Williams, who also emphasizes the nineteenth century, but for having developed the idea of culture as a counterpoint to the alienating and fragmenting forces of a modern division of labor. Eagleton stresses the exemplary force of theorists who are also poets or novelists, a characteristic that alleviates, as it were, the "foreign" and "abstract-alienated" taint of theorizing.

5. *Fin-de-Siècle Socialism* (New York: Routledge, 1988), 5, 12. A useful self-critique of what Lukács names "abstract synthesizing" (based on the hermeneutic circle) is found in Lukács's 1962 preface to *The Theory of the Novel* (Cambridge, Mass.: MIT Press, 1971): "It became the fashion [after Dilthey's *Das Erlebnis und die Dichtung*] to form general synthetic concepts on the basis of only a few characteristics . . . of a school, a period etc., then to proceed by deduction from these generalizations to the analysis of individual phenomena, and in that way to arrive at what we claimed to be a comprehensive overall view" (13).

6. Martin Jay, *Adorno* (Cambridge: Harvard University Press, 1984), chapter 4, "Culture as Manipulation; Culture as Redemption."

7. The polyglot itself, of course, or a sort of "Danny Kaye" talent for mimicry would not suffice. The second or "other" language code must produce a sensitivity strong enough to create a disturbance in the original cultural at-homeness. Jewish literary sensibility may have some

relation to the uneasy fact that the Yiddish *mammeloshen* was challenged by a higher cultural language (usually German or a revived Hebrew) and saw itself as *jargon*. Later, in the United States, especially after a Holocaust that destroyed it as a living tongue, Yiddish seemed more authentic (if also more sentimental) than the English to which writers like Henry Roth, Saul Bellow, or Cynthia Ozick assimilated it. The native English of many Jewish-American writers is questioned by that consciousness of a lost vernacular; this sense of loss also overshadows Paul Celan's German in "Conversation in the Mountains" (1959).

    8. Jay, *Adorno*, 160.

index